"Dr. Merida has produced a commentary that is faithful to the text, sensitive to voices of the past, and full of practical applications. Here we see exegesis and applications wedded in a beautiful and Christ-exalting way. This is the work of a pastor-scholar writing for the church within the church."

Edgar Aponte, Director of Hispanic Leadership Development and Instructor at Southeastern Baptist Theological Seminary

"Tony Merida has accomplished a rare achievement! His commentary on Philippians is skilled without being stuffy, clear without being simplistic, and at its core you will find a scholar's mind and a preacher's heart. He has provided a great gift to pastors and students of the Word."

Bernie A. Cueto, campus pastor and assistant professor of Biblical and Theological Studies, Palm Beach Atlantic University

"While many commentaries are written by scholars for scholars, Tony Merida and Francis Chan's *Exalting Jesus in Philippians* is written for preachers by preachers. (Two of the most prominent ones at that!) Like their sermons, Merida and Chan's commentary is informative and conversational, humorous and convicting. They seamlessly transition from a quip about Quarterback Tom Brady to a quote by New Testament scholar Gordon Fee, from a joke by comedian Jim Gaffigan to a citation of St. Cyprian. Sections of the commentary are punctuated with devotional questions to help readers reflect and discuss, which makes this book not only a priceless resource for pastors but also a viable option for small groups. In addition to their insights as preachers, Merida and Chan share Paul's fervent heart for church planting and his profound heartache for the lost, which provides a fresh, extraordinary perspective on Philippians."

Joseph R. Dodson, Associate Professor of New Testament, Ouachita Baptist University

"This commentary, like all in this series, does not disappoint. Tony faithfully takes us to the text, equipping us to faithfully take the text to our churches and to our streets. Exalting Jesus in Philippians will be a high-caliber addition to your arsenal as you joyfully seek to make Jesus known to all people in every circumstance as we look to the day when 'every tongue will confess that Jesus is Lord,' to the glory of God the Father."

Mike Hanafee, pastor, Restoration Church, Detroit, Michigan

"This commentary on Philippians is a gift to pastors because it blends qualities rarely combined in commentaries: faithful text-work, careful application, and winsome communication. Tony and Francis stay anchored to Scripture, model a heart for people, and most importantly, keep their eyes on Jesus. As preachers, we should always do the same, and this commentary will serve us well."

C. J. Mahaney, senior pastor, Sovereign Grace Church of Louisville

"Precise and diligent exposition of God's Word must remain a core value of God's people if the church is going to continue to fulfill God's purposes. This commentary will strengthen and encourage that value among the churches for years to come. It does an excellent job of unpacking the riches of Philippians in a way that is clear, Christ exalting, and gospel saturated. Filled with helpful illustrations and thoughtful applications, I am confident that this will be a powerful tool in the hands of those who love God's Word and desire to handle it rightly."

Kevin Peck, Lead Pastor of the Austin Stone Community Church, Austin, Texas

CHRIST-CENTERED
Exposition

NT / COMMENTARY

AUTHORS **Tony Merida and Francis Chan**
SERIES EDITORS **David Platt, Daniel L. Akin, and Tony Merida**

CHRIST-CENTERED
Exposition

EXALTING JESUS IN

PHILIPPIANS

HOLMAN
REFERENCE

NASHVILLE, TENNESSEE

SERIES DEDICATION

Dedicated to Adrian Rogers and John Piper. They have taught us to love the gospel of Jesus Christ, to preach the Bible as the inerrant Word of God, to pastor the church for which our Savior died, and to have a passion to see all nations gladly worship the Lamb.

—David Platt, Tony Merida, and Danny Akin
March 2013

TABLE OF CONTENTS

Philippians

ACKNOWLEDGMENTS

Just as Paul opens up by thanking God for the Philippians, I, too, want to express my gratitude to God for several gospel partners.

Thank you, Imago Dei Church, for being such a joy to pastor. The elders count it an undeserved privilege to shepherd such a Bible-loving, missionary-minded congregation. It was a joy to study Philippians with you.

I'm also indebted to Samuel Rogers, Ben Palka, and BreAnna Lewis for helping me put the finishing touches on the commentary.

To my bride, Kimberly, and our five children, thank you for your constant love, support, and prayers. May God continue to bless us as we seek to exalt Jesus together.

Finally, I want to say thank you to Sandra Schmid for tracking down the audio files of Francis Chan's sermons through Philippians. I was greatly edified and blessed by these messages. I have incorporated many of Francis's ideas into the body of the commentary. When a personal illustration is used, I try to identify to whom it is referring (me or Francis). Thank you, Francis, for the joy of partnering in this venture. I pray that this commentary will be used in the multiplication of disciples around the world, for the glory of our Lord Jesus Christ.

Tony Merida

SERIES INTRODUCTION

Augustine said, "Where Scripture speaks, God speaks." The editors of the Christ-Centered Exposition Commentary series believe that where God speaks, the pastor must speak. God speaks through His written Word. We must speak from that Word. We believe the Bible is God breathed, authoritative, inerrant, sufficient, understandable, necessary, and timeless. We also affirm that the Bible is a Christ-centered book; that is, it contains a unified story of redemptive history of which Jesus is the hero. Because of this Christ-centered trajectory that runs from Genesis 1 through Revelation 22, we believe the Bible has a corresponding global-missions thrust. From beginning to end, we see God's mission as one of making worshipers of Christ from every tribe and tongue worked out through this redemptive drama in Scripture. To that end we must preach the Word.

In addition to these distinct convictions, the Christ-Centered Exposition Commentary series has some distinguishing characteristics. First, this series seeks to display exegetical accuracy. What the Bible says is what we want to say. While not every volume in the series will be a verse-by-verse commentary, we nevertheless desire to handle the text carefully and explain it rightly. Those who teach and preach bear the heavy responsibility of saying what God has said in His Word and declaring what God has done in Christ. We desire to handle God's Word faithfully, knowing that we must give an account for how we have fulfilled this holy calling (Jas 3:1).

Second, the Christ-Centered Exposition Commentary series has pastors in view. While we hope others will read this series, such as parents, teachers, small-group leaders, and student ministers, we desire to provide a commentary busy pastors will use for weekly preparation of biblically faithful and gospel-saturated sermons. This series is not academic in nature. Our aim is to present a readable and pastoral style of commentaries. We believe this aim will serve the church of the Lord Jesus Christ.

Third, we want the Christ-Centered Exposition Commentary series to be known for the inclusion of helpful illustrations and theologically driven applications. Many commentaries offer no help in illustrations, and few offer any kind of help in application. Often those that do offer illustrative material and application unfortunately give little serious attention to the text. While giving ourselves primarily to explanation, we also hope to serve readers by providing inspiring and illuminating illustrations coupled with timely and timeless application.

Finally, as the name suggests, the editors seek to exalt Jesus from every book of the Bible. In saying this, we are not commending wild allegory or fanciful typology. We certainly believe we must be constrained to the meaning intended by the divine Author Himself, the Holy Spirit of God. However, we also believe the Bible has a messianic focus, and our hope is that the individual authors will exalt Christ from particular texts. Luke 24:25-27,44-47 and John 5:39,46 inform both our hermeneutics and our homiletics. Not every author will do this the same way or have the same degree of Christ-centered emphasis. That is fine with us. We believe faithful exposition that is Christ centered is not monolithic. We do believe, however, that we must read the whole Bible as Christian Scripture. Therefore, our aim is both to honor the historical particularity of each biblical passage and to highlight its intrinsic connection to the Redeemer.

The editors are indebted to the contributors of each volume. The reader will detect a unique style from each writer, and we celebrate these unique gifts and traits. While distinctive in their approaches, the authors share a common characteristic in that they are pastoral theologians. They love the church, and they regularly preach and teach God's Word to God's people. Further, many of these contributors are younger voices. We think these new, fresh voices can serve the church well, especially among a rising generation that has the task of proclaiming the Word of Christ and the Christ of the Word to the lost world.

We hope and pray this series will serve the body of Christ well in these ways until our Savior returns in glory. If it does, we will have succeeded in our assignment.

David Platt
Daniel L. Akin
Tony Merida
Series Editors
February 2013

Philippians

Partnership and Church Planting in Philippi

PHILIPPIANS 1:1-2

Main Idea: After planting the church in Philippi, Paul writes exhorting them to advance the gospel with joy in the face of opposition.

I. The Relevance of Philippians
II. The Back Story
   A. Flashback: Acts 16:6-40
      1. Submission to the Spirit
      2. Evangelistic encounters
   B. Let's do the work of evangelism and church planting.
III. The Big Picture: Six Challenges
   A. Recognize that gospel advancement will cost us, but Jesus is worth it.
   B. Fight for joy in Christ.
   C. Maintain the unity of the Spirit.
   D. Become a "Macedonian giver."
   E. Let's learn what gospel partnership looks like.
   F. Let's give the world a picture of the coming kingdom of God.
IV. The Beautiful Greeting (1:1-2)
   A. Grace is displayed in the life of the senders of the letter: Paul and Timothy (1:1a).
   B. Grace is displayed in the receivers of the letter: the Philippians (1:1b).
   C. Grace is displayed in this Trinitarian blessing (1:2).

Recently our kids (the Merida children) have been reading Scripture every morning and then journaling about their verses. They typically reflect on the passage and sometimes write a prayer. Then they give their journals to their mother, who writes back to them. The other day Joshua wrote a humorous but thoughtful thank-you to his mother, saying, "Dear Mom, thank you for making breakfast. You are a good cooker. I don't understand what this verse means. But thanks for breakfast, and for making my room look good!"—an honest and sincere thank-you note!

Have you written or received an affectionate thank-you letter lately? We're about to read one—Paul's thank-you letter to the church in Philippi. A guy named Epaphroditus brought a gift on behalf of the church to Paul, and Paul writes back to thank them for their support and partnership. He opens the letter, "I give thanks to my God for every remembrance of you" (1:3; cf. 4:14-20). He deeply loves this church. But Philippians is more than a mere thank-you letter. Paul also uses this occasion to encourage the believers to persevere together with joy in spite of opposition. Drawing on known military language of the time, Paul exhorts the Christians to advance the gospel bravely, as fellow servants of the true King, in the face of terrifying opponents. One must not miss this theme of partnership for the advance of the gospel. It's not just an epistle of joy. It's about fearlessly advancing the gospel with joy, working together in hardship.

Indeed, Paul's overarching concern is with the gospel, a word that appears more in Philippians than in any other letter (per hundred words), as scholar Gordon Fee points outs (Fee, *Paul's Letter*, 14, 82). Paul writes much about the glorious nature of the gospel that believers must defend and declare. He writes about the sovereignty of God in salvation, the person and work of Christ, the imputed righteousness of Jesus received by faith, sanctification, and our citizenship in heaven. He also touches on doctrines related to the kingdom, unity, generosity, and more. Perhaps you would say about this letter, like my son, "I don't know what these verses mean." Or perhaps you're very familiar with this letter. In either case, I invite you to study it carefully. For this letter isn't just a message from the ancient past (ca. AD 62). It's the living Word of God, written by the apostle Paul. It's only four chapters, 104 verses, and about 2½ pages in most Bibles. But there's gold here.

The Relevance of Philippians

Just how relevant is this letter? Let me ask you some questions to demonstrate its relevance. Is it easy to be a Christian in today's world? No. If we follow Christ, we will encounter opposition. This letter should encourage us to live for Christ courageously. Where are you going for true joy? Paul radiates a contagious joy here. Though he writes from a Roman prison, he can say, "I rejoice, so you rejoice" (paraphrasing 2:17-18). Paul reminds us that ultimate joy isn't derived from comfortable circumstances, but from a living, vibrant communion with Christ. He doesn't say, "Look at my house; now rejoice," or "Look at my wife . . . my kids . . . my bank account." No,

he says, "Look at Jesus, like I am doing, and rejoice with me." Where will
you find meaning and purpose in life? Welcome to Philippians. Paul says,
"For me, living is Christ and dying is gain" (1:21). Do you need deep and
encouraging Christian *friendships?* This letter provides marvelous application for building and sustaining true community. Does your church need
to grow in *unity?* What church doesn't? Then read this letter. Paul loves
the church at Philippi and refers to it as his "joy and crown" (4:1), but
disunity exists in the body (4:2). He provides wonderful instruction for us
as we seek to unite in the gospel. It isn't hard to understand why this letter is a favorite of many Christians. Just stop and consider how many "life
verses" are found in this little book:

> *I am sure of this, that He who started a good work in you will carry it
> on to completion until the day of Christ Jesus.* (1:6)

> *For me, living is Christ and dying is gain.* (1:21)

> *So then, my dear friends, just as you have always obeyed, not
> only in my presence, but now even more in my absence, work out
> your own salvation with fear and trembling. For it is God who is
> working in you, enabling you both to desire and to work out His
> good purpose.* (2:12-13)

> *My goal is to know Him and the power of His resurrection and the
> fellowship of His sufferings, being conformed to His death, assuming
> that I will somehow reach the resurrection from among the dead. . . .
> Brothers, I do not consider myself to have taken hold of it. But one
> thing I do: Forgetting what is behind and reaching forward to what is
> ahead, I pursue as my goal the prize promised by God's heavenly call
> in Christ Jesus.* (3:10-11,13-14)

> *Our citizenship is in heaven, from which we also eagerly wait for a
> Savior, the Lord Jesus Christ.* (3:20)

> *Don't worry about anything, but in everything, through prayer and
> petition with thanksgiving, let your requests be made known to God.
> And the peace of God, which surpasses every thought, will guard your
> hearts and minds in Christ Jesus.* (4:6-7)

> *I am able to do all things through Him who strengthens me.* (4:13)

And my God will supply all your needs according to His riches in glory in Christ Jesus. (4:19)

I didn't even mention the amazing Christ hymn in 2:6-11! Many Christians have built their lives on these rock-solid verses in Philippians, and rightly so. Perhaps you're new to the Bible, and you find some of this difficult to understand. I often tell my kids, "Keep reading. I didn't say to go understand all of the Bible. I said to go read it." Paul told Timothy, "Think over what I say, for the Lord will give you understanding in everything" (2 Tim 2:7 ESV). If you don't know what these life verses mean, you aren't alone. Many struggle to understand the Bible, but the biblical writers teach us that God opens up our minds to understand the message of the gospel. In fact, that's how it all got started in Philippi—God opened up the mind and heart of a lady named Lydia. Luke writes, "The Lord opened her heart to pay attention to what was spoken by Paul" (Acts 16:14). Our introduction to the book of Philippians is divided into three parts: (1) the back story (Acts 16:6-40); (2) the big picture (of the whole book of Philippians); and (3) the beautiful greeting (Phil 1:1-2).

The Back Story

In his excellent commentary, Peter T. O'Brien summarizes some significant aspects of the background of the city of Philippi, particularly its relationship to Rome:

> In 42 B.C. Philippi became famous as the place where Mark Antony and Octavian defeated the Roman Republican forces of Brutus and Cassius, the assassins of Julius Caesar. The victors settled a number of their veteran soldiers there and established Philippi as a Roman colony. . . . After the battle of Actium (31 B.C.), in which Octavian defeated Antony, more settlers, including some of Antony's disbanded troops and former supporters, were settled in Philippi by order of Octavian (Augustus), who renamed the colony after himself, and it finally became Colonia Iulia Augusta Philippensis. These settlers, along with some of the previous inhabitants, constituted the legal citizen body. Philippi was given the highest privilege possible for a Roman provincial municipality—the *ius Italicum*—which meant that it was governed by Roman law. . . . The citizens of this colony were Roman citizens. . . . Philippi itself was modeled on the mother

city, Rome: it was laid out in similar patterns, the style and
architecture were copied extensively, and the coins produced
in the city bore Roman inscriptions. The Latin language was
used, and its citizens wore Roman dress. Although not the
capital of the province, Philippi was a leading city and an
important stopping place on the Via Egnatia, the recently
constructed military road linking Byzantium with the Adriatic
ports that led to Italy. (O'Brien, *Epistle,* 4)

It was in this important city that Paul planted the first church on
European soil, which Luke recounts for us in Acts 16.

Flashback: Acts 16:6-40

How did the Philippian church begin? You could discuss its origins in
two parts: submission to the Spirit and evangelistic encounters.

Submission to the Spirit (16:6-10). First, Luke tells us that Paul, on his
second missionary journey, received a vision from a man saying, "Cross
over to Macedonia and help us" (v. 9). Just as Philip was led to the
Ethiopian and Peter was led to Cornelius, Paul was led to Macedonia.
In submission to the Spirit, Paul and his team broke on through to the
other side, in what becomes a momentous decision. How did Paul eventually start the church in Philippi? Paul and his little team "evangelized
them" (v. 10). Plant the gospel; plant the church. That's the pattern
here. God was working out His plan to get the gospel to the ends of the
earth, and He was using ordinary guys to fulfill His mission, directing
them by His gracious providence and the Spirit's leadership.

We should recognize that God in His providence often directs our
path by shutting doors. Paul was prohibited from ministering in Asia
and Bithynia (Acts 16:6-7). If you read missionary biographies, it's sur-
prising how some of the most influential ones wanted to go somewhere
other than where they ended up serving (e.g., Carey, Judson). So your
task is to faithfully carry out the work that God gives you day by day, and
to be ready and willing to change directions as the Holy Spirit leads.
Perhaps you're spending too much time trying to plan the next 10 years
of your life and not enough time planning the next 10 days. Don't wait
to live your life. Stop worrying about your "life plan" and simply follow
Jesus right now. Do you need to commend Christ to someone? Is there
a new work that the Spirit is leading you to start? Have you recently
shared coffee or a meal with someone who doesn't know Jesus? They
may not say it out loud, but many are pleading, "Come help us."

Evangelistic Encounters (16:11-34). In verse 12 Paul and his team arrive in Philippi (ca. AD 51). Luke points out that Philippi was "a Roman colony." Richard Melick writes, "Apart from Rome, Philippi was no doubt the most Roman of all the cities Paul visited" (*Philippians,* 24–25). In other words, if you had visited Philippi and were familiar with the mother city, you would have said, "This reminds me of Rome." Hang on to this idea. Finding no synagogue in Philippi, Paul found the closest thing, a women's prayer meeting by a river (v. 13). To some, I imagine this looked like nothing more than a little picnic. Some people may have walked right past them. Paul and his team of Silas (Acts 15:3-41), Timothy (Acts 16:1-5), and Luke (Acts 16:10) approached them humbly. But here, in this quiet, non-spectacular event, the first church on European soil came together! The kingdom of God breaks in like this—small, quiet, lowly—but then expands.

Interestingly, in the next chapter, when this little mission team is in Thessalonica, the people say, "These men . . . have turned the world upside down . . . saying there is another king—Jesus" (Acts 17:6-7). Ordinary and somewhat unimpressive believers were turning the world upside down with a distinct message and a distinct way of life.

We have three different types of evangelistic encounters described. The first meeting is with **Lydia** and some other ladies (Acts 16:11-15). Luke tells us of this very significant individual (v. 14). Apparently, Lydia was a woman of means (a "dealer in purple cloth") who "worshiped God," but that doesn't mean "Christian." She was probably a God-fearer. But when Paul began teaching, God opened her heart and mind to believe the gospel. She and her household (who apparently also believed) were baptized. After this, she showed hospitality by inviting Paul's team to stay with her. God opened her heart; she opened her home. Women played a very important role in the church in Philippi. She started her day as a non-Christian. She went to bed as a follower of Jesus. We should pray every Sunday for this type of thing to happen. Those who arrive like Lydia to the gathering may have their hearts opened to the gospel and go to bed that night as Christians. This is a very encouraging story because we see that when you share the gospel, you aren't on your own. The Spirit of God is at work. Trust in this fact. God opens up hearts. One might think, *These people will never believe!* Really? Paul went into a totally unreached area, preached the Bible, and people were saved.

Next, we read of **a slave girl** (16:16-24). Paul cast out a spirit from this tormented girl, and she was presumably converted. Because she had brought her oppressive owners a profit from fortune telling, her transformation didn't please them. In anger the owners took Paul and Silas before the magistrates and had them flogged and imprisoned. This story reminds us of the spiritual battle that goes on in ministry (2 Cor 10:3-4; Eph 6:12; Jas 4:7; 1 Pet 5:8-9) and the superior power of God. God can change the lives of even the most tormented people (see Mark 5:1-20).

Finally, Luke describes the conversion of the Philippian **jailer** (16:25-34). In a most impressive scene, Paul and Silas begin praying and singing hymns to God while in prison—what a remarkable example for us! Do you praise God in the midst of suffering? How can you? Tertullian said, "The legs feel nothing in the stocks, when the heart is in heaven" (*To the Martyrs*, 2). These men cared more about Jesus than about earthly comforts. This scene powerfully illustrates Paul's command to "rejoice always" (Phil 4:4). He didn't just write about rejoicing always; he did it!

As a result of their praise, God shook the earth and shook the heart of one particular individual. Everyone's bonds were unfastened. Then we read of the jailer. He initially feared for his life because he had failed to do his job (cf. Acts 12:19), but then, after Paul comforted him, the jailer eventually said, "Sirs, what must I do to be saved?" (16:30). Isn't that wonderful? God was at work in his life. The evangelists rightly told him that he didn't have to clean his life up; he needed only to "believe on the Lord Jesus" (cf. John 3:16; Acts 10:43; Rom 1:16; 10:10-11). After Paul and Silas explained things further, this jailer and his family believed and were baptized. Like Lydia, he, too, showed the men hospitality. He brought the evangelists to his house, fed them, and washed their wounds. Chrysostom said that he washed their stripes, and God washed his sins (*Homily on the Acts of the Apostles*, 36.2). That might be the way it happens sometimes. It may take enduring stripes to see people's sins washed away. In Acts 16:35-40 we read how the missionaries got an official release (after some drama!) and were asked to leave the city. But before they did, Luke writes, "After leaving the jail, they came to Lydia's house where they saw and encouraged the brothers, and departed" (v. 40). The church apparently had already grown, and we read that Lydia made her home available as a house church. She used her wealth and her home as a means of building up the church and advancing the gospel.

This is the story of the founding of the church in Philippi: Lydia and her family, along with some other ladies (Euodia and Syntyche?), a slave girl, a jailer and his family, and some new "brothers." When Paul left, he received generous and loyal support from this new church (2 Cor 11:7-9; Phil 4:15-16; see Silva, *Philippians*, 2–4). He also revisited them on his third missionary journey (Acts 20:1-6).

Let's Do the Work of Evangelism and Church Planting

We should be moved by the *evangelistic passion* of this band of missionaries. Paul told Timothy to "do the work of an evangelist" (2 Tim 4:5). Here we see them doing work. You can slowly become so inwardly focused that you stop caring about those who are perishing. You can start complaining about all sorts of things when you lose sight of the mission. But it's amazing how little you will complain about things inside the church when you're reaching out to lost people. Evangelism stirs up your passion for Jesus, produces holiness, and yields hatred for sin. And it's amazing who will say yes to Jesus when you speak the gospel! Let's pray for this passion, and let's pray for God to open up hearts as we do the work of evangelism. Also, pray for God to use you to help *plant churches*. Just as Philippi was a beachhead in Europe, we need new churches in many other parts of the world. We need some people to go and some to support the work, just as the Philippians supported Paul in his efforts elsewhere.

Why plant churches? Here are a few reasons. (1) The Great Commission points to church planting. When Jesus told the disciples to "baptize" and "teach" all nations, these commands pointed to church planting. Baptism is about people identifying not only with Christ but also with the body of Christ. In Acts 2 people are saved and baptized, and the church forms. They are also taught within the context of a church. (2) Paul's ministry methodology was urban church planting. He was the greatest missionary-evangelist. There is no better way to reach the world than by starting new churches. (3) There are many practical reasons to plant churches, such as the fact that new congregations reach more unbelievers, particularly new residents, younger adults, and various social groups. We need to plant more churches just to keep up with the population growth, particularly in cities.

We learn much about church planting from Acts 16. We should *be sobered* by the fact that it may involve suffering—it did for this team. But we should also *be encouraged* by the fact that Paul reached three different types of people, using three different approaches, with the one gospel. We should also *be instructed* by the various methods by which these unbelievers were reached. Consider the following chart adapted from Tim Keller, *Church Planter Manual*:

	Ethnically	Economically	Spiritually	Ministry Approach
Lydia	Asian	Wealthy	God-fearer	Words
Slave girl	Native Greek	Poor?	Spiritual turmoil	Deeds
Jailer	Roman	Blue collar	Practical and indifferent	Example

All ethnicities and classes of people can be saved, and people in all types of spiritual conditions can be saved. Some are really influenced by dialogue, argument, and teaching. Others are moved by deeds of mercy. And some are attracted to Christian example. All of them are saved through responding to the gospel (Rom 10).

Do you know some "Lydias"—people who have moved to your city because of business or vocation? We have a lot of them in our city. Do you know some tormented girls—those who are dealing with hurt, abuse, human slavery, and even demonic power? They need mercy, counsel, and freedom. Do you know some blue-collar dudes? Perhaps God will lead you to minister to them.

As a church, we need to find contexts where we can teach the Bible to outsiders like Lydia. For Paul, that was down by the river. For us, it might be on college campuses or in religious clubs on campuses or at a coffee shop. You might start a small Bible study and invite people to it. My friend Harvey started his church as a result of a Bible study that he launched simply to reach his friends in Reno. It grew to 60 guys quickly, and now he pastors a church of more than 2,000.

As a church, we want to practice deeds of mercy, helping those who are poor and oppressed. We are commanded to practice good deeds, and Peter tells us that it has a tremendous impact on outsiders (1 Pet 2:12). I was in Detroit this week meeting with a church planter who has gained massive respect in a rough neighborhood, serving the community and loving the people around him with hospitality and authenticity. The example of this church has made people ask, "Why are you doing this?"

As a church, we need to witness through our example—in how we suffer, in how we praise, in how we live (1 Pet 3:1-2,16). Do people find something attractive about our lives? Let them see a life that says, "In all of our pleasures, Jesus is better; in all of our sufferings, Christ is enough" (Steve Timmis, "Christ Is Enough").

The Big Picture

About 10 years after Paul established the church at Philippi, he wrote this letter to his partners in the gospel. He thanks them for their exemplary generosity (4:14-19). Before he does that, he makes them aware of his present situation (1:12-26); he explains why he had to send Epaphroditus back so soon (2:25-30); he appeals to them to unite in the gospel (1:27–2:11; 4:2-3); he warns them of the dangers of false teaching (3:2); and in all things, he urges them to persevere with joy in Christ.

Paul writes the letter with a warm, friendly tone. He loves this church. He calls them his "joy and crown" (4:1). But they were facing some adversity. They were experiencing problems stemming from false teachers (see 3:2), and they were also experiencing some disunity from within (see 4:2). As a result, Paul calls them to persevere, to unite around the gospel (see 1:27–2:4), and thereby to retain their joy (he refers to joy around 15 times). These dynamics are important. Our joy and our unity are found in Christ (cf. 2:5-11). When you get the gospel, you get joy. When you focus on the gospel, you get unity. But we must persevere in believing the true gospel, and we must persevere in cultivating harmony in our relationships around the gospel. We aren't told much about the disagreeing ladies in Philippians 4:2-3. They appear to be very faithful Christians. And the issue doesn't seem to be doctrinal. Disunity often appears over nonessential matters. Even the best churches have to work at unity (see Eph 4:3).

Six Challenges

So, what is the message of Philippians? I've already touched on some messages, but let me just mention six points of application from the book as a whole.

First, recognize that gospel advancement will cost us, but Jesus is worth it. This letter exalts the person and work of Jesus. He is the only Savior and Lord, whom we adore and proclaim to the world. He is the source of joy and unity. He is worth living and dying for. Paul speaks of the glorious "day of Christ" coming (1:6,10; 2:16), of being imprisoned for Christ (1:13), of honoring Christ (1:20), of the humility and exaltation of Christ (2:5-11), and of the imputed righteousness of Christ (3:8-9).

May this study make us love Jesus more and fill us with fresh courage to make Him known to the nations.

Second, fight for joy in Christ. The psalmist says, "Serve the LORD with gladness" (Ps 100:2). Paul gives us a picture of what joyful service to Jesus looks like, and he mentions it with some joy-related words about 20 times. This is "crazy joy" because it doesn't derive from pleasurable circumstances. It comes from Christ and is experienced even (or especially) in suffering. But it doesn't come naturally; we must pray for joy and fight for joy. We must fight against overvaluing things in this life and remember that Jesus is our greatest treasure and highest good. Beneath all of our sins is a lack of joy in Christ. We live out of the overflow of our hearts, and we must find our greatest pleasure in knowing Christ. I must admit some mornings are difficult. Do you agree? When I (Francis) was a child, my aunt [with broken English] used to ask me all the time, "*Why you never happy?*" I also remember once when my dad was cooking a fish—and we cooked the whole fish—I commented that the fish looked very sad. My dad said [with broken English], "That's how you always rook." He was right. I wasn't a very happy kid. Maybe you can identify. Joy is not always greatly present in our lives, but I want you to see your need for Spirit-produced joy, and to see how a joyful attitude glorifies God.

Let me illustrate how joy honors God. Imagine me (Tony) telling my wife this Valentine's Day that I want to take her to a nice restaurant and to watch *Les Misérables,* the musical. She might say, "That's sweet. Why do you want to do this, Tony?" The wrong answer would be, "Because I have to. It's Valentine's Day. Everyone else does stuff like this. I guess I have to also." Does that honor her? No. The right answer is, "Nothing gives me greater joy than serving you." That honors her. The other attitude doesn't.

We don't *have to* serve Jesus; we *get to* serve Him. Your motives and attitude matter to Him. You can dishonor Jesus by not serving Him with joy. Such joy flows from our union with Christ, for it is a fruit of the Spirit. You need to know Jesus to find joy, and as a Christian, you need to commune with Christ for fresh joy. This doesn't mean that you are silly or that you never grieve—not at all. It means that there's a profound contentment and satisfaction in Jesus that's authentic and compelling to others. It means that in your grief and hard times, you can truly say, "The joy of the LORD is my strength" (see Neh 8:10).

Third, maintain the unity of the Spirit. Paul addresses unity in several letters, including this one. It was important to him, and it must be important to us. Avoid disunity created by arguing over nonessentials and spreading rumors about others. Pursue unity by focusing on the gospel and forgiving and reconciling with others. The church in Philippi was a great church, yet they needed to seek unity. Even the best churches have to defend against gossip, forgive, and reconcile.

Fourth, become a "Macedonian giver." Paul thanks the Philippians for their generous, loyal, God-honoring support. In 2 Corinthians 8–9 Paul remarks on the exemplary generosity of "the churches of Macedonia" (Philippi, Berea, and Thessalonica). He writes,

> *We want you to know, brothers, about the grace of God granted to the churches of Macedonia: During a severe testing by affliction, their abundance of joy and their deep poverty overflowed into the wealth of their generosity. I testify that, on their own, according to their ability and beyond their ability, they begged us insistently for the privilege of sharing in the ministry to the saints, and not just as we had hoped. Instead, they gave themselves especially to the Lord, then to us by God's will. So we urged Titus that just as he had begun, so he should also complete this grace to you. Now as you excel in everything—faith, speech, knowledge, and in all diligence, and in your love for us—excel also in this grace. I am not saying this as a command. Rather, by means of the diligence of others, I am testing the genuineness of your love. For you know the grace of our Lord Jesus Christ: Though He was rich, for your sake He became poor, so that by His poverty you might become rich.* (2 Cor 8:1-9)

These churches weren't wealthy (though there were some exceptions), but they were sacrificial, generous, cheerful, and loyal. What moved them? They treasured Jesus above all (2 Cor 8:5,9). Here in Philippians, Paul says they gave as an expression of love and as an act of worship (Phil 4:19). They were loyal to Paul and the mission, and they were devoted to Jesus.

Fifth, let's learn what gospel partnership looks like. We will take a closer look at this later, but for now be ready to learn what it means to be coworkers in the mission.

Sixth, as a church, let's give the world a picture of the coming kingdom of God. Just as people looked at Philippi and said, "This looks like Rome," one should look at the church and say, "This looks like the coming kingdom of God." We should long to be able to say, "You want to know what the kingdom of God is like? Then look at the church." The church in

Philippi may not have looked spectacular, but Paul tells them they are an embassy of the kingdom, an outpost of the kingdom (see 1:27; 3:20).

In the coming kingdom many of the poor will reign with Christ. So the poor should be present and should often be leaders in the church. It shouldn't be a strange thing for a godly hotel maid to mentor a new Christian lady who is a CEO. In the coming kingdom there will be no class or color distinctions. Likewise, there should be none in the church. In the coming kingdom we will eat together with people from east and west. Therefore, the church should reflect kingdom hospitality. In the coming kingdom righteousness and justice will dwell. So, the church should be a community of justice. In the coming kingdom we will sing praise to the King. And so now, let the church exalt the Messiah. This church in Philippi was showing Rome what a better kingdom looked like; let's show our city and our world what a better kingdom looks like. We do this by submitting our lives to the kingship of Jesus, following His Word.

The Beautiful Greeting
PHILIPPIANS 1:1-2

Finally, consider Paul's opening words to the Philippian church in the first two verses. This is a beautiful greeting because it sounds the theme of grace. All of these things that we've been talking about are works of God's grace—joy, unity, partnership, conversions, new churches, generosity, and such. By God's grace we become Christians, servants of Jesus, and it's by God's grace that we live out the Christian life. The phrases "of Christ," "in Christ," and "from God" all highlight God's work in uniting us to Jesus. Notice three evidences of grace in this little greeting.

First, grace is displayed in the life of the senders of the letter: Paul and Timothy (1:1a). Paul had been a Jew who hated Christians. But then he met Jesus. Did he deserve this? No. It was grace. He explains his glorious conversion in Philippians 3:1-11. He explains how he was a very religious person, but he couldn't earn righteousness. Righteousness was given to him only by faith in Christ. It was a gift. Consequently, he was transformed. What about Timothy? His mother was Jewish, and his father was a Greek. He became a Christian by God's grace also. He heard the gospel and believed. Elsewhere Paul says that Timothy's faith was "sincere" (2 Tim 1:5). In chapter 2 Paul speaks joyfully of Timothy. He had been transformed by grace. These two men were now "slaves of Christ Jesus." There's humility here. They don't go on and on about their title. They are slaves or servants of Jesus.

What about you? What's your story? Are you a Christian? Do you think Christianity is about being religious? It's not. It's about Christ. It's about trusting that Jesus Christ has lived the life we couldn't live and then died the death we should have died. It's about embracing Jesus as your Savior, Lord, and Treasure. You can do that now. Lydia heard and believed. Timothy heard and believed. Will you believe?

Second, grace is displayed in the receivers of the letter: the Philippians (1:1b). Paul calls them "saints." How did they become saints? Was it by performing religious rituals? No! It wasn't because of their behavior. They became saints when they changed positions. They were once in Adam, but through faith in the gospel message they became "in Christ" new creations. Are you in Christ? That's different from being in a church building. You may be in a worship service but not in Christ. If you're in Christ, then you have every spiritual blessing. If not, then you're in Adam (1 Cor 15:22).

Further, some of the Philippian Christians even became "overseers and deacons." What about that? Remember how the church got started? A businesswoman, a slave girl, a jailer, and some other converts. And now, some of them are Christian leaders. Isn't that remarkable?

Sometimes when I (Tony) am on a plane or out on the town I eventually get asked, "So what do you do?" I like to play with inquirers and so I say, "Guess." They guess everything imaginable. But when I tell them I'm a pastor, their jaws drop. Apparently, I don't look like a pastor. I then proceed to tell them, "Oh, believe me, I'm far more surprised than you are!" I'm sure some of these Philippians were exceedingly surprised that they were called overseers and deacons. The mention of these church leaders in a greeting is unusual for Paul. Perhaps he makes a distinction among them either because of the need for them to assert their leadership in handling the disunity or because the disagreement was over leadership (or the lack of it?). What's important to note is that Paul mentions these two offices: overseers—who shepherd the flock by knowing, feeding, leading through the Word and prayer; and deacons—who not only serve but also help others serve well.

Finally, grace is displayed in this Trinitarian blessing (1:2). Paul reminds us of the fountain of grace and peace! Where do grace and peace come from? They come from our triune God. Paul mentions the Father and the Son, the Lord Jesus, but we know that such grace and peace come through the Holy Spirit's work in our hearts. Peter calls God "the God of all grace" (1 Pet 5:10), and rightly so. We have received grace from the Father, grace from the Son, and grace from the Spirit. Consequently, we have peace. We have rest. We have blessing. Out of this position, and out of this blessing, we are called to live a mission-oriented life of holiness. By grace, we are servants of Jesus and God's saints. Bless His holy name!

Let's finish with this phrase: "the Lord Jesus Christ" (Phil 1:2). In the first century one could be killed for saying Jesus, not Caesar, is Lord. Yet that's what Christians did. How was it that these ordinary people turned the world upside down? Luke writes that they were "saying that there is another king—Jesus!" (Acts 17:7). Is Jesus your King? Paul goes on to say that you will either bow the knee to Jesus now or do so later, when it's too late (Phil 2:5-11). Scripture implores you: bow to the King now.

Reflect and Discuss

1. Go back and read Acts 16:6-40. What do you find most encouraging in that chapter? What do you find most challenging?
2. Why should we plant churches? What can we learn about church planting from Acts 16?
3. Do you find it difficult to share the gospel with people? What encouragement can you find in Acts 16 regarding personal evangelism?
4. What are some common themes in Philippians? Which theme strikes you as being especially relevant for your life?
5. How would your church benefit from a study on Philippians?
6. Paul uses military language throughout Philippians. What sort of application should this have for us?
7. Philippians talks a lot about joy. Compare the joy Paul talks about to common references to joy in our culture.
8. What are some of the differences between a "partner in the gospel" and a casual attender on Sunday?
9. Take a moment to identify some verses or a passage that you want to memorize from the book of Philippians. Stop and meditate on this passage, and then write it out.
10. What do you find encouraging about Paul's greeting (1:1-2)? Stop and pray for the Lord to open up your heart and your eyes to behold wonderful things from this study.

The Happiest Man in Rome

PHILIPPIANS 1:3-8

Main Idea: Paul fills his opening words to his beloved partners in the gospel with expressions of thanksgiving, joy, and affection.

Finding Joy in Christ and Community

I. **Know the Joy of Prayer (1:3-4).**
   A. Gratitude despite internal conflict
   B. Great memories despite hardship
   C. Joy despite imprisonment
II. **Know the Joy of Partnership (1:5).**
   A. *Koinonia*
   B. Friendship
   C. Mission
   D. Cultivate gospel partnerships.
III. **Know the Joy of Anticipation (1:6).**
   A. Divine grace
   B. Human evidence
IV. **Know the Joy of Affection (1:7-8).**
   A. Heart-felt affection
   B. Appropriate affection
   C. Christ's affection

Popular comedian Jim Gaffigan, known for his bacon and Hot Pockets® jokes, wrote a book called *Dad Is Fat*. In it, he talks about a countercultural lifestyle: having lots of kids (he and his wife have five). Gaffigan says some onlookers have asked, "Don't you know what's causing that?" Others see him as some sort of alien, watching as his large family boards the subway in New York. He's even had people liken kids to pets: "Oh, you just had a baby? Yeah, we just got a puppy." Though *Dad Is Fat* is not a handbook on Christian parenting (though I found it encouraging!), it did remind me of how unusual Christians are in highlighting the value and glory of children. Many today devalue children. They see them as strange little distractions from their careers.

Christians not only have a countercultural view of children, but we also have a countercultural view of *joy*. We aren't against pleasure and satisfaction. We simply have a source other than sex, money, power, career advancement, and entertainment. What do you think will give you joy? The quest for it is built into the fabric of the United States: "life, liberty, and the pursuit of happiness." Yet many could take as their anthem "I still haven't found what I'm looking for." People look everywhere, and once they find something, they often end up saying like Solomon, "Vanity." Others commit suicide when they realize their functional god won't satisfy or when it gets taken away—as we've seen in recent years with the collapse of the economy. Dissatisfaction isn't new, though. According to the ancient historian Plutarch, Alexander the Great wept in his tent saying, "There are no more worlds to conquer." A modern example was seen in the honest confession of Tom Brady, who after three NFL championships, remarked, "Is this all there is?" Can you find joy? The answer is yes. St. Cyprian wrote to his friend Donatus in the third century:

> This seems a cheerful world, Donatus, when I view it from this
> fair garden under the shadow of these vines. But if I climbed
> some great mountain and looked out over the wide lands, you
> know very well what I would see; thieves on the high road, pirates
> on the seas, in the amphitheaters men murdered to please
> the applauding crowds, under all roofs misery and selfishness.
> It really is a bad world, Donatus, an incredibly bad world. Yet,
> in the midst of it, I have found a quiet and holy people. They
> have discovered a joy which is a thousand times better than any
> pleasure of this sinful life. They are despised and persecuted, but
> they care not. . . . These people, Donatus, are the Christians, and
> I am one of them. (Christensen, *Heroes and Saints*, 18)

Are you one of them? Consider the apostle Paul sitting in a prison. The happiest man in Rome was in jail! How could this be? Ancient Rome was a consumerist wonderland filled with games, sexual pleasures, lavish parties, theatre, and more; yet Paul had a joy a thousand times better. He writes a prayer of thanksgiving "with joy" (v. 4). This is the first mention of joy in Philippians, but it resounds through this section and throughout the book. Often in Paul's opening prayers he expresses key topics to follow, as well as setting the particular *tone* of the letter. This prayer is no different. Here's an overview of this idea of joy and the tone of the letter (*ESV Study Bible*, 2,280):

Reference	Paul . . .
1:4	prays with joy
1:18	rejoices that Christ is proclaimed
1:25	will remain living on earth, for the Philippians' joy in the faith
2:2	asks the Philippians to complete his joy
2:17-18	is glad and rejoices with the Philippians
2:28	sends Epaphroditus, that the Philippians might rejoice
2:29	tells the Philippians to receive Epaphroditus with joy
3:1	tells the Philippians to rejoice in the Lord
4:1	tells the Philippians they are his joy
4:4	tells the Philippians twice to rejoice in the Lord
4:10	rejoiced in the Lord at the Philippians' concern for him

That's a lot of joy! How could the happiest man in Rome be in jail? Joy is found in Christ, not in a trouble-free life or in a life filled with stuff.

I know the acronym is cheesy, but it's helpful. The secret to joy is in keeping things in this order: "**J**esus, **O**thers, **Y**ourself." As you scan through the letter to the Philippians, you see that Paul is all about *Jesus*, and his mind is filled with concern for *others*, namely, the Philippian believers. When contemplating the glory of death, he says, "I will remain and continue with all of you *for your progress and joy* in the faith" (1:25; emphasis added). Paul doesn't pretend he has no real needs, but the glory of Jesus and the needs of others occupy his heart and mind. He lives out his later exhortation: "Consider others as more important than yourselves" (2:3). Because this was the pattern of Paul's life, he was truly happy, even though he was shackled to a Roman guard! No Jesus? No joy. No relationship with gospel partners? You'll lack joy. Always focused on self—your stuff, your problems, and your calendar? You'll lack joy. Even Christian servants often misplace their cause for joy. They can turn inward too. When Jesus sent out the 70 missionaries, they came back "with joy" saying, "Lord, even the demons submit to us" (Luke 10:17). But Jesus rebuked them. He said, "Don't rejoice that the spirits submit to you, but rejoice that your names are written in heaven" (10:20). Don't derive your joy from your performance, your popularity, your gifting, or your accolades; rejoice in the fact that you have a relationship with God through Christ. Focus on Jesus and others, and you'll maintain joy.

In Philippians 1:3-8 Paul displays his vibrant communion with Christ and his personal love for the Philippian community, which results in his alien-like joy. Though Paul doesn't mention "joy" in each of the following verses, his tone is joyful. The phrase in verse 4, "with joy," strikes the chord that runs through the passage. Paul is brimming with joy in thankfulness to God and with love for the Philippians. To know the joy that Paul possessed, we, too, need to know the joy of (1) prayer, (2) partnership, (3) anticipation, and (4) affection. Let's learn from Paul here.

Finding Joy in Christ and Community

Paul's thanksgiving in verses 3-8 bears some similarities to his thanksgiving in other epistles, but there are differences. It's important to note that Paul didn't pray the same generic prayers for every church; nor did he pray in the same way. As you read through his epistles, you find specific thanksgivings and requests for each group of people. This prayer appropriately reflects Paul's special bond with the Philippians.

Know the Joy of Prayer
PHILIPPIANS 1:3-4

The opening verses are remarkable, especially when you consider the context of the book. As Paul prays for the Philippians, he is thankful, and his mind is filled with blessed memories. This leads him to joyful intercession. In prayer we can commune with God anywhere at any time. We can pray for our friends and colleagues. And in prayer we gain fresh perspective and strength.

Gratitude despite Internal Conflict

He begins his prayer, "I give *thanks to my God* for every remembrance of *you*" (1:3; emphasis added). Even though the church was not perfect, Paul was still grateful for them—*all* of them! Look at the phrase "all of you" in verses 4, 7, and 8. Based on chapter 4, some individuals needed a pastoral rebuke, yet overall Paul was grateful. The conflict didn't crush gratitude.

Do you give thanks to God in prayer for others? Kent Hughes says, "Paul rarely thanked God for things. Paul thanked God for people, who, despite whatever trouble they may have been to him, remained a source of joy and thanksgiving" (*Philippians*, 24). Paul even wrote a word of thanksgiving for the crazy Corinthians (1 Cor 1:4)! That's impressive. That's instructive. That's hopeful. If you're a super-critical person, always focusing on what's wrong, then you won't be a grateful person. Don't look for perfection before you show gratitude; look for evidences of grace in people's lives. Be quick to thank God for Christian virtues in others, and remember that sanctification is a slow process.

Do you allow conflict to crush your joy? Don't misunderstand: Paul doesn't overlook the conflict; he addresses it. He doesn't say he enjoys conflict. He simply is able to rejoice in the Lord despite the conflict. This again shows us that we had better have a well of joy that is much more satisfying and sustaining than a fountain filled with comfortable circumstances to stimulate joy. You must go to the gospel for this kind of joy.

Have you expressed thanks to God lately? Or do you think when blessings come that it's "God's job"—that He owes you? If you're an entitled person, you won't be a grateful person. May God help us to see that we deserve nothing but judgment, and every good gift we have comes from Him. And may we not take people for granted either. May we be quick to give thanks for people. One sure sign that you're growing in grace is that you're becoming a more thankful person.

Are you an interceding individual? The context for Paul's gratitude is in prayer for the Philippians. Many problems in the church would disappear if we genuinely prayed for one another. Let us learn to pray from Paul here—in joyful thanksgiving and faithful intercession.

Great Memories despite Hardship

Scholars point out that you could translate this opening phrase as "upon all your remembrance of me" (A. T. Robertson, *Joy in Christ*, 56; also Witherington, *Friendship and Finances*, 38). Both are certainly true. Paul remembers them prayerfully, and the Philippians constantly cared for him practically. In a fallen world we will have trouble, and surely some of Paul's memories were not good (e.g., the conduct of the magistrates and the populace toward him in Acts 16); but overall, Paul could be thankful. As he thought about the big picture, he gave thanks. Don't allow a few stumbles and struggles to rob you of gratitude and joy. Take a view of the big picture and learn to give thanks to God. Recognize that Jesus has already taken care of your greatest problem through His cross and resurrection. Realize that there's no condemnation for those who are in Christ. As you reflect on where God has brought you in His loving faithfulness and how He has reached down and rescued you, does it cause you to give thanks, and does it fill your heart with joy? As you think about people who have impacted you and the community of faith that surrounds you, does it cause you to give joyful thanks? That was the attitude of the greatest missionary in history.

Joy despite Imprisonment

Remarkably, Paul is filled with joy while in prison. Do you find this challenging? I do. Do you think you need something other than Jesus to find real joy? Better-behaved kids? A better job? A different address? More vacation time? In America we often think "bigger" is the answer—bigger house, bigger muscles, bigger church, etc.—but what we really need is a bigger vision of God. Nothing else is an ultimate source of joy. You can have all of those and never know this joy. If you have everything but Jesus, you will be longing for more. If you have nothing but Jesus, you have everything you need for joy. Look at the decadence and the excess of modern culture. None of it provides what people desire. On the flip side, consider what Paul says in 2 Corinthians 6, especially verse 10:

> But as God's ministers, we commend ourselves in everything: by great
> endurance, by afflictions, by hardship, by difficulties, by beatings,
> by imprisonments, by riots, by labors, by sleepless nights, by times
> of hunger, by purity, by knowledge, by patience, by kindness, by the
> Holy Spirit, by sincere love, by the message of truth, by the power
> of God; through weapons of righteousness on the right hand and
> the left, through glory and dishonor, through slander and good report;
> as deceivers yet true; as unknown yet recognized; as dying and look—
> we live; as being disciplined yet not killed; as grieving yet always
> rejoicing; as poor yet enriching many; as having nothing yet possessing
> everything. (2 Cor 6:4-10)

You can grieve and still rejoice. And you can have nothing but possess everything—if you have Jesus.

In Psalms 42 and 43 we find the psalmist wrestling through a period of despondency. Yet he begins to preach to himself, saying to his soul, "Hope in God!" He reminds himself of the goodness and grace of God to inspire hope and joy. That's what we have to do as well. You need to preach this gospel to yourself "instead of listening to yourself" (Lloyd-Jones, *Spiritual Depression*, 20–21). Stop listening to what your culture says you need. Dwell in God's Word daily, don't neglect meeting with the saints regularly, and sing songs of praise constantly—all in a spirit of prayer. Know the joy of prayer.

Know the Joy of Partnership
PHILIPPIANS 1:5

In verse 5 another distinctive in this thanksgiving stands out: gospel partnership. Paul provides one of the reasons for his grateful joy. This church had supported Paul and served as coworkers in the mission from the beginning. As a result, he was filled with joyful thanksgiving.

Koinonia

What does "gospel partnership" mean? To answer this, we need to consider the word *partnership*, from the Greek *koinonia*, a word that appears throughout Philippians (see 1:5,7; 2:1; 3:10; 4:14,15). We often translate it as "fellowship." It connotes a variety of relationships "involving mutual interests and sharing" (Hanson, *Letter*, 48). Hanson notes that marriage and family relationships, friendships, business partnerships, and common ownership of property were some of the examples of *koinonia* (ibid.). D. A. Carson states that in the first century if "Harry and John" bought a boat to start a fishing business, they entered into a "fellowship" (*Basics*, 16). He adds, "The heart of true fellowship is self-sacrificing conformity to shared vision" (ibid.). In Philippians *koinonia* refers to *gospel-centered friendship* (look at the affection words in verses 7-8) as well as a shared *mission* of *gospel proclamation* (e.g., 1:7,12). We do well to dwell on these two aspects of gospel partnership: *friendship* and *mission*.

Friendship

Christ established their friendship (3:10). They were bound together by the Spirit (2:1). Even though they may have been from different places (Rome, Greece, Asia), they could be brothers and sisters because of these spiritual realities. Unbelievers can have friendships. These friendships are the result of God's common grace to humanity. And you should have friendships with unbelievers, just as Jesus did. But spiritual friendships, gospel partnerships, are different. C. S. Lewis said friendships are discovered when you say, "What, you too?! I thought I was the only one" (*Four Loves*, 248). They're based on commonality. Gospel friendships are much deeper because there is a "You too?!" that's radically deeper.

We share in a common Savior, are united by the same Spirit, and are headed for glory together.

Gospel partnerships are also deeper and more abiding because not only do they have a deeper *commonality*, but they also have a means by which to deal with *conflict*: the gospel. When a couple gets married, two sinners become one! When a bunch of sinners come together, redeemed though they are, and form a church, then there will be trouble—just look at Philippi. But from the gospel we learn about sin, repentance, reconciliation, forgiveness, and service. We learn what is necessary to maintain relationships. When Paul calls the Philippians to unite in chapter 4, he mentions gospel concepts: "agree *in the Lord*," "true partner," "contended *for the gospel* at my side," "coworkers," "names are in *the book of life*" (vv. 2-3; emphasis added). These are gospel applications that maintain relationships. We are made for relationships. No dying person ever says, "Hey, bring me my diploma. I'm dying. And bring me my trophies from third grade too." Instead, he wants *people* at his bedside. Paul would have wanted the Philippians at his bedside because they were more than friends; they were gospel partners.

At least four obstacles will keep you from having such enjoyable and edifying relationships as a Christian: sensationalism, mysticism, idealism, and individualism. *Sensationalists* don't find Christian community scintillating enough to participate in it. However, the Christian life isn't about shock and awe, but lowly acts of service and love (Phil 2:3-4), which are extraordinarily significant. *Mystics* make the Christian life into a series of quiet times. They desire to live a "me and Jesus" kind of Christianity without the church. But Christianity is "we and Jesus," not just "me and Jesus." *Idealists* struggle in Christian community because they have, in the words of Bonhoeffer, a "wish dream" of what the church ought to be, and it never lives up to their expectations (*Life Together*, 27). *Individualists* fall prey to culture that only enjoys community online. Privatization coupled with this technological video-game culture kills people's ability to relate to others. We have a culture of "busy loneliness": people do a lot of stuff, but they remain extremely lonesome. It doesn't have to be this way. Get a new vision. You need gospel partners, those united together in Christ by the Spirit, from every tribe and tongue, who live on the gospel—friends that will fall and fail but who need the same grace and mercy of Jesus that you need. But you need more than friendships; you also need coworkers on mission with you.

Mission

Regarding their shared *mission* of gospel proclamation, Paul calls the Philippians to suffer for the gospel (1:27-30), and he goes on to commend them for "sharing" (*koinonia*) in his troubles for the sake of the gospel (4:14-15). You know what Paul is talking about if you've ever worked a job with other people. If you work in a good restaurant with others, a bond is created. You have a different relationship with coworkers than with customers. Paul saw the Philippians as coworkers who brought him great joy. Sadly, many see the church as an audience of customers to please rather than a group of coworkers who spread the gospel all week and then gather together to encourage one another.

Our concept of *fellowship* today is often watered down to mean little more than "hanging out." If you have coffee with a non-Christian, then you're just having coffee, but if you have coffee with a believer, we often call it fellowship (Bonhoeffer, *Life Together*, 27). While socializing is part of fellowship, there's much more to it. We share in the common mission of making the gospel known to the world. Through Christ, we are friends *and* coworkers with other believers. It's one thing to have gospel-centered friendships, but it's another to have coworkers on mission. If you get both, friendships and co-laborers, then you can enjoy what many never experience.

In his book *The Fellowship of the Ring*, J. R. R. Tolkien writes a thrilling story to illustrate this idea of gospel partnership. The fellowship is made up of radical diversity—little, resilient, pipe-smoking hobbits with big, hairy feet from the green Shire; a few warrior men; a wizard; an elf with amazing archery skills; and an out-from-under-the-mountains dwarf with an axe. Together they share a common mission of defeating the forces of darkness and saving Middle-earth. They were willing to die for one another and for the mission.

Paul says that in the fellowship of the gospel, we recognize our differences, but we celebrate our unity in Jesus and commit to give ourselves for the mission of making the gospel known. If you have partners in the gospel, you should celebrate! If you don't and you are a Christian, then you should cultivate these relationships.

Cultivate Gospel Partnerships

How might we enjoy such friendships? *We must put the gospel first.* Notice how many times "gospel" or "proclaim" appears in chapter 1. Because they loved the gospel, they were co-laboring, loyal friends. When you're together around the table, at a ball game, or doing a project, talk about Jesus. Talk about your time in the Word, about your prayer concerns, about who you are sharing the gospel with, and about how you can bear one another's burdens for the sake of gospel ministry. Center everything on Jesus.

The outworking of this Christ-centered unity between Paul and the Philippians manifested in at least three ways. First, they provided financial aid and personal care. Ben Witherington, renowned New Testament scholar, has a commentary on Philippians titled *Friendship and Finances in Philippi*. Financial aid was a major aspect of their partnership. Second, their partnership involved suffering alongside one another and encouraging one another. Third, their partnership involved praying for one another (cf. 1:19). These are good tests for whether or not you have gospel partners—generosity, suffering alongside and encouraging, and praying for one another.

What gives Paul joyful thanks? People—his friends and co-laborers in the mission. Christian joy comes from Christ and in community. If you don't have deep joy, then you might not know Jesus; or maybe you haven't cultivated such relationships or participated in the mission as you should.

Know the Joy of Anticipation
PHILIPPIANS 1:6

Paul gives a further but closely related reason for his joyful gratitude: confidence in God's nature and purposes. He writes wonderfully comforting words about God's unstoppable work of grace in believers' lives. The apostle is sure that God will continue and complete what He started in the Philippian believers. He bases this on his knowledge of God—God's saving grace—and his knowledge of the Philippians' faith. While many apply this verse to individual salvation, we should remember that Paul has been speaking of the *koinonia*, that is, the work of God to form *a people* for Himself. It seems best to apply this text to both dimensions, the personal and corporate aspects of God's saving grace. Both are gloriously true.

Divine Grace

Believers should rejoice in the fact that God will have a people that give honor and glory to Jesus. Paul tells the Thessalonians that Christ is coming "to be glorified by His saints and to be admired by all those who have believed" (2 Thess 1:10). "That day" is coming. And that day should give us joy this day. We learn here that salvation from beginning to end is *God's work*. God sovereignly *inaugurates* this work in us, opening up our hearts like He did for Lydia (Acts 16:14). We receive this salvation by faith alone, apart from works (Phil 3:9), as illustrated by the Philippian jailer (Acts 16:31). God sovereignly *continues* this work in us, as He was doing for the Philippians (cf. Phil 2:12-13). And God *will complete* this work in us "until the day of Christ Jesus" (1:6).

God started the work, continues the work, and will complete the work. Sometimes when students fail to turn in their assignments before the term ends, they receive an "incomplete." Perhaps you've had some incompletes. If not in school, what about incomplete projects around the house? I've started many things that I never finished! But God never receives an "incomplete." God always finishes what He starts. The psalmist says, "You guide me with Your counsel, and afterward You will take me up in glory" (Ps 73:24). Is there any better news than this? God will take us to glory if we're in Christ! It's a sure thing. You may not be sure of a lot of things in this life, but you can be sure of this if you're a Christian. We can be sure of it because this is God's Word, and this is God's work of salvation.

Not only is salvation God's work, but Paul also refers to it as "a good work." The work that God begins and completes is good because salvation flows from the very goodness of God. When you think about your salvation and how God has saved others whom you know, you should say, "This is God's work. And this is good work." Kent Hughes reflects on God's goodness in keeping us:

> As I reflect on my fifty plus years in Christ it is indeed God who has kept me. It is not my grip on God that has made the difference, but his grip on me. I am not confident in my goodness. I am not confident in my character. I am not confident in my history. I am not confident in my "reverend" persona. I am not confident in my perseverance. But I am confident in God. (*Philippians*, 28)

You can be confident too. This promise is for every Christian. No wonder Paul's heart is brimming with joy and praise!

A few years ago I (Tony) was teaching in Ukraine. Due to a volcano in Iceland, flights were grounded. This bizarre event hindered thousands of people from going to their destination. Every day I would call the airline to see if I could go home, only to be denied, leaving me with groanings too deep for words! Finally, about a week after my original departure time, I was able to get my boarding pass, but I would face some drama before getting home. Once I arrived at the airport in Kiev, the agent told me that I wasn't on the passenger list. After a period of discussion, I got on the plane. Then, in Amsterdam, I had to wait in line for three hours to get a boarding pass. People were storming off furiously after being told that the flights were full. So, when I got to the agent and he gave me my seat, needless to say, I was celebrating. I got on the plane, sat down, breathed, and worshiped.

Believers are going home one day. If you're in Christ, your destination is certain. You have something even more secure than a boarding pass to assure you; you have the promises of God and the Spirit dwelling inside of you. The waiting may be grueling, but soon it will be over. And we will worship.

Human Evidence

We must notice something else as it relates to assurance, namely, the "human evidence of assurance" (Motyer, *Message*, 45–46). Paul knew not only the nature of God who provides salvation, but he also knew that the believers' lives demonstrated that they belonged to Jesus. If we just peek into the next verse, or consider the whole letter, we see that Paul commends the Philippians for their faithfulness. Moisés Silva says,

> God is the only grounds of our confidence, but the apostle claims no insight into the eternal counsel. His assurance that the Philippians will persevere to the end arises from the external, visible evidence that their lives provided. (*Philippians*, 6)

In other words, when God works salvation into the lives of people, they bear fruit. They demonstrate a life of faithfulness. Paul could say, "It is right for me to think this way about all of you" (1:7), for there were observable qualities to their faith. Paul speaks of their partnership in the gospel (vv. 5,7) and of their support in the "defense and establishment of the gospel" (v. 7). He goes on to commend them for many other qualities. All of these fruits were evidences of God's amazing grace in their lives. John wrote, "I have no greater joy than this: to hear that my children are walking in the truth" (3 John 4). Paul, too, shared this joy of hearing that the Philippians were living out their faith.

Further, Paul later exhorts them to "work out your own salvation with fear and trembling" (2:12). Assurance of salvation is not an excuse for laziness. It should lead us to persevere, and we can do so with hope because God graciously provides the desire and power for endurance. The doctrine of assurance of salvation, then, should make us *happy* and *humble* people. We should praise God with great joy for His work of salvation in our own lives. And when we see believers giving evidence of God's grace, we should glorify God for His work in them. We should be humbled because we've done nothing to deserve such a great salvation. God alone receives the glory. He started it, continues it, and will complete it. Humility should also be expressed as we grow in the knowledge and grace of God—as we kill sin, stand in awe of God, set our minds on things above, live in biblical community, and dwell on God's Word.

So what are you anticipating? Does something other than the "day of Christ Jesus" fill your heart with better, more sustaining joy? An upcoming game? An upcoming vacation? Live with the anticipation of either dying, which is "gain" (1:21), or the return of Christ and the coming new heavens and new earth. Fill your mind with what's ahead!

Know the Joy of Affection
PHILIPPIANS 1:7-8

Paul digresses for a bit, and this digression highlights a fourth distinctive in this thanksgiving: his affection. He picks up his prayer again in verses 9-11. The material in verses 7-8 conveys Paul's emotion and intensity that he touched on in verse 5. From these verses, we see that the apostle Paul was neither an isolated saint nor merely an intellectual giant. Paul loved people deeply. Some academics may be embarrassed by such a display of emotion or dismiss it as mere exaggeration. But Paul says, "God is my witness"—he truly feels deep emotion and affection. We need not only to learn the theology and disciplines of the apostle but also to accept the importance of having deep affection for God and others. Paul's faith didn't have the appearance of a stuffy classroom or an empty ritual; there was passion.

Heart-Felt Affection (1:7)

Paul says that he holds the Philippians in his heart. A. T. Roberston notes that the text can be translated, "because you hold me in your heart" (*Joy in Christ*, 64). Both are surely true. A heart relationship exists between Paul and these believers. But the preferred translation is that Paul holds them in his heart; he delights in his friends at Philippi. This affection shouldn't be taken as mere sentimentalism. Hanson points out a similar expression, where Paul tells the Corinthians, "I have already said that you are in our hearts, to live together and to die together" (2 Cor 7:3). In Philippians 2 Paul says that he has poured out his life for the Philippians (v. 17). Paul and the Philippians model for us what it means to have Christian friendships centered on the gospel. It involves a willingness to sacrifice.

Appropriate Affection (1:7)

Paul moves from affection to appropriateness in saying that it is "right" to feel this way. Why was it right? It was right because they were "partners with [him] in grace, both in [his] imprisonment and in the defense and establishment [or confirmation] of the gospel." Paul uses the same word in verse 7 that he used in verse 5: "partners." As mentioned, being a partner in grace meant more than just saving grace; Paul has in mind sharing in the struggle for making the gospel known (see v. 29).

The Philippians displayed their partnership in loyalty to Paul and the mission. In his imprisonment they had supported him in prayer and with financial support. They didn't turn their backs on him. They weren't ashamed of him—imprisonment would have brought great shame in that time—rather, they supported him as he shared the gospel with the captors and judges over him. As Paul shared in these contexts, through his suffering, the power of the gospel was put on display, confirmed. The Philippians' loyalty to him in prison made this relationship especially sweet.

Christ's Affection (1:8)

As Paul thinks on his relationship with the Philippians, he makes a remarkable statement, saying that he longs for them with the "affection of Christ Jesus." He reminds them of Christ's affection for them and how God is at work in him to love them that way. The Greek word translated "affection" refers to the inward parts of the body; they served as referents for emotions of love and deep compassion. Paul is united to Christ, and he shares Christ's love for the church. It's a deep love that goes beyond sentiment. Once again, we need to think about our gospel partnership. Realize the love Christ has for you and the church, and resolve to share in this love. Express affection for gospel partners, and receive affection from gospel partners. Such affection leads to joy.

Conclusion

Paul's thanksgiving emphasizes joy, gospel partnerships, assurance, and affection. His skin is chafed from being chained to a Roman guard, but his heart is filled with thanksgiving because of these things. He's the happiest man in Rome, and he doesn't have a posh life. If you could bottle up Paul's joy, you could sell it to the world. Yet it's available for free.

What will rob you of this type of joy? If you are Christ-less, you won't find joy. If you are prayer-less and ungrateful, you won't find joy. If you don't have gospel partnerships, you won't find joy. If you don't have assurance of salvation, you won't have joy. If you don't have affectionate relationships, you won't have joy. So, let us look to Jesus, who went to the cross for us, bearing our sin and punishment, so that we may be reconciled to God and enjoy Him forever.

Reflect and Discuss

1. Where do people look to find joy? How is this different from Paul's view of joy?
2. How can prayer lead us to joy?
3. How do people think of "fellowship" in your local church? Does it involve mission or just hanging out? Compare it with Paul's view of fellowship.
4. Why do you need gospel partnerships?
5. What are some of the problems associated with trying to live out the Christian life apart from community?
6. What are some of the enemies of enjoying biblical community?
7. Does Philippians 1:6 encourage you? If yes, how so?
8. Compare Philippians 1:6 with Philippians 2:12-13. How do these passages complement each other?
9. Do you think much about "the day of Christ"? How can a daily reflection on this future event impact our daily lives?
10. We often think about Paul as a mighty theologian (and rightly so), but how does Paul talk about his "affections"? What might we learn from him regarding both thinking and feeling?

Praying for Your Partners in the Gospel

PHILIPPIANS 1:9-11

Main Idea: Paul intercedes for his partners in the gospel, expressing his desire for their increased growth in love, discernment, and fruitfulness so that God may be glorified.

I. **Six Observations from Paul's Prayer for the Philippians**
   A. Continuance
   B. Essence
   C. Reoccurrence
   D. Resemblance
   E. Uniqueness
   F. Relevance
II. **Praying with Paul**
   A. The petition (1:9)
   B. The purposes (1:10-11a)
   C. The praise (1:11b)

The opening section of Philippians is an explosion of joy and affection. Paul's thanksgiving to God and his warm, affectionate words to the Philippians are striking and exemplary. We should all affirm the importance of passion, expressing our love to God in thankful prayer and worship, and our affection to others in relationships. Why? We should worship with passion because Jesus isn't an object to be studied like a frog in biology class. He's the Creator and Redeemer who is to be feared and cherished. And we should express our love to other believers because we're family, and we became a family by a divine miracle! God has adopted us into His family and made us brothers and sisters in Christ. That should mean something to us.

Because the preaching event is also an act of worship, we should listen attentively and actively. Again, everyone can do this differently, but if God is speaking to us when His Word is accurately taught, then we shouldn't simply listen to a sermon the same way we listen to a lecture on robots. For some, active listening involves tears of joy and repentance. For others, it's a hearty "Amen!" For others, it's a "Yes!" For some, it means standing up and clapping (as a friend recently did during one of my sermons).

This past Wednesday night I (Tony) was preaching in Tampa at a missions conference. Because this particular night was youth emphasis night, I was challenging parents to release their kids for mission. Drawing from Psalm 127, I said, "Kids aren't antiques to be sheltered and protected but arrows to be sharpened and sent." I said it forcefully, and a lady yelled back from the third row, "But I don't want to!" Her response got everyone's attention! I actually appreciated her active listening. She wasn't disagreeing with me. She was confessing the difficulty of this challenge. She didn't listen to the Word dispassionately. And neither should we.

Paul was a deeply passionate man. When you read his writings, you notice moments in which he bursts into praise (e.g., Rom 11:33-36). Here in Philippians 1, he uses visceral terms to explain his affections. His passion flows into this prayer in verses 9-11. He was passionate before he was a Christian, and those passions got redirected after he became a Christian (Phil 3:1-11). But the Christian life is also about *the life of the mind*, as Paul often emphasizes (e.g., Rom 12:1-2; Eph 4:22; Phil 4:9). When you become a Christian, you should be a student of the Bible for the rest of your life.

In Philippians 1 in the context of talking about his emotions and feelings, Paul prays for a type of love that's growing in *discernment* and *knowledge* and *approving what is excellent*. Notice the cognitive words. This is instructive for us. We need to live wisely, being informed by the Word, and we need to live with deep love for God and others.

Paul's *informed affections* are evident in other passages as well. In his farewell speech to the Ephesian elders he recounts his commitment to truth through preaching the whole counsel of God. But it isn't passionless instruction. He reminds them that his biblical admonishments are filled "with tears" (Acts 20:31). After he speaks to the elders, his passion is revealed again as all the elders pray in a puddle of tears (20:36-37).

Nehemiah 8 is an Old Testament example of loving God with heart and mind. The people express great affection as they hear the Word of God; they lift their hands, they say, "Amen!" and they bow down and worship the Lord (Neh 8:6). They aren't lost in pure emotionalism; they express worship based on an understanding of the Bible. Be this type of Christian: *biblically informed* and *deeply affectionate*. Unfortunately, many Christians never pursue wisdom and knowledge, and consequently they make terrible choices and even follow false teachers who prey on gullible, emotion-driven people. Others affirm sound doctrine but have no genuine affection for Christ and for others. These two problems are reflected in the churches of Ephesus and Thyatira in the book of Revelation. Ephesus was doctrinally sound but lost its first love (Rev 2:1-7). Thyatira had love but lacked discernment and tolerated heresy (2:18-28). We must avoid these extremes as we grow in our pursuit of both knowledge and affection.

One reason I really love this prayer is it underscores the dual need for affection (love) and biblical knowledge and discernment. Before we examine the prayer in detail, let's fly above it and consider some big-picture features of Paul's prayer for his gospel partners in Philippi. These items should help us catch the essence of Paul's prayer and help us make some important applications.

Six Observations from Paul's Prayer for the Philippians

Allow me to give you six words to help guide our brief overview of the prayer. (I made them almost rhyme because I aspire to be a starving poet.)

Continuance

One shouldn't be surprised that each verse builds on previous verses since that's the way a letter works, but notice the tight connection here. In verse 4 Paul speaks of his "prayer" for the Philippians, and we get to that prayer in verse 9. The resumptive nature of the prayer is signaled by the opening word in verse 9, "And." In the same spirit of Paul's thanksgiving and "affection" (vv. 7-8), he now offers these requests.

I think it's worth pointing out that Paul's affection for the church leads into this prayer. This is what you do for people you love—you pray for them. Do you love people? If so, you'll pray for them. Paul loved the Philippians; they were family. Family meant something to Paul, and it should mean something to us. It means we are a band of brothers and sisters on mission, on our knees for one another. What holds gospel partnerships together is not location or affinity, but loving intercession. Perhaps you, like Paul, need to write a prayerful letter to your gospel partners.

Essence

What's this prayer essentially about? Silva says, "The object of Paul's prayer is the total sanctification of the Philippians; what they now have in part must be brought to full fruition" (*Philippians*, 52). The graces mentioned here are present in their lives, but partial. The Philippians are positionally righteous and pure (justification) and one day will be transformed into the image of Jesus (3:21, glorification). His prayer is that they will become what they are and, indeed, what they one day will be.

Sanctification is the theological term we often use to talk about spiritual growth, that is, growth in Christlikeness, conformity to Christ. Paul's concern for growth is evident in several ways. He prays for more love (1:9). He prays for preparation for the "day of Christ" (v. 10; cf. v. 6). He wants them to grow in wisdom and knowledge, and to bear fruit. The structure of the prayer also points to progress and growth. The clauses have a progressive nature. Paul provides a basic request in verse 9, then offers his immediate goals in verse 10, and then states the ultimate goal, "to the glory and praise of God," in verse 11.

This desire for total sanctification is also reflective of the whole letter. Already mentioned is Paul's forward looking to the "day of Christ Jesus" in verse 6. In 1:25 he commits to minister for their "progress and joy in the faith." Regarding his own life, Paul asks for the Philippians to "fulfill [his] joy" (2:2), again showing a virtue that's present but not complete. In 2:12, Paul exhorts the Philippians to "work out [their] own salvation." In 3:12-14 this concept is driven home with powerful athletic imagery.

> *Not that I have already reached the goal [of Christlikeness] or am already fully mature, but I make every effort to take hold of it because I also have been taken hold of by Christ Jesus.* (3:12)

In 4:9 he urges them to practice what they've "learned," "received," "heard," and "seen" in Paul. Therefore, this prayer for growth is consistent with the entire letter.

Reoccurrence

Related to the previous point, we should notice how the themes of this prayer reoccur later in the letter. The details of this prayer serve as a table of contents or a preview of coming attractions for the rest of the letter. "Love" is addressed in a number of places in the letter (e.g., 1:16;

2:1-4; 4:1). Paul later speaks of being pure and blameless (2:14-15), of fruitfulness and righteousness (1:22; 3:6-9), about power through Christ (3:10), of the coming day of Christ (3:20), and of the glory of God (2:11). Further, the prayer for insight and discernment probably alludes to the need to handle the conflict mentioned in chapter 4 in an appropriately loving way. The request to approve the things that are superior may relate to his instruction in Philippians 3:8 to gain "the surpassing value of knowing Christ."

Paul's prayer connects to his instructions, which is the basis of an important application for us. That is, we need teaching that's bathed in prayer. In other places, like Ephesians 1:15-21 and 3:14-21, Paul prays for the sorts of things that he's teaching. Before he instructs the Ephesians, he prays for them, and he tells them he's praying for them. Sound teaching is essential, but we should also pray that the teaching will transform hearts. If Paul thought information alone was sufficient to transform lives, then he would never pray in his letters. He knows the reminder we need, namely, we should teach and listen in a spirit of dependent prayer (cf. Acts 6:4).

Resemblance

Some of the features of Paul's intercessory prayer resemble other prayers, such as those we find in 1 Corinthians 1:4-9 (e.g., "blameless in the day of our Lord Jesus," v. 8), and in 1 Thessalonians 3:11-13 (e.g., "increase and overflow with love" [v. 12] and "May He make your hearts blameless in holiness before our God and Father" [v. 13]). But as Silva points out, its closest resemblance is to Paul's prayer for the Colossians. Both have a thanksgiving followed by a substantive intercession with an abundance of mental/cognitive words (Silva, *Philippians*, 59). References to knowledge, discernment, wisdom, and understanding are present along with statements about fruitfulness, good works, and God's glory. Here's Paul's prayer for the Colossians:

> *For this reason also, since the day we heard this, we haven't stopped praying for you. We are asking that you may be filled with the knowledge of His will in all wisdom and spiritual understanding, so that you may walk worthy of the Lord, fully pleasing to Him, bearing fruit in every good work and growing in the knowledge of God. May you be strengthened with all power, according to His glorious might, for all endurance and patience, with joy.* (Col 1:9-11)

The similarities between Paul's prayer for the Philippians and for the other churches show us that some petitions are worth praying for all believers. Occupy your prayers with spiritual matters like being blameless for the day of Christ, bearing fruit, increasing in love, and having knowledge and discernment. It's not wrong to pray for things that you need, but don't let that be all you pray for. Read Paul's prayers and pray with him for others.

Uniqueness

While Paul's prayer in Philippians is similar to those in other letters, it also has some distinctive qualities. One major distinctive is how Paul links growing love with knowledge and discernment here. Elsewhere he prays for love and for knowledge, but here it is a love informed by knowledge (more on this below). This type of informed, insightful, discerning love was needed in the Philippian congregation.

Relevance

This prayer is *applicable*. Nothing in this prayer should cause us to minimize its importance for our own lives today. These are transferable petitions. Every Christian should be concerned about growing in love, knowledge, purity, and righteousness, and about bringing God glory. Further, this prayer is *memorable*. What a wonderful gift this prayer is to us! It helps inform our prayer, and it's short enough for everyone to memorize it and pray it for themselves and others.

Praying with Paul

Let's walk through this prayer line by line and pause to pray these petitions. Paul first expresses the basic request in verse 9, and then, in verses 10-11a, he mentions the results he hopes God will produce in them as an answer to his prayer (Thielman, *Philippians*, 40). Finally, he mentions his ultimate goal: the glory and praise of God (v. 11b). Let's take a look at the prayer in these three parts: (1) the petition, (2) the purposes, and (3) the praise.

The Petition (1:9)

Paul's basic petition is for growth in love—a love that's informed by knowledge and discernment. Paul's prayer for their love to "keep on growing" or "abound" helps us to see that our love shouldn't be static.

While Paul recognizes that love is present in their lives (he's already thanked them for their partnership, and later thanks them for their gift), he prays for their love to increase. In 1 Thessalonians Paul is speaking about sanctification, and after discussing the need for purity, he exhorts the believers to grow in love. He writes,

> *About brotherly love: You don't need me to write you because you yourselves are taught by God to love one another. In fact, you are doing this toward all the brothers in the entire region of Macedonia. But we encourage you, brothers, to do so even more.* (1 Thess 4:9-10)

Paul loved the Philippians like he loved the Thessalonians, and he recognized the presence of genuine love, but he wasn't content with the status quo. Even though they were models in many ways to other churches, he still believed that their love could abound more and more.

Biblical love is not mushy gushy. The Bible is not a hippie manual ("All you need is love!"). Biblical love is sacrificial (*agapē*) love. It involves action (1 John 3:11-18). For the Thessalonians' love to have this type of reputation has to mean that their love was visible. Do you want your love to be known throughout the entire region? Their love was known by others, and Paul says, "Come on, let's love even more." You have to admire his zeal for more impact!

Consider four particular characteristics related to this love. *The object of their love.* Paul doesn't specify who is to receive their love. He just prays "that your love will keep on growing," but love for whom? Some think this neglected object is intentional. It's true that if Paul specified an object of this love, as in the parable of the Good Samaritan, we might try to justify ourselves. We might say, "Who's my neighbor? Oh, I have that covered." But if the command is to love everyone, including your enemies, then that's quite another task.

Paul probably has love for "one another" in view, though we shouldn't press this hard because our love for one another should also extend to everyone (see Gal 6:10). Hanson points us to three clues for this possible "one another" intent (*Letter*, 57). We should bear in mind the immediate context, which is occupied with the *koinonia* (1:5,7). It makes sense that Paul wants the fellowship to grow in love. Next, Paul just mentioned his comprehensive affection for the Philippians, saying "all of you" three times (vv. 4,7,8). He's concerned about the unity of all the saints. The fact that this prayer begins with the conjunction "and" is another big clue that his focus is on their love for one another. Paul's love for them (vv. 6-8) is a model of their love for one another, and Paul later tells them to imitate him in all these things (4:9). A final clue is that the rest of the letter deals with issues such as unity, rivalry, selfish ambition, and other internal struggles of the congregation. Again, it seems that Paul is praying about that for which he will later provide instruction.

As believers we're called to love our neighbor, the least of these, our enemies, and one another. The one-another love is very important for the watching world to see. Jesus said that they will know we are His disciples by how we love one another (John 13:34-35). John writes that this is one of the ways we know we have "passed from death to life," that we "love our brothers" (1 John 3:14). Do you love your brothers and sisters? It's a mark of a Christian. It's essential for unity. It's a powerful witness to the watching world.

The source of their love. From where do we get the power and strength to love people, especially those at odds with us? All the fruits in this prayer have the same root: Christ. It is "through Jesus Christ" that we love (Phil 1:11). Paul already touched on how his affection was related to "the affection *of Christ Jesus*" (1:8; emphasis added). Christ provides the example for love, as powerfully illustrated by the Christ hymn in 2:5-11, and Christ provides the power for love (3:10-11). The more you dwell on Christ's love for you, the more loving you become (see 2 Cor 5:14-15); ask God for power to love.

The foundation of their love. Not only do we need power to love, but we also need knowledge and wisdom to know how to love. Paul prays that their love would abound *in the sphere of knowledge*. Love is not blind. Love is biblically informed. Paul uses this particular word for knowledge (*epignosis*) 15 times in his letters. It has to do with spiritual knowledge, a knowledge of the things of God—as in knowing God and His will, or knowing His truth (e.g., Eph 1:17; 4:13; Col 1:9-10; 3:10; 1 Tim 2:4; Titus 1:1). Later in Philippians, he expresses his greatest desire, namely, knowing Christ (3:10). As we know Christ more and more through His Word—He who humbled Himself and went to the cross for us (2:5-11)—we will be transformed into compassionate people. We can conclude with Hanson, "Knowledge of Christ multiplies love" (*Letter*, 59).

It's true that Paul puts knowledge and love at odds in 1 Corinthians 8:1 ("Knowledge inflates with pride, but love builds up") and speaks of the futility of knowledge when it doesn't have love in 1 Corinthians 13:2, but here he puts knowledge and love together. It reminds us of Hosea:

Hear the word of the LORD, people of Israel, for the LORD has a case against the inhabitants of the land: There is no truth, no faithful love, and no knowledge of God in the land! . . . My people are destroyed for lack of knowledge. (Hos 4:1,6)

Apart from knowledge of God and His Word, we will not love in a way that glorifies God and blesses others. We must see the need for knowledge in all of our relationships. Put all of your relationships under the authority of God's Word and ask God these questions:

- What does Your Word say about this relationship?
- What does Your Word say about dating and marriage? (How many lonely single men and women have made a shipwreck of their lives because they didn't submit to God's Word and ended up making a terrible decision?)
- What does Your Word say about loving my enemies?
- How should I love my friends and coworkers?
- How should I love my kids?
- How should I love the nations?
- How should I love "the least of these"?

Then submit to the instruction of the Word of God, not to cultural opinion or your own feelings.

Love is rooted in the knowledge of God. Otherwise, we can't know how to love appropriately. We learn from Christ what it means to serve, forgive our enemies, and lay down our lives for others. Paul tells the Ephesians, "Walk in love, as the Messiah also loved us and gave Himself for us" (Eph 5:2). Knowledge of how He loved us is necessary if we want to walk in love.

In our day people want to separate knowledge of God's Word from love. Love today is more associated with tolerance and feelings than with truth and righteousness. Many operate by "If it feels right, then it's acceptable." If you try to correct someone, then you are labeled as intolerant and therefore unloving. But love must be tied to truth for it to be truly, distinctly Christian love. When the Bible rubs against your preferences, who wins? Be encouraged that this is a prayer! Pray for help in loving in a way that honors an accurate view of Christ and His Word. Know Jesus deeply and allow Him to soften your heart toward others.

The application of love. In addition to knowledge, Paul says that love should abound in the sphere of "every kind of discernment"

(v. 9). Knowledge asks the question, "What is *right?*" Discernment asks the question, "What is *best?*" Once you get the foundational question answered, you move to the application question. But don't pass up the foundational question! This term for "discernment" only appears here in the New Testament, but it is used 22 times in the Greek translation of the Old Testament (the Septuagint, aka LXX) in the book of Proverbs, where it refers to practical insights that inform choices and conduct (O'Brien, *Epistle*, 76–77). So it's closely related to knowledge but is even *more practical.*

It seems what Paul has in mind is praying for God to help you answer the question, What is the best way for me to love this person based on what Your Word says? In light of your knowledge of Christ and His Word, there may be several acceptable expressions of love for a person or a people, but you need discernment and wisdom to know the *best* way to love them. This idea is conveyed in verse 10: "to discern what is best" (NIV). For example, my knowledge of Scripture teaches me that I am to lay down my life for my bride. I'm to love in a way that's sacrificial. I'm also to remain with her in the covenant of marriage. I'm to avoid all forms of lust because of my devotion to her. That's clear. You need to *know* these foundational things in marriage. But there may be several other ways for me to carefully and appropriately love her, and I need discernment for that.

Relationships are complex. God didn't just upload a program into our brains for us to love people perfectly. We need to pray for wisdom, and God generously provides it (Jas 1:5). When it comes to choosing a spouse, the first question you ask has to do with spiritual condition. Is this person a Christian? That's the foundational question. Then you need discernment for determining compatability.

The Philippians needed to know of Christ's love for the church and how they were to unite together. They needed to know that they should love by putting the needs of others ahead of their own. Every church needs to know these foundational theological truths. But how can love be expressed in a way that puts the needs of others ahead of one's own needs? There could be many ways to express this. And we need discernment to choose the *best* way forward. As you follow Jesus, you should be praying for discernment. Should you plant a church in Buffalo or Birmingham? Planting a church is a wonderful thing, and neither would necessarily be wrong. But what's best?

Put the two together. You need a knowledge of Christ and His Word, and you need a discerning heart and mind in life and in your relationships. In this we see the great commandments of loving God and people. The two are tied together. Know God, know people; love God, love people. Let's stop and pray for these things:

> *Father, please increase our love for one another. Help us to love one another based on our knowledge of Christ and His Word. Grant us discernment to know how best to express Christ-centered love to one another, as well as how to express love to the outside world. Fill our hearts with the love of Christ. May our love for Him, who took hold of us, cause us to love others more sacrificially and genuinely. Through Christ we pray. Amen.*

The Purposes (1:10-11a)

Let's consider the two results or purposes now. These two petitions involve a Christian's growth in Christ-like character. Paul longs for these character qualities to grow in his friends as they live in view of Christ's coming.

Approving things that are superior (v. 10a). This idea is also very practical. The word for "approve" (*dokimazo*) means "put to the test, examine." O'Brien notes that it was employed of testing metals and money (*Epistle*, 77). It's used in Luke 14:19 for trying out oxen for their usefulness. It's also used in references to self-examination and testing leaders, doctrine, and one's works (1 Cor 11:28; 2 Cor 13:5; Gal 6:4; Eph 5:10; 1 Thess 2:4; 5:21; 1 Tim 3:10). Translators use words like "superior" (HCSB), "excellent," (ESV), and "best" (NIV) to convey the idea of things that "differ" (cf. Gal 4:1). In this context it refers to what differs because it's best or superior (Hanson, *Letter*, 60).

A few images come to mind, such as baseball tryouts, food/drink tastings, and auditions. In each of these, things or people are evaluated. The judges are examining all to determine which is best. Based on a growing, knowledgeable, and discerning love, Paul prays for the Philippians to choose the things that are best in this life and in their relationships. He prays for them to have discernment in order to properly distinguish between right and wrong, between the better and the best, between things that matter and things that don't matter. Later in the letter, he tells them to think on the things that are excellent and praiseworthy (Phil 4:8). He also urges them to distinguish between true and false teaching (cf. 3:1–4:1, Thielman, *Philippians*, 41).

In chapter 3 Paul speaks about his own ability to test things, as he speaks of "the surpassing value of knowing Christ Jesus my Lord" (3:8). He classifies his former religious life of works righteousness as garbage compared to knowing Christ. In knowing Christ—who is excellent, best, and superior—one finds a life that matters as well as the knowledge to inform and empower excellent love for one another. This petition should cause us to ask questions like these:

- Am I pursuing knowledge of Christ with passion?
- Am I valuing knowing Christ above everything else?
- Am I in a church that teaches the Bible faithfully?
- Am I doing what is best with my life, with my time, with my money, with my mind, with my kids, with my ministry, and in my relationships?
- Am I doing good things or gospel things with my life?

By knowing Christ and pursuing a life that matters, you are living in view of "the day of Christ." That's a wise life. That's a life like Jesus, who always did what pleased the Father.

Being pure and blameless (v. 10b). Paul desires to see his people fit and prepared for the coming day of Christ, and so he prays for them to be "pure and blameless." Paul often prayed for other churches to be prepared for the judgment day of Christ (1 Cor 1:7-8; Col 1:12; 1 Thess 3:13; 2 Thess 1:11-12). Jesus is coming, and we must be ready! Does this exhortation to live righteously contradict verse 6, that salvation is by grace? No. For God saves us *unto* good works, not *by* works (Eph 2:8-10). And God energizes us for obedience.

The fact that He's coming should change the way we think and live. We *will* see Him! It should cause us to be "pure" and "blameless." The former has more to do with inner character, while the latter has more to do with outer character. *Pure* means "sincere, without hidden motives or pretense" (Hanson, *Letter*, 61). The word may be derived from the word for "sunlight," which continues the idea of testing (Martin, *Philippians*, 68). "What you see is what you get" is a popular way to say this. This fits perfectly with the letter, as Paul later talks about those who have the wrong motives in ministry (1:15-17) and those who are filled with selfish ambition (2:2-3). True Christian discipleship is about being authentic and real.

The aspect of moral purity in view seems tied to the sphere of relationships. Grow in purity in your relationships, particularly in regard to killing the inner sins of envy, pride, jealousy, selfish ambition, complaining, and arguing. The word *blameless* means "without offense" or "not causing offense" (Martin, *Philippians*, 68). The only other occurrences of this word are Acts 24:16, where Paul tries to keep a "clear" conscience that doesn't offend anyone, and 1 Corinthians 10:32, "Give no offense." Paul doesn't want the Philippian believers to cause others to stumble by creating division. You can cause the church to stumble in unity when you commit outward sins like gossiping, complaining, and arguing (2:14). Don't minimize these supposedly "respectable sins"; they can be devastating! Also, realize that this prayer for purity and blamelessness is not a prayer for you to go clean yourself up to meet Jesus. It's a prayer for you who already trust in Jesus to grow in Christ-likeness, which flows from your union with Christ. The Philippians were already accepted by God in Christ. Paul is praying that they would become what they are. Are you growing in purity? Paul encourages growth in purity in two ways.

The day of Christ (v. 10c). The reference to the "day of Christ" should call us to self-examination. Live in view of that day. Are you trusting in Jesus as your righteousness? Are you pursuing what is pure and right? Don't go through your days trying to satisfy your sinful desires; live for the day of Christ (2 Pet 3:11-13). For some people, this is terrifying; it fills the hearts of others with motivation, hope, and joyful anticipation.

When I (Tony) was in high school, I got in a fight with a big football player. It was a dumb thing to do on many levels. We were to meet at a field at 4:30 or so. I got there first and had to wait on him to show up. It was terrifying. That's one analogy I have of the coming of Jesus. Those who are not in Christ Jesus need to realize that judgment is coming. And a skinny kid facing a big kid is nothing compared to a rebellious sinner facing the holy Lord of Hosts. But I have another analogy—my wedding day. At 27 years old, I couldn't wait to be married. Just before the ceremony, I remember being backstage with my best friends from college and seminary. We were laughing, telling stories, and talking about the upcoming honeymoon. Then while we were backstage, the band played three songs, and we all sang. Then my friend David preached for about 15 minutes. When he finished, we huddled up and prayed and then went to the stage. Then it happened. The doors opened, and my father-in-law brought out my bride. Tears of joy poured down my face. I had waited, hoped, and lived my previous days in light of that day. It reordered all my priorities. It affected all my decisions.

In Matthew 25 the parable is similar but different. It's still a marriage scene, but the groom is coming for the bride. The point of the parable is that we must be ready! And while the day is drawing near, we should encourage one another just as my friends were doing for me backstage. We should reorder our priorities in light of that day.

Being filled with fruit of righteousness (v. 11a). Paul expresses another way to talk about a life of purity with the phrase "filled with the fruit of righteousness that comes through Jesus Christ." This prayer for godly character seems to parallel "pure and blameless." The righteousness of God is given to the believer by faith alone (3:9). That is a "forensic righteousness." We are declared righteous and made acceptable to God through Christ. It's an "alien righteousness" in that it comes from outside ourselves. God reaches down and puts us in a position of righteousness. But I think Paul has practical righteousness, not positional righteousness, in view here. Out of our position of righteousness, through Jesus, the believer is called to live righteously. Paul is emphasizing the righteous fruit that should grow out of the relationship a believer has with Jesus (cf. Gal 5:22). When we plant our roots in the streams of Christ, fruit emerges.

In light of the whole prayer, the righteous fruit Paul has in mind is probably right relationships with one another (Hanson, *Letter*, 64). Are you doing what's right in your relationships? Paul provides an amazing word of hope with this wonderful phrase: "that comes through Jesus Christ" (11b). We aren't left to our own power for purity and righteousness. That comes through Jesus! As we abide in Him (John 15), we bear fruit. The most important part of your Christian life is the part no one can see, namely, your communion with Jesus. Let's pray this petition:

> *Father, grant us wisdom that we may pursue what matters most in life—knowing Christ, loving others, and making Christ known. Grant us purity of motives. Keep us from envying other Christians, complaining about people, gossiping, competing for praise and recognition, pursuing our own ambitions. Help us to love and serve in a way that's pure. In all our relationships, help us to do what is right and what is best. Through Christ we pray. Amen.*

The Praise (1:11b)

Why does Paul pray for all of these things? It is for the fame and renown of God. He ends with his ultimate goal: *the glory and praise of God.* This doxology concludes not just this prayer but also the entire opening section, including the thanksgiving. Paul opened by thanking God and expressing his deep affection for the Philippians, and he closes with the reason for it all—that God may be glorified. This grand reason for all things appears in two other places in Philippians: at the conclusion of the Christ hymn in 2:11 and at the conclusion of the letter in 4:20. Regarding the former, Paul says that all of history is moving to this climactic conclusion.

There is no higher purpose in life than to glorify God. You don't glorify God in order to do something else; the end of it all *is* the glory of God. This goal is consistent with Paul's prayers elsewhere for God to be glorified (e.g., Eph 3:20-21; 2 Thess 1:11-12). It's also consistent with the Lord's Prayer, which begins "Our Father in heaven, Your name be honored as holy" (Matt 6:9). Jesus taught us to pray with this God-centered vision. This longing to see God's name made great is present throughout the Old Testament as well. For example, when threatened by King Sennacherib of Assyria, Hezekiah prays, "Now, LORD our God, please save us from his hand so that all the kingdoms of the earth may know that You are the LORD God—You alone" (2 Kgs 19:19). Pray for God to be glorified in you and in His people, and for God to make His glory known through us to the nations.

In John 15 fruitfulness and the glory of God are tied together. Jesus said, "My Father is glorified by this: that you produce much fruit and prove to be My disciples" (John 15:8). Paul prays for essentially the same thing here in Philippians. He desires for them to grow in love, knowledge, and discernment—for them to be pure and blameless that they may bear fruit for the glory of God. And just like John 15, Paul says this happens "through Jesus Christ," or as we "remain" in Him (John 15:4).

We are dependent on Christ to glorify God and bear fruit. Apart from Him we can do nothing (John 15:5). That reminds me of a story I read somewhere. Lawrence of Arabia once brought a group of poor Bedouins to London and housed them in a beautiful hotel. The only kind of dwelling they had ever lived in was a tent in the desert. They quickly became fascinated with the faucets in the hotel. In the desert, water was hard to come by, but in the hotel, they merely had to turn a knob to get all the water they needed. When Lawrence helped them pack up to leave, he discovered they'd taken the faucets off all the sinks and put them in their bags! They believed that if they possessed the faucets they would also possess the water. We are like faucets. Unless we are connected to the pipeline of spiritual water, we are as useless as the faucets the Bedouins had in their bags.

Father, our greatest purpose in life is to glorify Your holy name. Fill our affections with a passion for Your glory. Through Jesus, give us power to glorify You in our lives, in our homes, in our church, in our city, and in our world. Grant us power to glorify You by the way we love, by the way we think, and by the way we live. Help us to live in view of the coming of Jesus, our righteousness, our Lord and King. In His name we pray. Amen

Reflect and Discuss

1. What does it mean to have "informed affections"? Are you pursuing this? Explain.
2. Paul moves from expressing his love for people to praying for them. Are you expressing your love for others by praying for them? Pray for some people now.
3. Read Colossians 1:9-11. Compare this passage to Philippians 1:9-11. How might these passages help shape our practice of prayer?
4. Paul prays for the Philippians' love to grow. How do people define "love"? How does Philippians describe *real* love?
5. Paul puts knowledge and love together in this prayer. Why is it important to keep these two virtues together? Are you submitting your relationships to Scripture and asking how you should love others based on the Word? Why or why not?
6. Have you ever prayed for discernment? Stop and pray for discernment for both yourself and for your church. Pray that you would not only do what is *right* but that you would also do what is *best*.
7. Paul wanted the church to be able to discern what really matters in life. Stop and pray for yourself and your church—that you all may be passionate about the things that really matter.
8. Stop and pray for purity in your life and in the life of your church, particularly in areas related to relationships.
9. Paul prays for the believers to be filled with the fruit of righteousness. What does this mean? What might this look like?
10. Paul reminds the church that these virtues and grace come "through Jesus Christ" and they should be done for the glory of God. Stop and thank Christ for being united to Him (if you're a Christian), and ask Him to empower you for faithful Christian living. Pray also that your life may be lived with a radical passion for God to be glorified.

How to Maintain Joy in Ministry

PHILIPPIANS 1:12-18

Main Idea: Paul maintains joy in ministry by staying focused on the gospel and the glory of Christ.

I. **Stay Focused.**
II. **Put the Gospel First (1:12-14).**
  A. God's mission is being accomplished (1:12).
  B. People are hearing the gospel (1:13).
  C. People are speaking the gospel (1:14).
III. **Love Christ's Glory More Than Your Own (1:15-18).**
  A. Check your motives (1:15-17).
    1. Beware of jealousy and envy in ministry.
    2. Beware of the temptation to promote yourself in ministry.
    3. Don't be surprised if others envy you.
    4. Pray for God to give you the grace to minister out of love for Him and others.
  B. Rejoice when Christ is proclaimed (1:18).

If your church supports missionaries, and if you have a close relationship with these individuals, then you know the value of getting a letter or an e-mail from them. With technology today, missionaries can possibly even Skype with their home church to give reports and pray together. The apostle Paul didn't have e-mail or Skype, but he was able to write a letter to his supporting church in Philippi, and they were eager to hear from him.

In verses 1-11 Paul thanks God for the Philippians, expresses his love for them, and then prays for them. In verses 12-26 Paul gives the church a report on his present situation and his outlook on the future. The present report is the focus of this study in verses 12-18.

The passage breaks down simply. Paul conveys his positive attitude in the first three verses. He can be positive because the gospel is advancing. He mentions two ways in particular it's advancing: people are hearing the gospel, and others are speaking the gospel boldly. Both are a result of his imprisonment. Then in the next four verses Paul addresses the motives of two types of evangelists. One group is made up of "envious evangelists," while the other group is made up of "empathetic evangelists." Regardless of their motives, Paul concludes, "Christ is proclaimed. And in this I rejoice" (1:18).

Stay Focused

This remarkable, Christ-centered perspective of Paul's, then, is on full display in this text. He isn't whining about his situation. He isn't complaining about not being able to labor in some ripe mission field, like Spain. He's not even complaining about his critics who are trying to afflict him in his imprisonment. He's stuck in prison, but he's able to rejoice. Paul cares about the gospel; he cares about Christ being proclaimed. Because the gospel is advancing and Christ is being preached, he rejoices.

This is one of the most relevant passages in the New Testament on how to maintain joy in the ministry. Ministry, whether vocational or nonvocational, can drain the joy out of you. I used to be a lot more critical of pastors until I became one! Now when I see a sincere gospel minister, I just want to hug him! It's often said that pastors think about quitting every Monday morning. Sometimes you go through seasons where every day seems like Monday morning. The pastor burnout rate is off the charts. The responsibilities are vast, and the burdens are exhausting. Paul knew this church pressure, and he experienced countless waves of opposition. Yet, while Paul knew these difficulties intimately, he could essentially tell the Philippians, "I rejoice; you should rejoice." How could he maintain joy in ministry?

Paul shows us that the key to maintaining joy in ministry is simple: stay focused on Jesus. Make the gospel the focus of your life and ministry. Is the gospel being preached? If so, then rejoice. Is Jesus Lord? Yes. Do you know Him? If so, then rejoice. Life may be hard, but when we keep our focus on Christ, we have reason to sing—even on Mondays, even when we're criticized.

Paul was dealing with critics, with people who were envious of him, and with the pressure of Rome itself, but in Philippians his eyes were fixed on the glory of Christ. We must keep our eyes on Him as well. Don't get overly concerned with what others are saying and doing. Don't get consumed with trying to measure up to someone else's church or ministry. Remember that comparison is an enemy of joy. It makes you unnecessarily distracted, can lead to either despair or pride, and will take your eyes off the King. Take your cue from Paul. Focus on Christ, and treasure His glory above all things.

Let's look at this passage in its two parts. Paul maintained joy by putting the gospel first and by caring more about Jesus' glory than his own glory.

Put the Gospel First
PHILIPPIANS 1:12-14

Having prayed for the Philippians, Paul gives his report. Epaphroditus surely filled the church in on some of the details not mentioned in the letter. Instead of going on and on about life in prison, Paul takes a different approach. He takes *a divine perspective* on the whole situation, reminding the church that God's mission is being accomplished, that people are being positively impacted by his imprisonment, and that Christians are being emboldened. His words highlight how he treasures the gospel and thus maintains joy.

God's Mission Is Being Accomplished (1:12)

Paul starts with a broad statement about how God was at work. When Paul says, "what has happened," he could be referring to everything that's taken place from Jerusalem to Rome. This would include a riot, a two-year imprisonment in Caesarea, an appeal to Caesar, the threat on his life, a shipwreck on the way to Rome, his house arrest with restricted freedom, and his impending trial (Melick, *Philippians*, 70). Whether Paul is speaking of all of these events or just his present situation in Rome, one thing is clear: it has served to "advance" the gospel.

The Greek term for "advance" was used of blazing a trail before an army, progressing in wisdom, and the progress of a young minister (Melick, *Philippians*, 70). Paul could survey the situation and see that the good news was making its way into new territories. The Romans thought they would quiet Paul down, but they only gave him a captive audience that he might not have otherwise addressed. Not only were the guards and Roman officials hearing the good news, but due to Paul's presence in the great city of Rome, many others were also being impacted by his witness. See the providence of God at work here. Instead of living freely and heading to places like Spain, the most powerful Christian missionary was allowed by God to be imprisoned. But it was through Paul's imprisonment that the Sovereign Lord was making the gospel known in Rome.

We never know how God might use suffering to advance the gospel. For example, I recently heard about the faith journey of Peter O'Brien (renowned Bible scholar—quoted often in the present work) in a sermon preached by D. A. Carson on the story of Joseph. When he was a youth, neither of O'Brien's parents were Christians. But his mother became greatly impacted by the faithful witness of a neighbor. This neighbor was a simple lady with sincere faith in Christ, who unfortunately lived with an incurable disease and suffered day after day. But she never complained. Her attitude and witness made a tremendous impact on O'Brien's mother, who eventually trusted Christ as Savior. Humanly speaking, it was because of this simple lady's faith that O'Brien's mother became a Christian. Because of that, O'Brien later believed. He would then go to seminary and get a PhD. Then he would go to India and make the gospel known for years. Then he would go to Australia, teach, and write several extraordinary commentaries. Now, suppose you had said to this simple, suffering woman: "Here's the deal: If you will glorify Christ in your suffering, then as a consequence Indians will be converted, pastors will be trained to teach the Bible, and countless sermons will be preached. Will you now suffer faithfully every day?" I'm sure she would have said, "Yes! Of course! I can endure for these reasons!" But she didn't know all of this would happen. When we're in the middle of our suffering, we never know what will happen, but we must trust that God is sovereign and that He can and often does advance the gospel through great personal hardships, such as imprisonment or cancer. Our job is to stay faithful, joyful, and Christ-centered through the suffering, confidently trusting in His wise, sovereign will (D. A. Carson, "The Temptation of Joseph").

Because God is sovereign and is advancing His gospel, we should also view circumstances as opportunities to share the gospel. Do you somehow think that where you live is only a stepping stone to what's next, and therefore you have no need to speak to your neighbors and really be on mission? Think again. Where you live is no accident. See your circumstances as God-ordained opportunities.

I heard of Matt Chandler coming to faith in Jesus in high school through a football teammate whose locker was providentially placed beside Matt's. The teammate said something like, "I'm going to share the gospel with you; just let me know when you're ready." When I (Tony) was in college, I went simply to play baseball and graduate with a degree. I had no spiritual life. But God used my double-play partner, the second baseman, Stephen, to lead me to Jesus. You may well have been converted through someone who was near to you. Embrace this pattern. Perhaps you will be used by God to make the gospel known to someone this week. See your circumstances as opportunities to speak the gospel.

In light of Paul's view of the providence of God, he could go on rejoicing. Live on mission in view of God's sovereignty, and experience this joy.

People Are Hearing the Gospel (1:13)

Paul can also rejoice because he has a captive audience. The first result of his imprisonment has to do with the gospel's impact on the "imperial guard." It's hard to know if Paul is talking about a *place* or a group of *people*. O'Brien notes several options. Possible places include (1) the prisoner's barracks, (2) the royal palace, or (3) the camp of the imperial guard. If he's referring to a group of people, then he's referring to (4) the elite imperial guard (*Epistle*, 93). Of the four options, most modern commentators go with option four.

As Paul lived and taught, the Roman guards were hearing the good news. There were about 9,000 of them (O'Brien, *Epistle*, 93), and Paul's message apparently impacted many of them, and probably many others in Rome, including officials and pagans. In this short book the term *gospel* appears as a noun nine times (Bruce, *Philippians*, 82, n. 47). Paul is consumed with the gospel. He has put the gospel first in his affections and priorities. What a lesson for us! Put the gospel first in your relationships, in your circumstances, and in your love for your neighbors. Talk about the good news of Jesus' death, resurrection, reign, and return all the time. Because Paul prized the gospel, he could praise Christ with joy despite being imprisoned.

Paul is putting the gospel first in this letter as he writes to Christians. We can easily talk about other things and fail to address this most important message. D. A. Carson writes,

> What ties us together? What do we talk about when we meet, even after a church service? Mere civilities? The weather? Sports? Our careers and our children? Our aches and pains? None of these topics should be excluded from the conversation of Christians, of course. In sharing all of life, these things will inevitably come up. But what must tie us together as Christians is this passion for the gospel, this fellowship of the gospel. On the face of it, nothing else is strong enough to hold together the extraordinary diversity of people who constitute many churches. (*Basics*, 19)

Perhaps our failure to talk about the gospel to unbelievers is tied to our lack of talking about the gospel to anyone, including one another! Paul is consumed with the risen Christ, and he is always talking about Jesus to the Roman guard and to his friends in Philippi—yet another way we should imitate him. While you may be involved in many noble and just causes, be a gospel person first. If you are fighting slavery, feeding the poor, or caring for AIDS patients, do it with the good news of Jesus on your lips. Take all of your opportunities to serve and love as occasions to speak—wisely, winsomely, compassionately, and fearlessly.

People Are Speaking the Gospel (1:14)

Speaking of fearlessness, Paul says that when others heard about his brave witness in the Roman prison, they were inspired to greater faithfulness. This is the second time in three verses that Paul mentions "the brothers" (v. 12). The first result of Paul's imprisonment related to those on the outside, but now Paul mentions how God has used his situation for those on the inside—the body of Christ. The family of faith was being built up by Paul's afflictions. Persecuted Christians often inspire otherwise timid believers. After Jim Elliot and his four missionary friends were brutally killed by the Auca Indians, a high number of Wheaton College graduates offered themselves as missionaries in the years following (Carson, *Basics*, 24). A similar thing was happening through Paul's sufferings. Christians were becoming more confident, more bold, and were speaking "fearlessly."

Don't miss the focus on courage and boldness in this verse, as well as in the rest of the chapter. In verse 20 Paul says that he will represent Christ with "all boldness," and in verse 28 he tells the church not to be "frightened." The book of Philippians should cause us to pray and pursue several Christian qualities, and one of them is courage.

I (Francis) had a pastoral staff member do something that I've only dreamed about. As my colleague was driving one day, the car in front of him accidently hit a guy on a bicycle and knocked him down. The cyclist got up. He then pounded on the hood of the driver's car. In his rage he then went over to the driver's side door, opened it, and began kicking and punching the driver—who happened to be a 75-year-old man! My friend was sitting behind this scene and was faced with a decision. What should he do? Should he get out and help? To make things more complicated, he also had a little baby in the back seat! Determined to help, our pastor proceeded to get out of the car and pull the cyclist off of the older man. As he did, the cyclist wouldn't stop. He got physical with our pastor, too, and even tore his shirt off in his effort to get back to assaulting the driver. So our pastor had to make another decision. Should he punch this guy? He decided yes. And with one upper-cut punch, he knocked this guy out! When the police came and verified the story from all the witnesses, who honked and clapped when this originally happened, the policeman asked our pastor, "How many times did you punch him?" He said, "Honestly, just once." The policeman said, "That's what everyone else said." Later, I told my wife—who knew I was impressed—that I've dreamed about doing this!

As I told this story, our congregation erupted into applause. Their excitement wasn't due to his mighty punch (though it did amaze many!) but the fact that he took up for this older man. So I asked our church, "How many of you would have gotten out of the car and tried to stop this assault, even if the guy was bigger than you?" Most nodded in affirmation. Most would get out and do something. They would have courage to intervene. Then I asked, "How many of you would go speak the gospel to a 75-year-old man who is sitting alone at a restaurant, if you knew that he was not a Christian? Would you even engage in spiritual conversation with him?" Why is it that we find it easy to be courageous in physical matters but difficult in this spiritual matter? Why are we cowards when it comes to speaking the gospel? Could it be because there's a deeper conflict going on? Could it be that speaking the gospel is warfare? I think so (see 2 Cor 4:3-4). Let us pray for great courage as we make the gospel known to people. Let us think on the affliction of other missionaries and pray for God to grant us boldness in making the gospel known.

In verses 12-14 Paul takes a divine perspective on his situation. He understands that God is using his imprisonment for the advancement of the gospel. The gospel was advancing through Paul's proclamation and through many others who were inspired by Paul's example. Because Paul put the gospel ahead of his selfish ambitions and his desire for comfort and ease, he wasn't freaking out. He was actually rejoicing and making the most of his opportunities. Let us follow his example.

Love Christ's Glory More Than Your Own
PHILIPPIANS 1:15-18

Paul shifts in these verses to talk about two different motives from different groups of evangelists. Even though some believers were inspired by Paul's imprisonment (v. 14), others were not. They looked at Paul's imprisonment differently. Eugene Peterson paraphrases this passage in a striking way:

> *It's true that some here preach Christ because with me out of the way, they think they'll step right into the spotlight. But the others do it with the best heart in the world. One group is motivated by pure love, knowing that I am here defending the Message, wanting to help. The others, now that I'm out of the picture, are merely greedy, hoping to get something out of it for themselves. Their motives are bad. They see me as their competition, and so the worse it goes for me, the better—they think—for them. So how am I to respond? I've decided that I really don't care about their motives, whether mixed, bad, or indifferent. Every time one of them opens his mouth, Christ is proclaimed, so I just cheer them on!* (Phil 1:15-18 MSG)

Let's compare the motives and the message of these two sets of evangelists and allow this passage to deal with our own motives.

Check Your Motives (1:15-17)

Paul states the motives of the two groups in verse 15, and then adds to this description in verses 16-17. The *envious evangelists* are filled with "envy and strife." The *empathetic evangelists* preach out of "good will." The former preach Christ out of "rivalry," while the latter preach out of "love." The envious evangelists look at Paul's imprisonment as an occasion to tear him down, to stir up trouble, and to elevate their ministries over Paul's. The empathetic evangelists care about Paul. They understand that Paul is in prison by God's sovereign will and not as a result of any disobedience or unfaithfulness. They serve out of goodwill toward Paul. They seek to continue his mission. So we have two groups of ministers with different motives. These ministers with bad motives seem to be believers, and so we shouldn't think that we can't fall into these same sins ourselves. Let's consider four applications for our ministries here.

Beware of jealousy and envy in ministry. While every Christian will be tempted with these sins (Rom 1:29; Gal 5:20-21), they are particularly active in the passions of ministers. Be alert to the presence of such temptations. Ask yourself, Am I constantly comparing myself with others in ministry? Do I rejoice when my friends succeed, or do I grow jealous? Do I resent it when others are praised? Paul was uniquely gifted and used by God. Instead of rejoicing in Paul's ministry, the envious evangelists resented him and couldn't rejoice in the Savior's work through him. Sadly, that sounds very familiar to our day.

If Satan can't corrupt your heart with a love of money or with sexual sin, he may try this tactic: envy and rivalry. Consider a story from the fourth century on the sin of envy. Some inexperienced demons were finding it difficult to afflict a godly hermit. They lured him with various temptations, but the man kept denying their allurements. The demons reported their problem to Satan. The evil one told them that they had been far *too hard* on the man. He suggested a more effective strategy: "Send him a message that *his brother has just been made bishop of Antioch. Bring him good news.*" The demons used the Devil's scheme, reporting "the wonderful news" to the pious hermit. On hearing this message, the godly hermit fell into deep, wicked jealousy (Kent and Barbara Hughes, *Liberating Ministry*, 100).

Does it bother you when others are praised, promoted, and more recognized then you? What about if they try to tear you down in order to build themselves up? Despite the fact that wrongly motivated preachers were using Paul's imprisonment as a means of tearing him down, Paul humbly said, "Christ is proclaimed. And in this I rejoice" (v. 18). The way you overcome your wicked jealousy is by caring more for Jesus' glory than your own. Let the glory of Christ be your chief concern.

Beware of the temptation to promote yourself in ministry. Paul says that some were guilty of "rivalry" (v. 17) or "selfish ambition" (ESV, NASB). They wanted to be recognized and made much of by others. Serving Jesus out of rivalry is warped motivation. Yet, it's sadly present today. Hanson notes, "Readers of Paul will observe that envy and rivalry are too often characteristics of preachers of Christ in our competitive churches" (*Letter*, 72). How sad it is to compete with others who are actually on the same team! How sad it is when we serve with selfish ambition while the heart of our message is about a Savior who emptied Himself for sinners. Avoid the sin of rivalry by caring for the glory of Jesus more than your own. Make it your ambition to make Christ known, not yourself (2 Cor 4:5).

Don't be surprised if others envy you. While you will never be the mighty apostle Paul, the Lord may grant you unexpected influence. That influence would inevitably serve as an occasion for others to grow jealous of you. Because of their jealousy, they might do a number of things. They might criticize you unfairly. They might disassociate with you. They might speak against you. They might disrespect you. You may think this will never happen to you, but you should think again. What should you do then? You should follow Paul. He doesn't try to defend himself. He doesn't really get wrapped up in it all. He knows God will ultimately judge the hearts and ministries of people. So he simply stays focused on proclaiming Christ, and he puts the gospel first. You can't control what others think of you; all you can do is finish your race with faithfulness.

Pray for God to give you the grace to minister out of love for Him and others. Paul recognizes that the message is more important than the motives, but he is clearly in favor of serving with good motives. Serve out of love and goodwill. The book of Philippians is filled with exhortations to loving, humble service that puts the needs of others ahead of our own. Why do you serve Jesus? Is it because you love Him and others? I don't want to be an envious evangelist; I want to be a goodwill gospel proclaimer. This will happen as we care more about Jesus' glory than our own, which Paul highlights in the next verse.

Rejoice When Christ Is Proclaimed (1:18)

Paul's exemplary Christ-centered focus continues as he summarizes his report. What matters most to him is the gospel. True, some were preaching the gospel with sinful motives, but still, the gospel was being proclaimed. Paul could rejoice in this (without condoning the twisted motives) because his ultimate desire was to see Christ proclaimed, known, and glorified. The message mattered more to Paul than the messengers. Notice how different Paul's attitude is here in Philippians compared to his words about the false teachers in Galatians.

> *I am amazed that you are so quickly turning away from Him who called you by the grace of Christ and are turning to a different gospel—not that there is another gospel, but there are some who are troubling you and want to change the good news about the Messiah. But even if we or an angel from heaven should preach to you a gospel other than what we have preached to you, a curse be on him! As we have said before, I now say again: If anyone preaches to you a gospel contrary to what you received, a curse be on him!* (Gal 1:6-9)

Does Paul's attitude here sound like his attitude about the envious evangelists in Philippians 1:12-18? No, it doesn't. Why then does Paul rail on the Galatian false teachers but not the envious evangelists? It's simple. The envious evangelists in Philippi were preaching Christ, but those in Galatia were not. The Galatian teachers were distorting the gospel. Paul never tolerates a false gospel. The message mattered more to Paul than the motives of the messengers. Granted, Paul would prefer to have both message and motive be pure, but he placed the highest importance on the message.

This is an important word for the Christian community, who are often quick to vilify people. There will be preachers and teachers who do things that make us cringe. But are they preaching Christ? If so, then we should rejoice. And then we should pray about their questionable motives. Our hearts are deceptive, and even the best of preachers can do dumb things for bad reasons. This doesn't excuse their sin. I just point it out for us to remember the centrality of the gospel and the weakness of human instruments.

Having said this, we should pray for and strive for both a clear, Christ-centered message *and* a Christ-honoring, people-loving motive. Paul told the Thessalonians about his suffering in Philippi, and then he went on to remind them of the purity of his message and his motive. Here is a model for us to pursue:

> *After we had previously suffered, and we were treated outrageously in Philippi, as you know, we were emboldened by our God to speak the gospel of God to you in spite of great opposition. For our exhortation didn't come from error or impurity or an intent to deceive. Instead, just as we have been approved by God to be entrusted with the gospel, so we speak, not to please men, but rather God, who examines our hearts. For we never used flattering speech, as you know, or had greedy motives—God is our witness—and we didn't seek glory from people, either from you or from others.* (1 Thess 2:2-6)

So let us speak the gospel that God has entrusted to us, and let us do it faithfully before God, who examines hearts. Let us pray for those who proclaim the gospel. And let us rejoice when people are proclaiming the gospel even if we find things about the messengers questionable.

Do you care more about Christ's glory or the one speaking about Christ? May it be the former. Because Paul was preoccupied with the Savior, not the speaker, he could rejoice! Surely Paul's joyful attitude displayed in front of the Roman guards had an impact on them. His consistent testimony of joy in the midst of suffering, coupled with the explosive power of the gospel, made an eternal difference in their lives. There's no reason to believe that such a strategy for evangelism won't work today—living an attractive and joyful life before people and proclaiming the good news to them. Jesus is better than comfortable circumstances and high-profile positions in ministry. He matters more than what others think about us. The proclamation of His gospel always matters most to Paul-like ministers. Let us care more about Jesus' glory than our own, and let us rejoice until we see Him—the One who bled and died for those with deceptive hearts.

I sometimes chuckle at halftime interviews with football coaches. There are many occasions for laughter at these sometimes awkward or heated interactions. What I often find most amusing is the simplicity with which the coach speaks. You will hear the multi-million dollar coach say things like, "We just need to run, block, and tackle better." You want to say, "Really? They're paying you all that money to say that?" Of course there are all sorts of things he could say to expound on these fundamentals, but he keeps it simple and focused. That's what we must do as well in order to advance the gospel and maintain joy in ministry. We need to keep our focus on Jesus. We need to put the gospel first. We need to care about people and the glory of Christ more than our own glory. Stay focused.

Reflect and Discuss

1. What factors may cause people to lose their joy in ministry?
2. What might we learn from this passage about how to deal with critics?
3. Does Philippians 1:12 encourage you? How so?
4. Why should Philippians 1:12 give us added incentive to speak the gospel to someone?
5. In what ways can you "put the gospel first" in your relationships?
6. Why is it easier for us to be courageous in physical ways than in speaking the gospel to someone who is spiritually lost?
7. Why do you think the sins of envy and jealousy are so prevalent among church leaders?
8. What's most important to Paul: motive or message? Why?
9. Do you love Christ's glory more than your own? Pray for God to help you treasure Christ more than the approval and applause of others.
10. How could Paul "rejoice" and tell others to "rejoice" even though he was in prison? How should his example impact us today?

A Life Worth Living and a Death Worth Dying

PHILIPPIANS 1:18B-26

Main Idea: As Paul gives the Philippians a report on his situation and his outlook on the future, he shows them how to live and die for the glory of Christ.

I. **Fill In the Blank.**
II. **The Christian's Ambition: Honoring Christ (1:18b-20)**
    A. By rejoicing in Christ consistently (1:18b)
    B. By relying on Christ completely (1:19)
    C. By representing Christ courageously (1:20-21)
III. **The Christian's Vision: Being with Christ (1:22-26)**
    A. Paul's dilemma (1:22-23a)
    B. Paul's desire (1:23b)
    C. Paul's decision (1:24-26)

In 1993, while fishing in St. Mary's Glacier, Colorado, Bill Jeracki got his leg pinned under a boulder. Snow was in the forecast, and he was without a jacket, a pack, or communication. In a desperate attempt to survive, he used his flannel shirt as a tourniquet, and then used his fishing knife to cut off his own leg at the knee joint! He used hemostats from his fishing kit to clamp the bleeding arteries. He then crab-walked to his truck and drove himself to the hospital! In 2003 Aron Ralston had a similar experience. While hiking in Utah, a boulder fell and pinned his right arm. After various attempts to get free, on the sixth day of being stuck there, he amputated his right forearm with a dull multi-tool. Exhausted and dehydrated, he then rappelled down a 60-foot cliff and hiked eight miles before finding a Dutch family who guided him to a rescue helicopter. He eventually made it to the hospital and survived. He wrote an autobiography titled *Between a Rock and a Hard Place*. An appropriate title!

What do these two stories teach us? Aside from providing some basic tips for adventure recreation, they teach us that *humans will do remarkable things in order to live*. We will spend money on the best doctors, take up disciplined eating habits, move to particular climates, and even cut off body parts to live. The whole world has witnessed this fight for survival in various ways, including the media's coverage of the horrific events of 9/11 and Hurricane Katrina.

But there's a big question we must answer: What do you live *for*? In this short life, we don't know how long we will live. What will you live for? Writing from a Roman prison, a chained man tells us about the meaning of life and the glory of death. The apostle Paul tells us about a life worth living and a death worth dying. Verse 21 summarizes it: "For me, living is Christ and dying is gain." This is one of the most quoted verses in the entire New Testament, and for good reason. This is what living and dying are about: Christ. Living is about serving Christ; dying is about being with Christ.

Fill In the Blank

Unfortunately, English translations can't capture the full beauty of this verse. There's no verb in the Greek. We usually supply it with "is." But other verbs could be supplied to describe this idea of purpose, meaning, center, foundation, or power. Living *means* Christ. Living *depends on* Christ. Living *honors* Christ (Hanson, *Letter*, 81). The English translation does try to get at the cadence of the verse, but it really comes out in Greek. Hanson calls this the "drumbeat repetition of the same sounds" and says that "Paul's own heartbeats are heard in the rhythm of these words" (ibid.).

To zēn—Christos	Living—Christ
To apothanein—kerdos	Dying—gain

That's Paul's heartbeat. While you may not get the full literary effect in an English translation, you can get the full heart effect, and that's the main thing! Do you see the glory of this truth?

The application of this verse appears with the little phrase at the beginning, "For me." Paul resolved that he would live for Christ. Everyone must fill in this blank personally. How would you complete this sentence, "For me, living is _____"? It often gets filled in with cheap substitutes: money, sexual pleasure, power, beauty, entertainment, etc. But using the logic of this passage, notice what fills the second blank, "Dying is _____," if you fill the first with one of these substitutes. If you say, "Living is *money*," then you would fill in the second blank with "Dying is *being broke*." After all, you can't take it with you. If you say, "Living is *sexual pleasure*," then you would conclude, "Dying is *having no more pleasure.*" What about power? The second blank would be, "Dying is *being powerless.*" What about saying, "Living is *beauty*"? You must conclude, "Dying is *losing all beauty and rotting.*" If you live for *entertainment*, then your gravestone would read, "Dying is *having no more fun.*"

In your short life, what will you live for? What will you die for? You don't want to live merely for money, sex, power, beauty, or entertainment. These are gifts from God, to be stewarded properly, but they aren't our aims in life. They often turn into idols. Instead, you want to spend your life on something that not only matters now but will also matter in a billion years: Christ. If you say, "Living is Christ," then you can joyfully say, "Dying is gain." Living for Christ not only takes the sting out of death but also makes death gloriously attractive.

While many are wasting their lives pursuing empty treasures in life, you can still find examples of people living out this Christ-centered vision of life. In my own local church (Imago Dei Church), we have an extraordinary number of people preparing to do long-term missions. We have 80-plus people in the next five years leaving to make Christ known among the nations. In their going, they're saying (I hope!), "For *me*, living is Christ and dying is gain." They're saying, "Jesus is my everything. And death is no enemy." Of course, you don't have to go overseas to say this, but you have to fill in the blank: "For me, living is _____." How do you fill it in?

Philippians 1:12-26

The apostle Paul has been telling the Philippians about his present situation. You can imagine your pastoral leadership going on a mission trip but not returning. If they sent you an e-mail after about a month, you would probably want to open it!

The Philippians were concerned for Paul. But he doesn't say to them, "Hey, you guys, please contact the Roman officials and all your political leaders, and please work the system to get me out of prison." Instead, Paul spends verses 12-26 comforting the Philippians. He essentially tells them not to worry about him because his suffering has led to the advance of the gospel, the whole palace guard is hearing, and others are boldly proclaiming Christ (vv. 12-15); he tells them not to be concerned with the envious evangelists since they are proclaiming Christ (vv. 16-18). And now he says they shouldn't be worried about him since Christ will be exalted in his life and death. They have no need to be worried, no need to be ashamed. He's comforting his friends before launching into his exhortations and encouragements, which begin in verse 27 and extend through the rest of the book.

Let's consider these verses in light of Paul's ambition and his inspiring vision. We see his *ambition* of honoring Christ in verses 18-20. He expounds his *vision* of being with Christ, specifically in verse 23, as he relates his win-win situation (vv. 22-26). Later in the letter Paul says, "Do what you have learned and received and heard and seen in me" (4:9). As Christians, we need to look at the words and example of Paul and follow them.

The Christian's Ambition: Honoring Christ
PHILIPPIANS 1:18B-20

Paul provides three ways the Christian should seek to honor Christ: by rejoicing in Christ, by relying on Christ, and by representing Christ. In these ways we find a life worth living. There's a great difference in making a living and making a life. Let's learn how to live.

By Rejoicing in Christ Consistently (1:18b)

Paul concluded the previous section with "I rejoice," but now he turns his eyes to the future, "I *will* rejoice" (emphasis added). After reporting his present situation, Paul tells them his plans for the future, and they include rejoicing in Christ. He is confident and joyful despite his situation because his sufferings can't drown his joy. In life, suffering, or death, Paul will rejoice.

"So what are your plans for the future?" Have you heard this question lately? Maybe you have great plans; maybe you have no idea. Whether you plan on going to the nations, planting a church, or planting corn, make this your plan for the future: "I will rejoice in Christ all my days." Rejoicing, especially in suffering, greatly honors Jesus. You rejoice in what you value. When you rejoice in suffering, it really shows people that your treasure isn't anything in this world. Everything can fall apart, and you can still sing because Christ is your treasure.

God's people have passed on this legacy to us. The prophet Habakkuk demonstrated this steadfast commitment to rejoice in the Lord despite having no food in the fields and no cattle in the stalls (Hab 3:17-20). Job could say, "Praise the name of Yahweh," despite losing everything (Job 1:20-21). Hanson notes, "The prospect of [Paul's] trial drove him to prayer, but not to despair" (*Letter*, 77). What are your trials causing you to do: pray or pout? Praise or protest? Let us look to Jesus in our difficulty and find Habakkuk-like, Job-like, Paul-like joy.

By Relying on Christ Completely (1:19)

In verse 19 Paul speaks of the source of his joyful confidence. He's relying on the prayers of the Philippians and the sufficiency of the Spirit of Christ. Commentators point out that Paul exactly quotes Job 13:16 from the Greek translation of the Old Testament. And he may have been reflecting on the life of Job, who also suffered even though he committed no crime. Here's what he quotes:

> *Even if He kills me, I will hope in Him.* . . . *Yes,* this will result in my deliverance. (Job 13:15a,16a; emphasis added)

What exactly does Paul mean by *deliverance*? Does he mean release from prison? Or does he mean deliverance in the sense of final salvation? The former seems like a legitimate interpretation based on verses 25-26, where Paul states his confidence that he will survive and be reunited with the Philippians. In verse 19 he says, "I know," and in verse 25 he says, "I know," showing an apparent consistency of thought. In addition to this clue, the term itself can speak of preservation and deliverance from temporary crises (see Acts 7:25; 27:31).

However, I tend to side with Silva, Hanson, Witherington, and others that Paul is probably referring to final salvation and ultimate *vindication*. Even though he does express his belief that he will be delivered in verses 25-26, that doesn't mean that this reference in verse 19 has to mean release from prison. It still could mean deliverance in an ultimate sense, as Paul is talking about in the following verses, particularly in verses 20-21, 23, and 28. In addition to these references, another compelling argument for this interpretation is the context of the Job 13 reference. Witherington says,

> The context of Job is important there. The issue is Job's standing before God and his vindication. . . . Presumably, then, "this" [Phil 1:19] refers to all the things that have happened to Paul, both good and bad, and he is reflecting on his own experience in light of that of Job. God will work these things out for Paul's ultimate good, and if things go badly, humanly speaking, God can provide a bountiful supply of the

Spirit's aid so that Paul can endure and remain a good witness to the end. (*Friendship and Finances*, 46)

Witherington goes on, "*Soteria* surely does not mean personal safety here, for v. 20 suggests that Paul will obtain *soteria* whether or not his trial turns out favorably" (ibid.; cf. 2:12; 2 Tim 4:18).

What I want to emphasize here is not only Paul's confidence in the sovereignty of God (though we could linger on that!), but also how Paul plans on being sustained in the trial—namely, through *the prayers of the Philippians* and *the Spirit of Christ*. We, too, will endure hard times and ultimately arrive at our final destination in the same way: by relying on the sufficiency of the Spirit of Christ. How can you honestly say, "For me, living is Christ"? You need the Spirit of Christ to say this and live this. Otherwise, you will live for something else.

Notice two applications related to prayer. First, note the relationship between prayer and God's provision of the Spirit (Rom 8:26). Don't think your prayers don't matter! God uses means, and one of the means for sustaining His servants is the prayers of His people. Don't presume on a strong degree of the Spirit's presence either! Such power comes through prayer. The omnipresence of God isn't synonymous with the effects and influences of the Spirit. While we can't presume on these influences even when we pray, we know that prayer is the normal means that God uses to provide abundant help to the believer.

James reminds us that prayer is effectual (Jas 5:16). In the book of Acts we have numerous examples of the church praying for boldness and endurance in trial (e.g., Acts 12). Paul told the Corinthians that God was using their prayers to help them in his great trials (2 Cor 1:5,8-11). He also implored the Romans, the Ephesians, the Colossians, and the Thessalonians to pray for him (Rom 15:30; Eph 6:18-19; Col 4:3-4; 1 Thess 5:25; 2 Thess 3:1). So this reference to the Philippians isn't some passing comment. Paul really believed, like the other apostles and early saints, that God uses the prayers of His people to provide strength to His servants. So then, let's ask others to pray for us. And let's pray for others. What an encouragement it is to know that people are praying for you, and how important it is that you are praying for others.

Second, notice Paul's apparent meditation on Scripture and his prayer. It seems that Paul was reflecting on the life of Job, which led him to trust God and pour out his heart in thanks, praise, and prayer. If Paul meditates on Scripture in the midst of suffering, how much more should we? Don't think you can go without Scripture; you need God's Word to sustain you in your trials.

By Representing Christ Courageously (1:20-21)

By the power of the Spirit of Christ, Paul confidently asserts his goal for the future. When Paul uses the word *hope*, he doesn't mean it the way we often mean it. "I hope the Tigers make it to the World Series." "I hope it doesn't rain tomorrow." Paul isn't uncertain; rather, he is confident that he will represent Jesus because of the sufficiency of the Spirit and the sovereignty of God.

His goal is quite simply to honor Christ. His desire is to represent Christ both in his living and in his dying. Paul says that he will not be ashamed but will do this with all boldness. Imprisonment was a shameful thing in Paul's day, but he knows that God is using his imprisonment for gospel purposes. He isn't concerned about his reputation, but about Jesus' reputation. So he will courageously represent Christ before the world in his defense of the gospel.

This is how you honor Jesus above all things: you care more about His glory than your glory, and you live this way with courage. Will you seek to honor something or someone other than Jesus? Will you live as a coward or with courage? In Philippians 1:12-30 the theme of courage appears in several ways (vv. 14,20,28). Such boldness comes from the Spirit of Christ, as illustrated by the early church in the book of Acts (e.g., Acts 4:29-31). As we think about representing Jesus courageously, look again at verse 21: "For me, living is Christ and dying is gain." Consider (1) the public nature of this statement, (2) the grace of this statement, and (3) the unstoppable mentality of this statement.

First, Paul isn't saying this is his private goal—living for Christ. His ambition in life made its way into the public square; his ambition was visible to others. You are showing what's most important to you by how you live. In verse 22 he speaks of "fruitful work." Don't say that you're living for Christ if there's no labor for Christ. If you're going to represent Him, go public!

Second, we find grace later in the letter where Paul says that he has not yet attained this goal (3:12-15). Will we always live perfectly for Christ? No. Paul didn't achieve perfection. There's grace here. There's also grace in the fact that our work for Christ is "fruitful" work. This indicates that our life flows from our union with Christ. We need His grace in order to represent Him. Each day we must saturate ourselves in His grace and then resolve to live for Him faithfully before a watching world.

Third, when we are living in the grace of Jesus, empowered by His Spirit, we can share Paul's unstoppable mentality. You can live courageously for Christ because if they kill you, then you will be with Christ! This verse has inspired countless Christians through the years, particularly those who have laid down their lives for the cause of Christ. But to be clear, Paul isn't promoting martyrdom, though his words truly encourage persecuted Christians. Further, Paul isn't saying that he wants to escape from life. He knows that his life, even in suffering, is filled with joy and fruitful labor. It's not escape that he's emphasizing; it's eternal enjoyment. Paul says that in death there's *more* of what satisfies him *now*. The "now" is amazing because it's about serving Jesus, which brings meaning and joy. But he knows that the "later" is better because it involves face-to-face communion with Christ (1 John 3:1-3).

This outlook truly made Paul unstoppable, and I suppose it was aggravating to his opponents! You can imagine his conversations with the guards:

Guards: "Hey, Paul, we don't like you and your Messiah. We're going to kill you."

Paul: "That'd be great! Dying is gain! Bring it on!"

Guards: "On second thought, we're going to allow you to live."

Paul: "Fantastic! Living means fruitful, joyous labor!"

Guards: "Well, we're going to let you live, but we're going to make you suffer."

Paul: "Hey, guys, I consider the sufferings of this present world not worth comparing with the glory that is to be revealed. It would fill me with joy to suffer for the Name!"

Do you see the power of this perspective? Kill me? I'll be with Christ. Let me live? I'll live for Christ. Make me suffer? I'll experience joy and get rewarded by Christ. This is the unstoppable mentality of the apostle Paul, and it can be ours as well *if we treasure Christ above all things*.

In verses 12-26 you can't miss the Christ-centered passion of Paul. It's all about Jesus—rejoicing in Jesus, relying on Jesus, and representing Jesus. It makes me think of the oft-quoted prayer of St. Patrick, an evangelist to Ireland, who represented and relied on Jesus in the fifth century:

As I arise today, may the strength of God pilot me, the power of God uphold me, the wisdom of God guide me. May the

eye of God look before me, the ear of God hear me, the word
of God speak for me. May the hand of God protect me, the
way of God lie before me, the shield of God defend me, the
host of God save me. May Christ shield me today. Christ with
me, Christ before me, Christ behind me, Christ in me, Christ
beneath me, Christ above me, Christ on my right, Christ on
my left, Christ when I lie down, Christ when I sit, Christ when I
stand, Christ in the heart of everyone who thinks of me, Christ
in the mouth of everyone who speaks of me, Christ in every
eye that sees me, Christ in every ear that hears me. Amen.

That's a Christ-centered prayer, and that would be a Christ-centered life.
Is that your ambition?

The Christian's Vision: Being with Christ
PHILIPPIANS 1:22-26

Paul continues to open up his heart to the Philippians, allowing them
to hear how he's processing his situation. It's truly a win-win situation.
To live means honoring Christ with fruitful labor, and to die means pos-
sessing Christ in the fullest sense. He found a love greater than life itself,
and this vision of being with Christ inspired him to endure. Let's consider it in three parts.

Paul's Dilemma (1:22-23a)

Paul is torn between the options. Paul's rhetorical question demon-
strates the value of both. This is why he is "torn" or "pressured." This
is an interesting term. It's used in a variety of ways to convey strong
feelings, like the pressure of crowds, the controlling power of a fever, or
fear (Luke 8:45; 4:38; 8:37), and being compelled by love (2 Cor 5:14).
The Christian shares in this dilemma. We know that life is about fruitful,
meaningful, and joyful labor. But we know that death is better. That's
why it's a win-win situation. It's like saying, "Would you like a filet or a
rib eye?"

Paul's Desire (1:23b)

Paul states his ultimate preference. Why did he prefer dying? It meant
being with Christ, and that was better. Paul doesn't mention desire
for reward, but for Christ Himself, who is the ultimate reward. Dying

means more of Christ—a more complete, close, and intimate relationship with Him.

When I (Francis) go out of town—even if it's to Hawaii—without my wife, Lisa, I will feel like something is missing. Hawaii isn't my home. And I am always ready to come home to be with her. That's the way you feel when you're in love. Paul couldn't wait to see Jesus. I often hear people talk about heaven without mentioning Christ. That's not what Paul envisions. When he thought about death, he thought about being in the presence of Christ (cf. 2 Cor 5:8). Some people never desire heaven because they've built a pretty comfortable life right here.

The Greek word for "depart" used here was a nautical term in Greek literature, used to describe a ship setting loose its mooring. Death is not an enemy for the Christian. Death is like a boat; it takes you where you want to go. This past year my wife (Kimberly) and I (Tony) went on a cruise to celebrate our 10-year anniversary. It was my first cruise, and I thoroughly enjoyed it. One of my favorite memories relates to this idea of departing. As we set off from Ft. Lauderdale you could see the lights in the distance, slowly fading away. Then we were in the dark, and soon we would go to bed. The next morning, however, was stunning. We had a room with a window, and I looked out and saw the amazing blue waters of the Caribbean and this beautiful island.

Death is kind of like that. The person dying sees the light slowly fading away, and then it's gone. But the best is yet to come because when Christians die, they awake to see something more glorious than the Caribbean: they see the Galilean, Jesus! They experience the glory of God in a way that they have never experienced it. Paul knew death was better, but not just better—better by far! It's far better in every way: from your new body to the new heavens and the new earth, and most of all because we will dwell with the Savior. Do you want to be with Him?

There's a relationship that supersedes all of your relationships, a love like no other. And if you know Christ personally, then you can look at death and say that it is better than life because it means being with Christ. Do you long for this? Endure with hope, Christian. Soon the war will be over, and we will see Him. We will be with Him.

Paul's Decision (1:24-26)

Even though Paul knew that Christ's eternal presence was better, he resolved to live out his days for the sake of the church. Even though death is better, Paul decided that he should stay for the benefit of the body of Christ. He doesn't tell us why he has this confidence. On a human level, perhaps he knew that Rome had no real reason to punish him (Melick, *Philippians*, 86). From a spiritual perspective, he believed God had more work for him to do. There was a necessary and unfinished task, and part of that involved laboring for the progress and joy of the Philippians (v. 25) and for their boasting in Christ (v. 26). He must do these things before going to be with Christ. With this in mind, let me ask you four questions aimed at believers, with the first three coming out of verses 24-26.

Are you serving others (v. 24)? Paul says that it is "necessary" for the Philippians that he stay alive. Think about this. Is it necessary for you to stay at your church? If you left, would people really miss you? Please understand, Paul isn't saying that the whole world will fall apart if he leaves, and the world wouldn't fall apart if we left either. Jesus is Lord over His church, and we believe in the sovereignty of God. But I'm asking with the body in mind, which is often used regarding the church. If you take off my arm, I'm going to miss it! If you take my ear, I will miss it! Paul could say that the church needs him, and the church needs everyone in the body doing their part. The question is really, "Are you serving?" If you get a job transfer, would people in your group, your neighborhood, or your church say, "We really will miss you"? Sadly, some people give the church a bad name with their sin, and it would improve the church's witness if they weren't present anymore. Paul says, "I'm going to stay and serve. That's why I'm living." Can you say this?

Are you serving for the progress and joy of others (v. 25)? Hanson points out that the words *progress* and *joy* are united by the same preposition and are both modified by the phrase "in the faith" (*Letter*, 91). He adds, "Real progress in the faith will result in genuine joy in the faith" (ibid.). In other words, these two go together: progress in the faith and joy in the faith (cf. Rom 15:13). This is why Paul wants to stay on planet earth: so people can grow in their faith and grow in their joy. He says something similar to the Corinthians:

> *I do not mean that we have control of your faith, but we are workers with you for your joy, because you stand by faith.* (2 Cor 1:24)

What a wonderful way to think about ministry: striving so that others may rejoice in all that is theirs in Christ. Can you identify with this mission? Do you think about living daily for the benefit of others' progress and for the increase of their joy? This is another way we make much of Jesus.

Are you serving so that others may boast in Christ (v. 26)? The ultimate purpose of Paul's reunion with the Philippians had to do with their growing in their confidence in Christ. Through his ministry, he wants them to make much of Jesus. Put this together. What's life about? It's about fruitful work. What does that mean? It means doing our part. It means helping people grow in their faith. It means helping people have more joy in Christ. It means ministering so that others glorify Jesus more and more. That's why Paul wanted to stay around a little longer. He was willing to postpone ultimate joy for the joy of serving others.

How can you have this life? How can you have a life filled with meaning like this—honoring Christ by rejoicing in Christ, relying on Christ, and representing Christ? And how can you have a death like this—dying with the great joy of knowing you will forever be with Christ? How did Paul get this passion? He actually tells us in Philippians 3:

> *If anyone else thinks he has grounds for confidence in the flesh, I have more: circumcised the eighth day; of the nation of Israel, of the tribe of Benjamin, a Hebrew born of Hebrews; regarding the law, a Pharisee; regarding zeal, persecuting the church; regarding the righteousness that is in the law, blameless. But everything that was a gain to me, I have considered to be a loss because of Christ. More than that, I also consider everything to be a loss in view of the surpassing value of knowing Christ Jesus my Lord. Because of Him I have suffered the loss of all things and consider them filth, so that I may gain Christ and be found in Him, not having a righteousness of my own from the law, but one that is through faith in Christ—the righteousness from God based on faith. My goal is to know Him and the power of His resurrection and the fellowship of His sufferings, being conformed to His death, assuming that I will somehow reach the resurrection from among the dead.* (Phil 3:4-11)

Paul met Jesus and was changed. He was previously a religious person—an extremely religious person—but he didn't know Christ. When he traded religion for the righteousness of Jesus and the new life that Jesus gives, he found life. Consequently, everything else was inferior to the surpassing greatness of knowing Christ.

This is the good news. If you don't have meaning in life, and if you don't have this outlook on death, grace is available to you in the person of Jesus Christ, who came to us, as Philippians 2 says, and humbled Himself. He died the death we deserved, paying the penalty for sinners like us. Then He rose on our behalf, and He's now reigning over all things. He says, "There is a righteousness that depends on faith not works—My righteousness. Turn away from your own efforts and trust Me alone; I will forgive you, give you My righteousness, and change your current passion and your eternal destiny."

Everyone wants to live, and everyone will die. But there's only one way to have a life worth living and a death worth dying, and that is to look to the One who conquered death, the One Paul desired to see above all things. If you see Him as He is, you, too, will say, "To be with Christ is far better."

Reflect and Discuss

1. How do others fill in the blank: "Living is _____"? What are you living for? Why does this matter for you today?
2. In verse 18 Paul says that he "will" rejoice in the future. How does this challenge you?
3. Do you allow your trials to cause you to pout or to pray? What trials can you take before God in prayer now?
4. How does the story of Job relate to Paul's situation in prison? What encouragement can we take from both of their stories?
5. What does this passage teach us about the importance of intercessory prayer?
6. Paul had an unstoppable mentality. Can we share this perspective? If so, how would this outlook affect our daily lives?
7. Stop and pray St. Patrick's prayer (p. 69).
8. How could Paul view death as "far better"? Do you view death this way? Explain.
9. For what purpose did Paul say he would remain on the earth?
10. How does this passage motivate you to serve others?

Living Worthy of the Gospel Together

PHILIPPIANS 1:27–2:4

Main Idea: Paul exhorts the Philippians to live worthy of the gospel by standing together against opposition and by serving one another in humble compassion.

I. **Just One Thing**
II. **Stand Together against External Opposition (1:27b-30).**
 A. Teamwork (1:27b)
 B. Purpose and fearlessness (1:27c-28a)
 C. A sign (1:28b)
 D. Suffering (1:29-30)
III. **Serve One Another with Humble Compassion (2:1-4).**
 A. The basis for unity: fourfold motivation (2:1)
 B. The command for unity (2:2a)
 C. The expressions of unity (2:2b-4)

You might call this a John Wayne passage. "The Duke" was known for being tough and tender. In the first paragraph (1:27-30) Paul emphasizes the need for the Philippian Christians to be tough or courageous as they stand against opposition. In the second paragraph (2:1-4) he emphasizes the need to be affectionate or tender in their humble love toward one another. Both paragraphs emphasize unity and togetherness. Faithful Christians have always displayed this combination of courage and tenacity mingled with humility and compassion. These virtues are the results of living out the gospel. We are made courageous and compassionate by God's grace.

When sin entered the world through our first parents, Adam was told that he would be tempted to drift toward either passivity or abuse. These traits sadly typify many men today. But the gospel makes us both courageous (not passive) and humble (not abusive) at the same time. It liberates us to live in the freedom of the gospel, fearing no one (courage), and it reminds us that we are unworthy recipients of grace. Therefore, we should extend tender love to everyone (humility). If we want to turn the world upside down, like the early Christians who lived for King Jesus, not Caesar (Acts 17:6-7), then we must heed this passage of Scripture and pursue courageous, humble service together.

Just One Thing

For those who like things simple, set your eyes on verse 27. After Paul gives his report on his present situation (1:12-18) and his outlook on the future (1:19-26), he turns his attention to exhorting the Philippians. The following verse serves like a topic sentence over Philippians 1:27–2:18. Some versions translate the opening word as "Only" (ESV, NASB), but I like the way the HCSB expresses it: "Just one thing." O'Brien says, "The word introduces an admonition 'lifted like a warning finger,' as Barth puts it" (*Epistle*, 145).

Paul is making one very important, serious, and comprehensive point, and we should pay attention to it. What is it? He exhorts the Philippians to live "worthy of the gospel of Christ." Believers are making a statement about the gospel not only with their lips but also with their lives. The gospel is about love; therefore, we should be known as loving people. The gospel is about justice; therefore, we should be justice-seeking people. The gospel is about life; therefore, we should display visible vitality and joy in our gatherings and in our relationships. The gospel is about liberty; therefore, we should not live as stuffy legalists. The gospel is about humility; therefore, we should be a humble people, gladly serving others.

Paul has already filled his report with references to the gospel (1:5,12,16,18). Now he turns to exhort the Philippians about keeping the gospel central in their lives. The gospel should shape our lives, and it should be on our lips. We, too, must remember just this one thing! This type of life flows out of our identity as kingdom citizens. This emphasis on the kingdom is implied in verse 27. The phrase "your life" doesn't capture the idea of *citizenship* imbedded in the verb *politeuesthai* (the verb is built on the noun *polis*—city). He essentially says, "Live *as citizens* in a manner worthy of the gospel of Christ." The same idea is conveyed later in Philippians 3:20, where Paul reminds the church that they're citizens of heaven.

Paul uses this political word only here in Philippians. He probably uses it because of the Philippians' pride over their Roman citizenship. If someone visited Philippi, they would have been reminded of Rome. It was a little colony of Rome. Whenever someone visits a Christian congregation and observes their way of life, they should be reminded of Christ's kingdom. Churches are little outposts of the kingdom of God.

Our love, life, liberty, humility, and other values of the kingdom should be on display. We should seek to make known in the present what life in the future will be like.

Just as Roman citizens enjoyed certain privileges and responsibilities, so do kingdom citizens—much greater privileges and responsibilities. We have the unspeakable privilege of being part of the kingdom! Paul reminds us of the gospel that brought us into the kingdom: "He has rescued us from the domain of darkness and transferred us into the kingdom of the Son He loves" (Col 1:13). And we have the awesome responsibility of living out the gospel and making known the gospel. As kingdom citizens, let's not only live in such a way as to make the King known, but let's also remember that this world isn't our home. We can move to India and leave it all behind because we treasure Christ and because our citizenship is in heaven.

In exhorting the church to this end, there is an implicit encouragement: the gospel has changed them. For it would do no good to tell them to live worthy of the gospel if they hadn't experienced salvation through Christ. Thus, believers have the power to live out this command (cf. 2:12-13). We aren't trying to earn acceptance before God, but rather, out of our acceptance before God through Christ, we must now live in a way that's consistent with the gospel.

In 1:27b–2:4 Paul gives us two concrete ways kingdom citizens can live worthy of the gospel, both of which emphasize our *unity*. This is not all that's involved in living worthy of the gospel, but it's the first subject Paul emphasizes, and indeed, much of the letter highlights this issue. We must live worthy of the gospel *together*, as good solders on mission of gospel advancement. One can pick up the strong military language of Paul in this central section. Many scholars have alluded to the similarities between Paul's vocabulary and phrases and those of ancient military commanders.

In 1:27b-30 Paul focuses on unity for the purpose of withstanding external pressure. In 2:1-4 he focuses on internal care for one another. So let's seek to apply this text in these two parts: stand together against external opposition, and serve one another with humble compassion.

Stand Together against External Opposition
PHILIPPIANS 1:27B-30

In urging the Philippians to stand together, Paul uses several word pictures in this section that draw attention to unity, teamwork, and fearlessness for the mission. Following this, he explains the nature of Christian suffering and his own suffering. These ingredients—teamwork, fearlessness, and willingness to suffer for Christ's sake—are essential for a unified stand against opposition.

Teamwork (1:27b)

Paul exhorts the church to live consistently on mission together. One mark of effective leadership is being able to leave without things collapsing. In the church, pastors are called to develop future leaders and to labor alongside other leaders so that if they do have to leave for some reason, for any length of time, continuity and progress remain. Paul tells the Philippians, "Hey, you don't need me in order to move forward in the mission. Whether or not I'm there, keep pressing on."

In addition to this note of consistency, Paul reminds the church that their unity isn't superficial, but spiritual. Notice first these foundational expressions of unity: "one spirit" and "one mind." Paul reminds the church of the deep unity they share as believers, and he elaborates on this fundamental unity in 2:1-4. We must always remember this about Christian unity. What binds us together isn't age, similar economic category, or preferences, but the gospel of Jesus and the Spirit of God. We are more like magnets than a bag of marbles; there's an internal unity among believers.

Paul then provides two word pictures illustrating Christian teamwork: "stand firm in one spirit" and "work side by side." Believers are like *soldiers* and like *athletes*, fighting and contending together as they make the gospel known to the nations.

As soldiers. The metaphor "stand" was taken from the military (Melick, *Philippians*, 89). This word *stekō* means "to stand firm and hold one's ground." The term indicates the determination of a soldier who stands his ground, not budging one inch from his post. The Philippians were attacked for believing in Christ as King. Consequently, Paul urges them to remember that they're engaged in a war. They must not disavow their loyalty to Jesus, but must instead faithfully stand firm in the face of intimidation.

We have strength to stand firm because of our union with Christ. In Philippians 4:1 Paul says, "So then, my brothers, you are dearly loved and longed for—my joy and crown. In this manner *stand firm in the Lord*, dear friends" (emphasis added). Here Paul grounds his exhortation in what God has done for us in Christ. We find our power to stand through our Warrior-King, Jesus. We are His. He loves us. He has purchased us. He has sent His Spirit to empower us. Now, stand together against external conflict in His power.

Perhaps you've read about the famous battle of Thermopylae (or saw one of the movies about it). In 480 BC an alliance of Greek-city states, led by King Leonidas of Sparta, fought against the mighty Persian army. The battle took place at the pass of Thermopylae in central Greece. Vastly outnumbered, the Greeks held back the Persians for three days in one of history's most famous last stands. A small force led by King Leonidas, including his famous group of 300 Spartans, blocked the only road through which the massive army of Persia's Xerxes the Great could pass. Likewise, the Philippian congregation may have felt vastly outnumbered, but they were called to stand courageously against hostile forces. And they were to do this together, under the kingship of Jesus, who has already won the ultimate battle.

As athletes. Paul adds to this image the call for "working," "contending," "laboring," or "striving" (ESV) side by side. The word is *synathleo* (cf. 2 Tim 2:5). You can hear the word *athleo* in there, from which we get the word *athlete*. So, Paul shifts to the realm of athletics, a world with which he was familiar. This phrase is only used twice in the New Testament (here and in 4:3). Melick points out, "If the Roman military element appreciated the military associations with the word 'stand,' the Greek population would identify with the necessity of 'contending as one man' as was demanded in athletic games" (*Philippians*, 90).

Many commentators make a connection not only with athletic games but also with the gladiator arena. It's like Paul envisions Christians in the arena of faith, with himself as a part of the contest (see O'Brien's discussion, *Epistle*, 150). Others suggest that it's a word descriptive of wrestling, but not wrestling as we know it—rather, a competition that involved a whole team wrestling together against another team. They battled in a united front. In contemporary sport, you might think of football, especially the linemen. They block, side by side, for the same purpose. In team sports, each person must do his or her part. You need the whole team contributing. So it is with the church. We advance the gospel side by side, working, contending, laboring together.

Let's pause and make a few applications regarding teamwork. *Remember you're in a battle.* What sort of images come to mind when you think of a Christian? Someone who spends all day in a library? Someone removed from society like a monk in a desert? Do you think of a celebrity? Notice what Paul thinks about: soldiers of the King and determined athletes. He uses images that denote warfare, perseverance, teamwork, and tenacity. He uses such metaphors often (cf. 2 Tim 2:3-5). We need to remember that this is the nature of the Christian life. You're an athlete. You're a soldier.

Why do athletes practice multiple times a day and go on disciplined diets? Why do soldiers put themselves through difficult training? Because the prize or the goal is worth it. We must engage in the war and contend faithfully because Christ is worth it. Paul tells Timothy that the aim of a good soldier is to "please the recruiter" (2 Tim 2:4). He goes on to tell him, "Keep your attention on Jesus Christ" (2 Tim 2:8). Remember Him when you go on those mission trips filled with unidentifiable bites, parasites, and sleepless nights. Remember Him as you go with that church-planting team to the urban core. Remember He is worth it when you keep serving and counseling that wayward brother or sister. He is worth it, and He is enough.

Realize that we don't engage in this battle on our own. There's nothing like being part of a local church on mission together; no group, no team, no organization is like the church, the fellowship of the gospel. Don't be a secret agent, a little ninja running off by yourself! Be part of the unit! Be part of the team! Pray, give, go, encourage, invest, and support. Be a soldier. And do so in Christ's power.

Fight alongside other believers, not against them. Unfortunately, some in the Philippian church started fighting each other. Such sideways energy output does no good in our efforts to advance the gospel in the face of the real enemy, Satan. Look at what Paul says regarding this matter, as he uses some similar language in chapter 4:

> *I urge Euodia and I urge Syntyche to agree in the Lord. Yes, I also ask you, true partner, to help these women who have contended for the gospel at my side, along with Clement and the rest of my coworkers whose names are in the book of life.* (Phil 4:2-3)

Previously, these two ladies were contending alongside Paul in the mission, but something happened, and they swerved off mission. How common this is in the church! *Remember the Titans* is one of my favorite sports movies. It's the story of a high school football team in Virginia in their first season as an ethnically integrated unit. They had to overcome some serious internal strife before they could win games against their opponents. They resolved many of the tensions at a two-week training camp at Gettysburg. Before they could win, they had to become a unit. Don't spend your energy on foolish debates and on things that don't center on advancing the gospel. We have a mission field to engage; we don't need fighting in the barracks and in the locker room!

Purpose and Fearlessness (1:27c-28a)

Paul says the Philippians must contend in two complementary ways, which he explains both positively and negatively. The positive exhortation addresses our purpose, and the negative addresses the issue of courage. Positively, the church should contend "for the faith that comes from the gospel." Just as Paul made it his ambition to advance the gospel in spite of opposition (v. 12), so must the church. This is the purpose for which we take our stand and for which we strive together as one. We want to make the gospel known. We are united both in the gospel and for the gospel.

Paul doesn't call the church to make an ideology or a political party the main thing. He tells them to make the gospel—the good news about Jesus Christ, described in 2:5-11—the main thing. We, the church, must avoid foolish arguments that distract us from the mission—questions like, "Will all of our toenails that we've clipped in our lifetimes be put back on at the resurrection?" Like Jude says, let's earnestly "contend for the faith" (Jude 3). Are you striving to make the gospel known through hospitality? Are you striving to make the gospel known by giving out books or inviting friends to worship gatherings? Let's be committed to this mission of advancing the gospel.

Negatively, he says "not being frightened in any way by your opponents" (1:28). Paul uses a term that appears only here in the New Testament to speak of being startled like a horse. Whoever these opponents were, the Philippians were not to be intimidated by them. They were to stand boldly and seek to spread the gospel faithfully (cf. vv. 14,20). They were probably not the Judaizers mentioned in chapter 3, since Philippi had a small Jewish population. These bullies were probably their pagan neighbors, perhaps even the authorities (O'Brien, *Epistle*, 153).

Paul spoke of adversaries and opposition often. To the Corinthians he said, "But I will stay in Ephesus until Pentecost, because a wide door for effective ministry has opened for me—yet many oppose me" (1 Cor 16:8-9). Effective ministry doesn't mean a ministry devoid of conflict. Paul says that "many oppose me," and we, too, will have our adversaries. After all, the chief adversary hates everything we do in Jesus' name. In light of the battle that we face, we need to stand together.

John Knox, a preacher in Scotland who showed remarkable courage, endured much opposition from the crown. During the dark reign of Bloody Mary in 1553–58, she burned some 280 Christians, including some of Knox's friends. He was a small man with a weak constitution, but he had a burning desire to serve God. In view of his fearless ministry, one person said at his funeral, "Here lies one who never feared the face of man" (in Stott, *Between Two Worlds*, 304–5). You won't fear the face of man if you fear God more than man. Jesus told His disciples, "Don't fear those who kill the body but are not able to kill the soul; rather, fear Him who is able to destroy both soul and body in hell" (Matt 10:28). If you're a Christian, you've already been accepted by the only One who ultimately matters. You don't have to fear condemnation, so what can a human do to you? Don't fear them. Your Father is with you. Live in the freedom of your acceptance before God through Christ, and never fear the face of man.

Let me encourage you to speak the gospel fearlessly and to be prepared for conflict when you do. While some will be drawn to the grace of Jesus, others will not only reject it but may also deeply oppose you. We shouldn't be surprised by hate, conflict, or persecution. We don't go looking for it. We shouldn't bring it on ourselves by non-gospel-reflecting conduct. But we must remember that we will suffer for proclaiming the message of a crucified, risen, reigning, and returning King. And we don't do this alone; we do this together, by the Spirit.

A Sign (1:28b)

As Paul describes the nature of Christian suffering in the mission, he says, "This is a sign of destruction for them, but of your deliverance." Paul offers this as a word of encouragement to the Philippians, which is also a word of warning to unbelievers. When Christians are standing together in the face of external pressure, something is happening: a sign is given. It's a "two-way sign." It's a sign pointing to destruction *and* salvation, to confrontation *and* confirmation, to judgment *and* assurance. Unbelievers are confronted with their unbelief and their impending judgment if they don't believe. Believers have a word of confirmation, as God assures them in the struggle that they really are God's people and they will be saved on the last day. Notice how non-politically correct this statement is. Contrary to what you hear, not everyone is going to heaven. We don't all believe the same thing. Like the judge in the gladiator games, we give a "thumbs up" to some and a "thumbs down" to others. Therefore, the decisive issue is, What will you do with that man on the cross?

Paul encourages the saints with these words. While those on the outside may mock and torture them, they will be saved. And he reminds them of who saves, pointing them to the source: "This is from God." God began the work of salvation in them, and He will sustain and keep them until the end. Paul tells them that their suffering is giving evidence of God's glorious salvation, which they experience in the present, and of the final salvation they will one day enjoy.

We need to remember that our opponents won't win. We shouldn't live hopelessly. God the Judge will have the last word. Some Christians live this life in a very sad, hopeless way. But we shouldn't. The wicked prosper only for a season (Ps 73). People may oppose you, but that doesn't mean you should live in discouragement. Many of the pagans in Philippi probably looked at the small band of Christians and thought, *We're winning*, and from the surface, the church may have looked like a small, weak, pathetic band of people. But God will have the last word; a sign is given, and it's a "thumbs down" to those who persecute you and a "thumbs up" to those who take a stand for the gospel. Don't panic. God is reigning, and God's glory will cover the earth as the waters cover the sea (Hab 2:14). Go on speaking the gospel, and don't be deterred by what you read in popular literature or online.

Suffering (1:29-30)

Paul rounds out this paragraph by touching on the nature of Christian suffering. What he says may surprise some believers. Most Christians understand salvation as a gift from God (John 1:12-13; Eph 2:8-9), but Paul points out that *suffering* for Christ's sake is also a gift. Suffering for the sake of Christ is a privilege. Paul's words are worth a careful, prayerful reflection. Do you recall how Peter rebuked Jesus for saying that He, the Christ, was going to die on a cross? At that time, Peter's gospel didn't have a cross in it, so he was rattled by this notion. Jesus then effectively told Peter, "You must follow Me to the cross" (see Mark 8:31-38). Peter had a hard time accepting this basic fact about following Jesus. How much more do we who live in relatively safe environments lose sight of this reality?

To be clear, we don't suffer in the same way as Jesus; His death was an atoning death. But our symbol for life and ministry is a cross, not a recliner, not a flat screen, not first-class tickets on the airplane, and not plush golf courses. You may have those things, and they may be enjoyed appropriately at times, but let's not forget that the call to follow Jesus is a call to follow Him down the Calvary road. And Paul adds this: It's a gift to suffer for Him like that!

How exactly is suffering for Christ a gift? According to the previous verse, it provides a sense of assurance that we belong to Jesus. Suffering also brings you closer to Jesus. Paul relates this idea in 3:10-11. This attitude regarding suffering appears throughout the book of Acts. At one point, after the apostles had been beaten, Luke says, "Then they went out from the presence of the Sanhedrin, rejoicing that they were counted worthy to be dishonored on behalf of the Name" (Acts 5:41). They did not just tolerate suffering, they rejoiced in it! They saw it as a gift.

You will enjoy a special intimacy with Jesus as you identify with Him through courageous Christian witness. Suffering for the sake of the mission doesn't mean He is abandoning you; rather, suffering is a sign that He is with you. Jesus calls us all to obey Him, and that will lead to varying degrees of conflict. You may face a mild form of opposition, like being mocked, insulted, or ignored. You may face severe opposition, like being tied up by Islamic extremists. In every situation, see your suffering as a privilege. We get to suffer for His name.

In verse 30 Paul tells the church that they were following his own way of life. They knew of his sufferings in Philippi and now in Rome, and he calls on them to share in these sufferings for the sake of the King. Paul and the church both received this gift of suffering. Full citizenship involves the grace of believing and the grace of suffering, together in the cause of Christ. Now let us live in a manner worthy of the gospel together, as we stand against external conflict.

Serve One Another with Humble Compassion
PHILIPPIANS 2:1-4

Unity is still on Paul's mind, though the focus shifts to internal unity. The church must not only take a stand against outside pressure, but they should also pursue particular attitudes and actions within the body of Christ in order to overcome division. Let's consider this classic passage on unity in three simple parts: the basis for unity, the command for unity, and the expressions of unity.

The Basis for Unity: Fourfold Motivation (2:1)

Paul opens with a series of "if" statements that may be better understood as "since" statements or "because" statements. They could be stated, "If, as is indeed the case" (O'Brien, *Epistle*, 165). The "if" refers to *certainties*, not possibilities. Together, these motivations remind believers of the cords of love that bind them together as God's people (Hanson, *Letter*, 106).

The first reminder is that there is encouragement in Christ. We have the blessing of knowing Christ (3:10) and being found in Him (3:9). We have been given the gift of faith (1:29). Does anything lift our spirits more than knowing we are in Christ? In the midst of trial and suffering, find encouragement in your relationship with Jesus.

Second, we have the consolation of love. This is presumably a reference to the love of Christ that comforts us. He is ours, and we are His. What comfort! It may also be a reference to mutual love for one another that flows from this relationship with Jesus. This connection was made in Philippians 1:7-8. Paul loves the church "with the affection of Christ Jesus" (1:8). We know God's love, and His love makes us love others.

Third, we're reminded that we share in the fellowship with the Spirit. The Greek word translated "fellowship" (*koinonia*) is the same word as in 1:5. The Spirit unites us as brothers and sisters (1:27), partners in the gospel, and the Spirit helps in our weaknesses (Rom 8:26). Later Paul says that Christians worship God "by the Spirit" (Phil 3:3). Paul is aware that disunity threatened the Philippian congregation, so he reminds them of the Spirit-produced fellowship they share.

Fourth, we share affection and mercy. This affection (cf. 1:8) or "tenderness" (NIV) flows from our union with Christ. Christ has loved us with amazing tenderness. He has shown us infinite affection. Mercy or "sympathy" (ESV) or "compassion" (NIV) has also come to us from the source of all compassion, our great God (see Ps 103; Rom 12:1; 2 Cor 1:3). We share in a common experience of being the objects of God's compassion. This tender care should cause us to look out for the interests of others (Phil 2:4) and serve sacrificially as illustrated by the life of Epaphroditus (2:25-30; 4:18).

We enjoy these amazing blessings as fellow believers. Notice Paul's approach with the Philippians. He's not only warm and pastoral, but he's also quick to first mention the blessings of the gospel before giving certain exhortations. If all you ever do is tell people what they're supposed to be doing, then they will get burned out. Remind people of the blessings while giving them the imperatives. Do this for your own soul, and do this for other Christians.

The Command for Unity (2:2a)

Technically, the one imperative in verses 1-4 is found here in the beginning of verse 2. The imperative is "fulfill my joy." Paul wanted the church to be like-minded in order to complete his joy. This may sound strange, but not if you think about it. A minister's well-being is always tied to the unity and growth of the church. John says, "I have no greater joy than this: to hear that my children are walking in the truth" (3 John 4). If you're a parent, you know this as well. Proverbs says, "A wise son brings joy to his father, but a foolish son, heartache to his mother" (10:1). Parents' well-being is tied to the maturity and growth of their kids. Paul, like a father to the Philippian church, naturally longs for the church to be unified, and so he requests like-mindedness.

The Expressions of Unity (2:2b-4)

To be united, Paul says, the church must have **the same mentality**. Instead of having petty squabbles and rivalries, they should get their heads on straight and remember their identity and common mission. Also, to be united, Paul says, we must pursue **Christlike humility.** This virtue had a negative connotation in Greek thought, carrying with it the notion of a slave, but Christians elevated it rightly as the soil of all virtue (see Luke 14:11; Eph 4:2; 1 Pet 5:5; cf. Col 3:12). Of course, the Old Testament extols this virtue, and the proud are regularly rebuked. The humble person will avoid "rivalry and conceit." Paul just spoke about the wrongly motivated preachers who are driven by rivalry in 1:17, and now he tells the whole church to avoid this attitude. Rivalry will divide congregations in a terrible way. Every church member should beware of the presence of rivalry and seek to put it to death. They should seek the glory of Jesus instead of their own glory and rejoice whenever someone is being used by God to advance the gospel.

The Greek word for "conceit" is translated as "vain glory" or "vain conceit" in some versions. It's an empty glory, a glory that doesn't exist. People are literally conceited over nothing! The opposite of this is the person of Christ. He didn't have vain glory; He had all glory, and yet He made Himself nothing for our sake. Follow the way of Jesus, not the way of our culture. We should ask ourselves some questions here: Am I competing for people's attention and approval? Do I find it difficult or easy to rejoice in the success of others? Am I conceited? Do I think I'm superior to people? Am I concerned with the needs of others?

There will never be unity in a congregation apart from people walking in humility. Paul puts it like this to the Romans: "Be in agreement with one another. Do not be proud; instead, associate with the humble" (Rom 12:16). Catch the connection with agreement and humility. A humble person contributes to the unity of the church, and humility is a key theme of chapter 2 of Philippians. It will be at the heart of a gospel-centered church. Paul goes on to give us the amazing Christ hymn in 2:6-11. There we see the ultimate picture of humility. Jesus, who had every right to be conceited, instead emptied Himself and associated with us, the lowly. He's our model for humility, and He gives us power to live out an others-oriented lifestyle.

Third, to be unified, we must live with **sensitivity** toward the needs of others. In verse 4 Paul tells the church not just to consider their own interests, but also "the interests of others." In your conversation with others, do you really listen to them? Are you really concerned about others? In this age of taking selfies, such a lifestyle of thinking about others is uncommon. It was rare in Paul's day, and it's rare in our day.

I (Francis) remember waking up one Sunday unable to get a thought out of my head for about an hour. Do you know what it was? I was thinking about me. I was thinking about poor, pitiful me. I was feeling a bit sick. I got in from San Diego the night before at 1:00 a.m., and I had to get up and preach four services. Then I was convicted as I realized that I was about to preach on Philippians 2, which is all about considering others more than yourself. It's so easy to think about ourselves and not others, isn't it?

The practice of thinking about the needs of others flows from the attitude of humility Paul mentioned in verse 3. Others have pointed out that humility is not thinking less of yourself; it's thinking of yourself less. I've always enjoyed C. S. Lewis's description of a humble person as he paints a picture of verses 3-4:

> Do not imagine that if you meet a really humble man he will be what most people call "humble" nowadays: he will not be a sort of greasy, smarmy person, who is always telling you that, of course, he is nobody. Probably all you will think about him is that he seemed a cheerful, intelligent chap who took a real interest in what you said to him. If you do dislike him it will be because you feel a little envious of anyone who seems to enjoy

life so easily. He will not be thinking about humility: he will not be thinking about himself at all. (*Mere Christianity*, 128)

Only when we possess the grace of humility will we serve others with spiritual sensitivity. A humble person thinks of others. An arrogant, self-absorbed person thinks only of himself.

In light of the importance of humility, John Stott says, "At every stage of our Christian development and in every sphere of our Christian discipleship, pride is the greatest enemy and humility our greatest friend" ("Pride, Humility and God," 2–3). Therefore, for the good of our own souls, for the unity of the church, and for the good of our witness before a watching world, we should want to know how to grow in humility. Drawing from other passages of Scripture, allow me to list a few disciplines necessary for cultivating humility. I'm not listing them as one who has mastered the art of humility; I list them as one who needs this grace as much as anyone!

Grow in humility by reflecting on the cross of Christ. After giving these exhortations, Paul immediately takes us to the cross. There is no room for pride at the cross. As the hymn says, "It was my sin that held him there, until it was accomplished" (Getty and Townend, "How Deep"). We see the holiness of God, the sinfulness of man, and the grace of our Lord on display at the cross.

Grow in humility by reflecting on the glory of Christ. After describing Christ's incarnation in Philippians 2:6-8, Paul points us to Christ's exaltation in vv. 9-11. He reminds us that Christ is now ruling and reigning and that one day everyone will bow before our glorified King. Allow Christ's all-sovereign lordship to create in you humble adoration before Him.

Grow in humility by reflecting on God's Word, which reveals to us Christ's humility and exaltation. Studying the Bible can be an act of humility in itself if you're going to the Bible with the attitude, "I need Your Word more than bread." It is the arrogant person who thinks he or she doesn't need to hear from God's Word. Of course, some read in order to fill their pride, and that's wrong. God is looking for people who humbly seek and submit to His Word. He tells Isaiah, "I will look favorably on this kind of person: one who is humble, submissive in spirit, and trembles at My word" (Isa 66:2). As you study, meditate on the greatness of God. Like Asaph in Psalm 73, get before God and realize that He rules over all; stand in the way of His greatness and regain your perspective on yourself and all of life.

Grow in humility through prayer. One reason for our prayerlessness is lack of humility. Prayer is a very hard thing to do because it seems like we aren't doing anything. But it's also hard because it's a humble act. We must humble ourselves before God's mighty hand regularly and cast our cares on Him (1 Pet 5:6-7).

Grow in humility through serving others. By doing humble actions, like serving without being noticed, you may begin to grow in humility. Paul encourages the church to think on the interests of others. So serve people humbly. As you do this, pray for God to cultivate in you the spirit of humility that was so gloriously displayed in our Lord.

How did the early Christians turn the world upside down? They obeyed a different King. They lived lives that reflected the values of the kingdom, lives that were worthy of the gospel. That involved standing together against external opposition with courage and serving one another with humble compassion. Let's go and do likewise in humble dependence on our Savior.

Reflect and Discuss

1. How does Philippians 1:27 encompass much of what follows?
2. What does it mean to live as a citizen of the kingdom, not just a citizen of your country?
3. How does this passage encourage churches to be "teammates"?
4. What do you make of the military language in this passage? How is the Christian life like a war?
5. What does this passage say about suffering?
6. What kind of motivations does Paul give for the church to serve one another with compassion in 2:1-4?
7. How does the command for unity in 2:2 strike you?
8. Do you find it challenging to avoid rivalry and to put the needs of others ahead of your own? How would your church be different if everyone faithfully lived out Philippians 2:3-4?
9. How does Jesus show us the Philippians 2:3-4 kind of life?
10. How does this passage show us our need for the Savior?

A Christ-Centered Mind-set

PHILIPPIANS 2:5-11

Main Idea: In this amazing passage, Paul magnifies the humility and exaltation of Jesus, which should lead us to emulate Jesus' example and adore Him as Lord of all.

I. The Mind of Christ (2:5)
II. The Humility of Christ (2:6-8)
    A. His humble renunciation (2:6)
    B. His humble incarnation (2:7)
    C. His humble crucifixion (2:8)
III. The Exaltation of Christ (2:9-11)
    A. His exalted position (2:9)
    B. Everyone's adoration and confession (2:10-11)

Last week, I (Tony) went into a store to grab a bottle of water, and the cashier asked, "Where are you from? You don't look like you're from here."

I said, "I live in North Carolina."

He said, "You look like Pitbull. You know him?"

I said, "No."

He went on to describe this pop icon. Then he asked, "Are you married?"

I said, "Yes, happily."

He said, "Why you married? How old are you?"

"I'm 37," I answered.

He said, "You're too young to be married. You need many women."

I said, "No, that's so overrated, man."

He said, "Really? I think you need many women."

I said, "I think you need Jesus, and you need a wife." Then I said, "I've gotta run, but you need to rethink your outlook on life."

In Philippians 2 Paul exhorts the Philippians to adopt Jesus' death as their central outlook, their central mind-set, for life. Instead of living to get and get and get—more women, more praise, more money—the Christian is called to imitate Christ, who came to give and give and give.

Philippians 2:5-11 is one of the most amazing passages in the Bible. We are on holy ground here. It appears to be an early hymn or poetic creed, perhaps used liturgically in ancient worship. It seems to have a unified structure, starting with God in eternity and ending in the same way, but hinging on verse 9. Think V-shape, with verse 9 being the bottom angle—"even death on a cross." Some propose that it was written by an early Jewish community in Jerusalem and sung during the Lord's Supper. One could certainly write a whole book on this passage; our approach here is more telescopic than microscopic. This text is both doctrinal and ethical in nature. It emphasizes the stunning humility of Jesus, who became a servant and died on behalf of sinners to the glory of God. As a result of His cross-work and resurrection, He is now exalted as the true King. He is our Savior and our example.

D. A. Carson points out that the cross can be viewed from five perspectives. From *God's perspective*, Jesus died as a propitiation for our sins (1 John 2:2). He absorbed God's wrath and turned away God's anger from us. From *Christ's perspective*, Jesus obeyed His Father perfectly, saying, "Not My will, but Yours, be done" (Luke 22:42). He carried out His assignment to "give His life—a ransom for many" (Mark 10:45). This text in Philippians highlights Christ's perfect obedience (also a major theme in John's Gospel). He became "obedient to the point of death— even to death on a cross" (2:8). From *Satan's perspective*, the cross means the accuser's defeat (see Rev 12:11). From *sin's perspective*, the cross is the means by which our debt is paid. Finally, from *our perspective*, while acknowledging all of these truths, treasuring the love and justice of God as well as the substitutionary life and death of Jesus—His victory over Satan and sin—we must also note that the cross serves "as the supreme standard of behavior" (Carson, *Basics*, 42). It's the primary point that Paul makes here in Philippians 2:5 (ibid.).

Notice where this passage is located in Philippians. It looks back to the previous verses (specifically vv. 1-4), and it also looks ahead through verse 18. In verses 1-4 Paul tells the Philippians to avoid rivalry and conceit and to instead pursue humility and selfless care for the interests of others. Then in verse 5, he draws their attention to the attitude and actions of Jesus, the supreme example of thinking about the needs of others in humble love. There are several word links with verses 1-4 and 5-11, such as: "same/one mind" and "mind" (cf. v. 2 ESV with v. 5 ESV), "consider" (cf. v. 3 with v. 6), and "humility" and "humbled Himself" (cf. v. 3 with v. 8). Jesus gives the perfect example of the mind-set we need and the humility we should pursue, as well as the ultimate picture of considering the needs of others.

So while Philippians 2:6-11 is filled with theological hot points that we must consider closely, we must remember that Paul's purpose for penning it isn't to stimulate debate. It's not here for argumentation; it's here for our adoration and emulation. As a result of adoring Christ and emulating Christ, we will experience unity as a people. Unity isn't the result of preaching on unity; it's the result of people adoring and emulating Jesus. The more we behold His glory and imitate His character, the more unified we will be as a church.

Additionally, this hymn reminds us not only of the pattern we have to follow but also of the power we possess to emulate Christ. Not only do we need Jesus' example, we also need His death and resurrection. We fail to serve God and others perfectly, but Christ died for self-absorbed, self-glorifying people like us. He rose on our behalf and now empowers us to follow His example (see vv. 12-13). Let's look at this passage in two parts—the mind of Christ and the hymn to Christ—and then collect some points of application.

The Mind of Christ
PHILIPPIANS 2:5

This opening verse is translated in various ways (emphasis added):

- Make your own **attitude** that **of Christ** Jesus. (HCSB)
- Have this **mind** among yourselves, which **is yours in Christ** Jesus. (ESV)
- You must have the same **attitude** that Christ **Jesus had**. (NLT)
- Have this **attitude** in yourselves which **was** also **in Christ** Jesus. (NASB)
- Think of yourselves the way Christ Jesus thought of himself. (MSG)
- In your relationships with one another, have the same **mind-set as Christ Jesus**. (NIV)

Whether translated "this mind," "mind-set," "frame of mind," or "attitude," it's essentially saying the same thing. The main exegetical question is which verb should be supplied after this first phrase: "Have this mind among yourselves" (ESV). We are left with varying renderings of the latter clause, literally translated, "which also in Christ Jesus." The ESV translates it, "which *is yours* in Christ Jesus," but provides a footnote: "Or which *was also* in Christ Jesus." But there's a difference in "is yours" and "was in Christ." One gives a theological interpretation, emphasizing our position in Christ ("is yours in Christ"), and the other gives an ethical interpretation, emphasizing emulation of Jesus' example ("was also in Christ").

While "is yours in Christ Jesus" makes sense theologically, I concur with others who say that many interpreters overreact to the "idealized ethic" of following Jesus' example, and they overlook the context, namely, that we're dealing with an analogy of Christ as our example. The fact that Paul doesn't detail the stages of Christ's exaltation (e.g., His resurrection) also adds to the argument that he intended to use this hymn as an example for Christians to follow. More likely, Paul intended his readers to supply the verb "was," rendering it, "Have this mind among yourselves which *was* also in Christ Jesus." I think this latter view, the ethical interpretation, fits better than the former view. Paul is commending the attitude that Jesus had in order to stimulate humility and unity among the congregation. Even so, both options are true. And it is because of the fact that we are *in* Christ Jesus that we can live out this ethical exhortation. We are united with Christ, and we must now walk after Him.

There's also a corporate element to this example. Some translate it as "yourselves," and others give a more dynamic equivalent or paraphrase, "in your relationships with one another" (NIV). Paul isn't simply speaking to the private experience of individuals. He is writing about unity in the church, which comes through adopting a humble, Christ-like mind-set. He wants to see "a community mindful of Christ" (Hanson, *Letter*, 118). To summarize, Paul exhorts the Philippians to pursue the attitude and actions of Jesus. As we prepare to look at the hymn to Christ, keep this point in mind. As you reflect on it, ask yourself, Is this my attitude, my mind-set? Is this my way of life? Do I seek to get, get, and get, or to give, give, and give? And ask, Is this our mind-set as a community? Are we known for humility and compassion?

Imitation is a theme of Philippians. Later in the chapter, Paul holds Timothy and Epaphroditus up as examples worthy of honor and emulation (2:19-30, esp. 20-21,30). In chapter 3 Paul tells the church to follow his example and to "observe those who live according to the example you have in us" (3:17). While we may emulate many role models in life, we must remember that Jesus is the *example par excellence*. The following verses unpack His humility, His perfect life, His crucifixion, and His exaltation.

Most teachers break down the text into two main stanzas, Christ's humiliation (2:6-8) and Christ's exaltation (vv. 9-11). Paul extolls Jesus,

> *who, existing in the form of God,*
> *did not consider equality with God*
> *as something to be used for His own advantage.*
> *Instead He emptied Himself*
> *by assuming the form of a slave,*
> *taking on the likeness of men.*
> *And when He had come as a man*
> *in His external form,*
> *He humbled Himself by becoming obedient*
> *to the point of death—*
> *even to death on a cross.*
> *For this reason God highly exalted Him*
> *and gave Him the name*
> *that is above every name,*
> *so that at the name of Jesus*
> *every knee will bow—*
> *of those who are in heaven and on earth*
> *and under the earth—*
> *and every tongue should confess*
> *that Jesus Christ is Lord,*
> *to the glory of God the Father.* (2:6-11)

The following image illustrates the nature of this hymn:

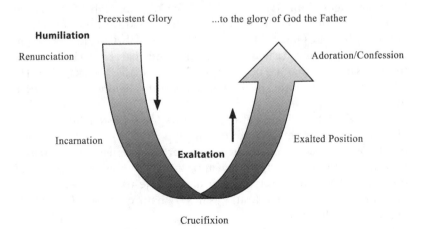

In verses 6-8 Paul speaks of the remarkable humility of Jesus. He set aside His divine prerogatives and incarnated Himself, being obedient to the Father all the way down to the cross. But God exalted Him. One day every knee will bow and every tongue will confess that Christ is Lord. Jesus accomplished His work and was exalted "to the glory of God the Father" (v. 11).

The Humility of Christ
PHILIPPIANS 2:6-8

Let's consider the humility of Christ in three parts: (1) humble renunciation, (2) humble incarnation, and (3) humble crucifixion. Allow these truths to lead you to adoration and emulation.

His Humble Renunciation (2:6)

Jesus enjoyed His preexistent exalted position, but He laid it aside.

"*Who, existing in the form of God*" (*v. 6a*). Notice, in these opening phrases, some very important doctrinal points. When Paul uses this first phrase, he touches on both the *preexistence* of Jesus and the *divine nature* of Jesus. The divinity of Jesus is also expressed in the second half of the verse: He "did not consider *equality with God* as something to be used for His own advantage" (v. 6b; emphasis added). John writes that Jesus was "calling God His own Father, making Himself equal with God" (John 5:18).

Other biblical writers highlight Jesus' preexistence in many different passages (John 1:1-2,14; 8:58; 17:5; Col 1:15; Heb 1:2-3). There never was a time when Jesus didn't exist. He had no point of origin. He is Alpha and Omega. John says, "He was with God in the beginning. All things were created through Him, and apart from Him not one thing was created that has been created" (John 1:2-3). He is Creator; He wasn't created. We differ from many cults and religions on this fundamental point.

Regarding His divine nature, Paul says Jesus existed "in the form of God." He isn't saying that Jesus only "appeared as God." He is saying that Jesus continues being in the very nature or essence of God. *Morphe* ("form") doesn't speak of external appearance or outward shape but of the essential attributes and the inner nature of Jesus. Paul uses the same word in verse 7 to say that Jesus was in very nature a slave. He was fully human and fully divine.

Church history is littered with debates over the nature of Jesus. We read of the famous Council of Nicea that took place in AD 325. Arius believed that Jesus was the first and greatest created being, but Athanasius won the day, defending the biblical position that Jesus is fully God, being of the same essence as the Father. Today we still confess the magnificent creed adopted in this historic debate:

> [We believe] in one Lord Jesus Christ, the only begotten Son
> of God, begotten of the Father before all worlds; God of God,
> Light of Light, very God of very God, begotten, not made,
> being of one substance with the Father, by whom all things
> were made.

Indeed, there have been many alternative positions through the years. Ebionism denied the divine nature of Christ. Arianism denied the fullness of the deity of Christ. Docetism denied the humanity of Jesus. Apollinarianism denied the full humanity of Jesus. Nestorianism denied the unity of the natures in one person. Eutychianism denied the distinction of the natures. In AD 451, leaders in Chalcedon wrote a creed affirming both Jesus' full humanity and His full deity, united in one person. In so doing, they rejected all six of these Christological heresies.

In every generation, we must contend for the biblical view of the person and work of Christ. We still hear things like "He was a prophet," "He was a good man," "He was a fine example," "The idea of Jesus is what matters." Like Athanasius, we must boldly defend the glory of Christ. We must also teach these things to our children, who are growing up in a world that is fine with a phantom Christ, Christ as a mere man, or Christ as a funny, religious sage. In the spirit of Deuteronomy 6, as you sit down, walk, and lie down, teach your kids about the person and work of Jesus.

"[He] did not consider equality with God as something to be used for His own advantage" (v. 6b). This phrase highlights the astonishing giving nature of Jesus. He did not consider being God grounds for getting but for giving. "The Messiah did not please Himself," Paul says to the Romans (Rom 15:3). In that context, like Philippians, he encourages the church to follow the example of Jesus' service in their relationships with one another. I like the translations that use the phrase, "a thing to be grasped." He could have clutched His rights, His blessings, and His benefits as King of glory. But He lived open-handedly, showing us what benevolent generosity and service look like. Do you have a hard time

letting go of your possessions? Do you find it hard to relinquish your rights to be mad at someone for the good of preserving a relationship? If we applied Jesus' mind-set to marriage and other relationships, imagine what our lives would be like. Here, Jesus shows us the way to live.

Our fallen nature wants to snatch, not offer. Stop and think about the differences between Adam and Christ:

Adam	Jesus
was made in God's image.	was and is the very essence of God.
wanted to be like God.	took on the likeness of man.
wanted to exalt himself.	emptied Himself.
was discontent being God's servant.	assumed the form of a slave.
arrogantly rejected God's word in sinful disobedience.	humbly submitted to God's word in perfect obedience.
succumbed to temptation.	overcame temptation; crushed the tempter.
brought the curse on the world.	took the curse for the world.
was condemned and disgraced.	was exalted by the Father.

How can you go from being a grasper to a giver? How can you adopt a mentality of downward mobility instead of upward mobility? You need the gospel. You need the second Adam, Jesus. Through His perfect life and atoning death, He gives Adam's race forgiveness and new life, empowering us to live like Him.

His Humble Incarnation (2:7)

Paul speaks of Jesus' coming in the flesh. *"Instead He emptied Himself"* (*v. 7a*). Some render this, "he made himself nothing" (NIV). Christ refused to hold onto His divine rights and prerogatives. He veiled His deity, but He did not void His deity (Tozer, *The Knowledge of the Holy*, 22). Sometimes we say, "remaining all that He was, He became what He was not." He added humanity; He didn't surrender deity. The wedding of the two natures was permanent. "Jesus will remain fully God and fully man, yet one person, forever" (Grudem, *Systematic Theology*, 543).

O'Brien says that four of the five New Testament occurrences of the verb *kenoō* ("emptied") bear a metaphorical sense; the balance of probability lies in favor of a figurative connotation at Philippians 2:7 as well

(*Epistle*, 217). Here is a good comparison: "For Christ did not send me to baptize, but to evangelize—not with clever words, so that the cross of Christ will not be *emptied* of its effect" (1 Cor 1:17; emphasis added). Christ didn't empty Himself literally of His deity, but figuratively. Some translate the text this way to convey the idea: "He made Himself nothing." So, our beloved hymn "And Can It Be" should be tweaked. The phrase "He emptied Himself of all but love" presents some problems. It seems to imply that Jesus emptied Himself of other attributes. If He did, He wouldn't be God. Perhaps we should sing, "He emptied Himself in humble love." Jesus didn't relinquish His deity; He surrendered His rights and prerogatives.

Bryan Chapell illustrates the idea of Jesus "emptying Himself" by relaying a story from an African missionary. Let me paraphrase it. In this particular part of Africa the chief is the strongest man in the village. As the chief, he also wears a very large headdress and ceremonial robes. One day a man carrying water out of the shaft of a deep well fell and broke his leg, and lay helpless at the bottom of the well. To get down to the bottom, one would have to climb down, using the alternating slits that go all the way down the deep well, and then climb back up. Because no one could carry the helpless man up like this, the chief was summoned. When he saw the plight of the man, he laid aside his headdress and his robe, climbed all the way to the bottom, put the injured man on himself, and brought him to safety. He did what no other man could do. That's what Jesus has done for us. He came to rescue us. And He laid aside His heavenly glory, like the chief did with his headdress, in order to save us. Now, did the chief cease being the chief when he laid aside his headdress? Of course not. Did Jesus cease being God when He came to rescue us? Of course not (Chapell, *Using Illustrations*, 11–12).

"By assuming the form of a slave" (v. 7b). The slave in the Greco-Roman world was deprived of most basic rights. Jesus gave up His sovereign rights and became a slave. The sovereign Creator made Himself nothing. He identified Himself with the lowest of society. Christ "did not come to be served, but to serve" (Mark 10:45). In John 13 we have a powerful illustration of Jesus' servant mentality:

> *Jesus knew that the Father had given everything into His hands, that He had come from God, and that He was going back to God. So He got up from supper, laid aside His robe, took a towel, and tied it around Himself. Next, He poured water into a basin and began to wash*

His disciples' feet and to dry them with the towel tied around Him.
(John 13:3-5)

While the disciples jockeyed for positions in the coming kingdom, comparing themselves to one another in rivalry, the One with all authority began to wash their feet. You can imagine what the disciples would have said if asked to do this task (which was reserved for slaves). "I'm not washing Peter's feet. Look at those feet!" "I'm not washing John's feet; he never washed my feet." "I'm not washing any of their feet; whenever we buy the fish sandwiches, I always pay for them. I'll let someone else wash feet." "I'm not washing Philip's feet. I'm so sick of Philip and all his dumb questions." But Jesus, in the very nature of God, begins to wash the feet that He made, with the water that He made. He humbled Himself, taking the form of a slave. Let this attitude be in you!

Imagine what would happen to the Philippian church if Euodia and Syntyche were to empty themselves and give up their rights and preferences for the good of the church. Imagine what would happen if we all took this posture in the church—if each person sought not to be elevated to higher positions but to humbly serve others as Jesus did.

"Taking on the likeness of men. And when He had come as a man in His external form" (v. 7c). This phrase, "taking on the likeness of men," doesn't mean that He merely became *like* a human being. Rather He, who always was God, became what He was not, a human being. The simple point in this hymn is that when people saw Jesus they saw a man. People recognized Him as a human. Jesus was not some alien. In fact, if not for the testimony of Scripture, His own words, and His works, few would have believed that He was God. He didn't have some silly halo over His head or a glow about Him. He was like us, yet without sin (Heb 4:15). With that said, regarding the language, "He had come as a man in His *external form*" (v. 7c HCSB; emphasis added), Paul uses *schema* here instead of *morphe* as in 6-7a. It's rendered in the ESV, "and being born in the likeness of men" (v. 7 ESV). It may be intended to leave some room for the idea that there was more to the story than Jesus' humanity. Jesus often left people asking questions like, "What kind of man is this?" (Matt 8:27).

His Humble Crucifixion (2:8)

Paul now takes us all the way down in this text.

"He humbled Himself by becoming obedient to the point of death" (v. 8a). Christ's whole life was marked by humility. Look at His birth. He wasn't

born in an influential city like Alexandria, Rome, Athens, or Jerusalem. He was born near a feeding trough in Bethlehem. He lived for 30 years in relative obscurity. Then, in His earthly ministry, He was known for loving unlovable people and humbly serving others. At His death, He was nailed to a cross alongside two criminals.

Christ humbled Himself voluntarily. Neither Herod, Pilate, nor the Romans humbled Him; no one can humble Jesus. Jesus humbles us. He chose to empty Himself. Therefore, don't look at this passage and feel sorry for Jesus, as if He were to be pitied. Jesus stands over you; you don't stand over Jesus. He humbled Himself. We must humble ourselves now before Him. We, too, must choose humility. In the New Testament the act of "humbling yourself" is active (Matt 18:4; 23:12 [twice]; Luke 3:5; 14:11 [twice]; 18:14 [twice]; 2 Cor 11:7; 12:21; Phil 2:8; 4:12; Jas 4:10; 1 Pet 5:6). This is the way of the kingdom.

"Even death on a cross" (v. 8b). Paul adds that He demonstrated this humility by becoming obedient to the point of death, and that death was the most vile of all—crucifixion. This phrase serves as the rock bottom of Christ's humility and the most gripping part of His obedience. Roman citizens couldn't be executed, and Jews believed a person was cursed if he died by crucifixion (Gal 3:13). For some, the cross was a total embarrassment. Paul goes on to say that some live as "enemies of the cross" (3:18). Yet here is Jesus, the preexistent One, the Lord of glory, dying on the cross for sinners. He endured the physical agony of the cross, the abandonment, the shame, and He received the wrath of God in the place of sinners.

It's quite possible that the Servant Song of Isaiah 53 loomed in the background of this hymn. He came having no "impressive form or majesty that we should look at Him, no appearance that we should desire Him" (53:2). He went to the cross, taking our place, "and the Lord has punished Him for the iniquity of us all" (53:6). "He submitted Himself to death" (Isa 53:12). In this most degrading of all deaths, we find the hope of salvation. Peter says, "He Himself bore our sins in His body on the tree, so that, having died to sins, we might live for righteousness; you have been healed by His wounds" (1 Pet 2:24).

C. S. Lewis writes in his book *Miracles* that the central miracle asserted by Christians is the incarnation (143). He explains the descent and ascent of Christ vividly:

In the Christian story God descends to re-ascend. He comes down; down from the heights of absolute being into time and space, down into humanity. . . . But He goes down to come up again and bring the whole ruined world up with Him. One has the picture of a strong man stooping lower and lower to get himself underneath some great complicated burden. He must stoop in order to lift, he must almost disappear under the load before he incredibly straightens his back and marches off with the whole mass swaying on his shoulders. Or one may think of a diver, first reducing himself to nakedness, then glancing in midair, then gone with a splash, vanished, rushing down through green and warm water into black and cold water, down through increasing pressure into the deathlike region of ooze and slime and old decay; then up again, back to color and light, his lungs almost bursting, till suddenly he breaks surface again, holding in his hand the dripping, precious thing that he went down to recover. (*Miracles*, 111–12)

Having considered Christ descending down, down, down, let's consider how the Son ascends up to the highest place.

The Exaltation of Christ
PHILIPPIANS 2:9-11

Christ's humility follows the spiritual principle, "Whoever humbles himself will be exalted." His incomparable self-humiliation leads to His super-exaltation. Let's look at His exaltation in two parts: His exalted position and everyone's adoration and confession.

His Exalted Position (2:9)

"*For this reason God highly exalted Him and gave Him the name that is above every name*" (*v. 9*). This verse begins by showing the results of Christ's humility. Some translations begin with "Therefore" (NIV, ESV) or "For this reason" (HCSB, NASB) to show the link. As a consequence of Christ's work, the Father "highly exalted Him." The phrase "highly exalted" means to "super-elevate." No one else is exalted like this. Jesus is in an exalted class by Himself. He reentered the glory that He enjoyed with the Father before the world existed (John 17:5). And for all eternity, we will join the millions in giving Him praise.

The phrase "and gave Him the name that is above every name" raises the question, What name? Some say it's *Jesus*, but the majority of commentators say it refers to *Lord* (or *Yahweh*). The former say that *Jesus* fits the context better (see Silva, 110–11). The next verse begins, "so that at the name of Jesus" (v. 10). Some in this camp say that the name *Jesus* took on a new significance after His exaltation.

But others are unconvinced for a variety of reasons. Let me point out four reasons. First, the name *Jesus* doesn't fit the upward shift of this passage, which climaxes in verse 11, where Christ is declared *Lord*. Second, *Jesus* was His name at birth, but this seems to be a new name. Hanson says, "At the incarnation, the name *Jesus* was given; when God exalted Jesus he then gave him the name *Lord*" (*Letter*, 162). Gordon Fee points out that Jesus was "graced" with a name, which implies that He didn't previously have it (*Pauline Christology*, 396). Third, there's an apparent intertextual connection between Isaiah 42:8, "I am Yahweh, that is My name; I will not give My glory to another," and Philippians 2:11, "Jesus Christ is Lord." Some point out that God's personal name *Yahweh* is in view in Philippians 2:11, which in the Greek version of the Old Testament is translated as "Lord." They also point out the connection between Philippians 2:10-11 and Isaiah 45:23: "Every knee will bow to Me, every tongue will swear allegiance." Finally, *Lord* carried deeper meaning to the Philippians. To hear that someone other than Caesar is Lord would be shocking (Hanson, *Letter*, 162–63).

If forced to pick, given the aforementioned reasons, and the following argument from John Piper, I would side with "Lord." Piper says,

> What name did Jesus receive after his resurrection that he did not have before? Not "Jesus." Jesus is precisely the name of the humble Servant who went to Calvary. In Acts 2:36 Peter says, "Let all the house of Israel know assuredly that *God has made him both Lord and Christ*, this Jesus whom you crucified." It was his *lordship* and *Messiahship*—his messianic lordship— that was bestowed on him at his exaltation. Not that he wasn't Messiah and Lord before his resurrection. He was. But he had not fulfilled the mission of Messiah until he had died for our sin and risen again. And therefore, before his death and resurrection, the lordship of Christ over the world had not been brought to full actuality. The rebel forces were yet undefeated, and the power of darkness held the world in its grip. In order to be acclaimed Messiah and Lord, the Son of God had to come, defeat the enemy, and lead his people out of bondage in triumph over sin and Satan and death. And that he did on Good Friday and Easter. . . . The name that is above

every name, therefore, is *Lord*—the Lord victorious over all
his enemies; the Lord who has purchased a people from every
tribe and tongue and nation. ("And All the Earth Shall Own
Him Lord"; emphasis added)

Even if you aren't persuaded to see the name as "Lord," the point is
the same essentially. Jesus has the same exalted lordship as the Father
(v. 11). He went all the way down to the cross and all the way up as King
of all. To the Ephesians, Paul says that Christ was exalted above "every
title given, not only in this age but also in the one to come" (1:21). In
his Pentecost sermon Peter tells us that following Jesus' death, resurrection, and ascension, Christ was "exalted to the right hand of God"
(Acts 2:33). The fact that Jesus is exalted means that He rules and reigns
over all (Heb 1:3). He has universal lordship. Jesus is Lord, not Caesar,
and everyone must give an account to Him.

What's astonishing for us who are believers is that we know Him!
We know the King of glory. My friend Rodney recently did some work
for the Charlotte Hornets NBA team. He was on a conference call with
the upper management, which included Michael Jordan. At one point
he heard the king of basketball say, "Hey Rodney, it's M. J." Rodney's
jaw dropped. He couldn't help but marvel that M. J. knew him. That
was astonishing because "M. J." is in a class by himself. The wonder of
it all is that Jesus, the Lord of glory, who is in a class by Himself, knows
us, and He loves us. Fall on your face, Christian. Lift up your voice in
praise and adoration to the King who has lavished you with astonishing
grace and mercy.

Everyone's Adoration and Confession (2:10-11)

*"So that at the name of Jesus every knee will bow—of those who are in heaven
and on earth and under the earth—and every tongue should confess that Jesus
Christ is Lord" (vv. 10-11a).* In response to Christ's universal lordship,
everyone will bow and confess His lordship. As in Isaiah 45, all will bow
to Yahweh, and here in Philippians, all will bow to Jesus and confess that
He is Lord. By giving Jesus the name *Lord*, God declared the deity of
Jesus. The phrase "Jesus Christ is Lord" is probably the earliest Christian
confession, and it is shorthand for the gospel (cf. Rom 10:9; 2 Cor 4:5).
Every week when we gather for worship and encourage one another
in the gospel, we are uniting with Christians who have gone before us.
And as we make our confession, we are anticipating the future, in which
everyone affirms this declaration.

Paul says everyone will bow and confess His lordship, including those "in heaven and on earth and under the earth." Melick says, "Thus the hymn includes every conceivable habitation of personal beings" (*Philippians*, 108). Some will confess Him as Lord with great joy and humility. Others will confess Him as Lord with despair and anguish. Pilate, Caiaphas, Stalin, Hitler, and every other evil dictator will confess Him as Lord. Everyone from every age will do the same. The hymn has this "already/not yet" dimension. We confess Him as Lord now, but we also look forward to the future day when all acknowledge the lordship of Jesus. History is not like a treadmill, going nowhere; rather, it's all moving toward that day. Sadly, it will be too late for some. If you don't acknowledge and confess that Jesus is Lord in this life, it will be too late after death. So, bow now! Confess Him as Lord now!

To confess Jesus as Lord in the first century meant that Caesar was not Lord. And as a result of such confessions, many were persecuted and killed. The same fate exists for many today around the world who claim that Jesus is their Lord and Savior. But those who confess Christ as Lord now will not regret it when they see Him. Contrastingly, those who refuse to bow to Him now will wish they had heeded the message.

"To the glory of God the Father" (v. 11b). Jesus' life, death, resurrection, ascension, and exaltation bring glory to God the Father. Here we see that there's no rivalry in the Godhead, only delight and honor. This text points out the remarkable fact that Christ doesn't keep glory for Himself, and even in His exaltation He remains the model of humbly honoring the Father. Paul writes elsewhere,

> And when everything is subject to Christ, then the Son Himself will also be subject to the One who subjected everything to Him, so that God may be all in all. (1 Cor 15:28)

The glory of God the Father is a fitting conclusion to this hymn, for this is what the heart was made to do: glorify God, not self. Humility involves following the pattern of Jesus for the glory of God.

Concluding Applications

Allow me to give a few final points of application regarding this amazing passage. It's truly a Christological goldmine.

Memorize this passage. It's a hymn. See the importance of poetry, music, and creeds. We are always in need of good writing of sound doctrine. When we write well, people can remember and rejoice in the truths of the gospel. Songs and creeds serve as portable theology. We get to take them with us. What a gift we have in Philippians 2! It's memorable, and because it's memorable, we can dwell on it regularly. And we should dwell on it regularly.

Believe this passage. Do you believe that Jesus Christ is Lord? You will—either now or later. Don't wait until it's too late. Say with the saints from all ages, "Jesus Christ *is* Lord."

Follow the lifestyle presented in this passage. This is the attitude and the lifestyle that we should pursue. Philippians contains a good word about following various people, but no one gives us a better model than Jesus.

Tell the world about the message of this passage. Our mission is to tell the world that Jesus is Lord, and if they will confess and believe in Him as such, they will be saved (Rom 10:9,13). Let us adore Him. Let our minds be on Him. Let our attitude be like His. Let our actions reflect Him—all of this is to the glory of God the Father.

Reflect and Discuss

1. Which of the five perspectives on the cross does D. A. Carson say that this passage magnifies? Do you agree? Explain.
2. What does it mean that this passage should stimulate "adoration and emulation"?
3. How is Christ's humility displayed in this passage?
4. What would happen in our relationships if we lived out Philippians 2:5-11? How can you go from being a "grasper" to a "giver"?
5. How is Jesus' model of leadership different from a worldly view of leadership? How can you put this type of life in practice today?
6. Stop and read Isaiah 53, and marvel at the humility of Christ and at His atoning work.
7. Why should we be overwhelmed by the fact that we (Christians) know Christ and that He knows us?
8. How is the exaltation of Christ displayed in this passage?
9. Why is the exaltation of Christ important for you today?
10. The passage ends by saying that Christ's work was done "to the glory of God the Father." How does this move you? Is your great aim to live a humble, others-oriented life for the glory of the Father, through Jesus? Pray for a deeper desire to live for God's glory by following Christ's example.

Shining Like Stars

PHILIPPIANS 2:12-18

Main Idea: Paul exhorts the Philippians to work out their salvation by the power of God's enabling grace and to shine like stars in a dark world.

I. **Work Out (2:12-14).**
    A. Commending (2:12a)
    B. Commanding (2:12b)
    C. Comforting (2:13)
II. **Shine (2:14-16).**
    A. Avoid grumbling and arguing (2:14).
    B. The reasons to avoid grumbling and arguing (2:15-16)
III. **Rejoice (2:17-18).**

In a recent sermon at our church, my (Tony's) friend, and hip-hop pioneer, William Branch, also known as "The Ambassador," talked about an aspect of hip-hop culture:

> Hip-hop knows glory. They know that glory is meant to
> be seen; glory is meant to be displayed. Hip-hop has an
> embedded conviction: if you come from nothing, and finally
> get "everything," flaunt it. Thus [we hear] slang terms like
> "floss," "swag," and "shine." So if you got it, flaunt it. Or in the
> words of the New Orleans-based rap crew Cash Money, "Get
> your shine on!"

In this passage Paul tells the church, "Get your shine on" by making the glory of Christ known in a dark and perverse culture.

How do you follow the amazing Christ hymn in Philippians 2:6-11? It's majestic, isn't it? The truths found in it and the scope of it leave us in awe and wonder. But there are also practical implications of this hymn, as Paul points out in this passage. Notice the link from the hymn to this passage. Paul says, "So then" (v. 12) or "Therefore" (ESV). He's looking back to what was just said and preparing to make some strong exhortations. Paul exhorts the Philippians to work out their salvation with fear and trembling and to shine like stars in the sky.

Indeed, Paul teaches us much about Christian discipleship in this passage. The whole tone of this passage is pastoral. Paul begins with "my dear friends." He loves the Philippians. And he loves them enough to exhort them with strong words in the spirit of a shepherd. Notice also *three connections* in this passage. Paul connects *God's work* and *our work* in verses 12-13. Then in verses 14-15 he connects *avoiding grumbling* with *shining as lights in the world*. In verses 16-18 he connects *sacrifice* and *rejoicing*. Let's consider these three connections under three simple headings: "Work Out," "Shine," and "Rejoice"—all ways we should live before the Lord Jesus Christ.

Work Out
PHILIPPIANS 2:12-13

Verses 12-13 provide us with a wonderful starting point for understanding what we call in theology "sanctification," that is, the lifelong obedience of believers, which leads us to growth in Christlikeness. This passage is not about works-based righteousness. Paul doesn't say, "Work *for* your own salvation." We can't earn salvation (Eph 2:8-10). Paul says, "Work *out* your salvation." That's a huge difference. God has worked salvation *for* us by His sovereign grace alone. *Christ* has done the work on the cross to bring us "justification." Sanctification is about living in light of this gracious gift of salvation, living in light of our new position and our new identity. As Paul teaches us about sanctification, he *commends* the Philippians, then he *commands* the Philippians, and he then *comforts* the Philippians.

Commending (2:12a)

Paul opens up by commending the Philippians for obeying Jesus consistently. He says that the church obeyed in his presence and his absence. Before Paul commands the Philippians, he commends the Philippians. This is a good pattern for making disciples. Commend and command. Encourage and exhort. Notice the mingling of commending and commanding in Thessalonians, as Paul teaches about sanctification:

> *Finally then, brothers, we ask and encourage you in the Lord Jesus, that as you have received from us how you must walk and please God—as you are doing—do so even more.* (1 Thess 4:1; emphasis added)

About brotherly love: You don't need me to write you because you
yourselves are taught by God to love one another. In fact, you are
doing this *toward all the brothers in the entire region of Macedonia.*
But we encourage you, brothers, to do so even more. (1 Thess 4:9-10;
emphasis added)

In both of these texts Paul drops in an encouragement, "you are doing
this," as he tells them to "do so even more." This is a sweet, pastoral
motivation that we should practice with those under our instruction.

We, too, should find fresh encouragement and motivation here. If
you find yourself growing in Christian maturity, realize that it's evidence
of God's grace. We aren't what we ought to be or what we will be one
day, but by God's grace, we are not what we used to be! Let us now press
on to obey "more and more" with great joy.

Commanding (2:12b)

Paul continues by saying, "Work out your own salvation with fear and
trembling." Paul doesn't say that because the Philippians are justified
they should just passively coast along in their Christian journey. He
urges them to what Eugene Peterson calls "a long obedience in the
same direction," which will be a difficult endeavor in this fallen world
(Peterson, *A Long Obedience*). Paul also doesn't say (based on v. 13) that
once we become Christians, we are left entirely to our own power to live
this life of obedience. We can work out our salvation *because* God is at
work within us.

What does it mean to work out one's salvation? Surely there are
hundreds of implications of working out the life-changing salvation that
God has wrought in our souls. But to work out your salvation simply
means to follow the example of Christ. In the Christ hymn, Jesus has
given us the pattern for obedience. He has shown us what humble,
others-focused, God-glorifying obedience looks like. That's the kind
of life that we are called to live as believers. Does your life look like
Philippians 2:6-8? Are you praying and striving for growth in humility,
personal holiness, selfless service, and sacrificial mission by the power
of God's enabling grace?

We might wish we could find a shortcut, some special diet to grow
in Christlikeness, but following in the footsteps of Jesus requires daily
taking up our cross. My (Tony) son James once looked at the picture on
a particular cereal box and asked me, "If I eat this cereal, will I become

a football player?" I said, "You need a bit more than cereal to become an athlete." The fact is, there are no shortcuts to becoming a professional athlete. It requires discipline and long workouts. So it is with the Christian's growth in Christlikeness. We can't take a pill or eat kale and automatically turn into perfectly sanctified individuals. We must work out our salvation every day by the grace of God.

This is a challenge—a long obedience in the same direction. We live in a fast-paced, fast-food, microwave, Internet culture, but sanctification is a slow process. We are often drawn to mega conferences and flashy events, but God has called the Christian to the day-in, day-out process of growing in Christlikeness. It's easy to show a spark of enthusiasm at an event; it's quite another thing to live faithfully and consistently when no one is watching and when no one cares. May God rekindle in us a passion for ordinary obedience, day to day, following the pattern of Jesus.

We must point out one other note before moving on. We tend to view verse 12 in a merely individual sense. Work out "your" salvation. But as with many passages in the New Testament, we should not merely highlight the personal dimension of salvation; we should also see the *corporate* dimension of it. Hanson provides a fine explanation of this personal and corporate dynamic:

> The plural form of the verb *work out* and the pronoun *your* can be seen as corroboration that Paul's command should not be interpreted in a merely individual sense as a requirement for each individual to work [out] personal, eternal salvation but in a corporate sense as a call for the whole community to rebuild social harmony. Paul's consistent emphasis on the unity of the church in this context compels us to see that Paul's call to *work out your salvation* has an ecclesiological reference: it is a call to restore harmony in the church by serving one another. This contrast between an individualistic sense and a corporate sense to the command *work out your salvation* does not posit an antithesis between individual responsibility and corporate responsibility. Restoring unity in the church by serving one another is the responsibility of each individual Christian. Paul's command in verse 14 to *do everything without grumbling and arguing* confronts each member with the challenge to desist from attitudes and words that tear apart the social fabric of the community. (*Letter*, 172–73; italics in original)

So, work out your own salvation—and do so with brothers and sisters in the context of the local church.

What does it mean to work out our salvation with "fear and trembling"? Obviously, this implies that the Christian should live in awe of God. It has to do with living in humility before God and in submission to His will. Based on the previous Christ hymn, this makes perfect sense! One way to cure selfish ambition and vain conceit (2:3) is by living with an awareness of the holy presence of God. That should put us in our place. That should compel us to live lives of holiness. While Christians should not be terrified of God, since we have found secure refuge in Christ, we should live in awe of Him (cf. 2 Cor 5:11). This is a fundamental concept of Christian discipleship. In the Old Testament, God commanded His people to fear Him (e.g., Deut 10:2), and we learn, "The fear of the LORD is the beginning of wisdom" (Prov 9:10). In the presence of our great and awesome God, let us work out our salvation.

Comforting (2:13)

Following this heavy imperative, Paul provides a comforting encouragement, reminding the Philippians that they aren't called to obey in their own power. Instead, he says, "For it is God who is working in you, enabling you both to desire and to work out His good purpose" (2:13). What will prevent us from burning out and giving up? It is knowing this fact: God is at work in us! D. A. Carson notes,

> God is not working merely to strengthen us in *our* willing and acting. Paul's language is stronger than that. God himself is working in us both to will and to act: he works in us at the level of our wills and at the level of our doing. But far from this being a *dis*incentive to press on, Paul insists that this is an incentive. Assured as we are that God works in this way in his people, we should be all the more strongly resolved to will and to act in ways that please our Master. (*Basics*, 62; emphasis in original)

Indeed, this is an incentive—God is at work in us at the deepest of levels. God is working in us to bring our salvation to completion (1:6). We work because God works (Hanson, *Letter*, 178). The psalmist says of our dependency on God, "Unless the LORD builds a house, its builders labor over it in vain" (Ps 127:1). Paul writes of God's working empowering his working in several places. To the Colossians, he writes, "I labor for this, striving *with His strength* that works *powerfully in me*" (Col 1:29; emphasis added). To the Corinthians he says, "But by God's grace I am what I am, and His grace toward me was not ineffective. However, I worked more than any of them, yet not I, but God's grace that was with me" (1 Cor 15:10). Based on this massively comforting truth—that underneath our work is God's work—work out your salvation with fear and trembling.

Paul says that God is working in us for "His good purpose" (2:13). God fulfills His good purposes in us by His mighty power. Isn't this comforting? You aren't alone, Christian. God is at work in you, and He is accomplishing His good purposes in and through you.

Let us step back for a moment now. If you're a genuine Christian, then receive a sweet commendation, embrace this commandment, and press on with joy based on this comforting truth: God is at work in us to will and work for His good pleasure.

Shine

PHILIPPIANS 2:14-16

What does it look like to work out our salvation with fear and trembling practically? While it certainly means living like Jesus, Paul moves on in the next paragraph to describe the attitude one should have as he or she obeys Christ and pursues likeness to Him. Indeed, working out our salvation is a comprehensive concept; as Paul says, "Do everything" without complaint. Following Jesus involves following Him in every area of life. His challenge brings us to the second connection, namely, between *complaining* and *shining*.

Avoid Grumbling and Arguing (2:14)

It might surprise you to see that Paul chooses the avoidance of "grumbling and arguing" as his concrete expression of working out our salvation. He gives a comprehensive application, "Do everything," with this particular command, "without grumbling and arguing." What's in view? Everything. Live all of life, doing everything you're called to do, without grumbling. Paul issues another all-inclusive imperative to the Corinthians like this one, only in a positive sense: "Therefore, whether you eat or drink, or whatever you do, do everything for God's glory" (1 Cor 10:31). Instead of grumbling, glorify God in all that you do.

Why would Paul mention this temptation to grumble? One reason is obvious: Christian perseverance is difficult. Discipleship isn't an easy road. Pursuing holiness, giving generously, practicing hospitality, loving one's spouse and kids appropriately, sharing the gospel, and other facets of Christian discipleship could tempt one to complain and murmur. The temptation to complain and argue is not only a temptation personally; it's a big temptation corporately as well. Remember the context: the Philippian church had some internal strife (4:2-3; see also 1:27–2:4). They also had external pressure (1:28). These problems could lead one to complain both to God and to one another. Complaining is a temptation for anyone in a local church because people often can't live up to the expectations of others. At some point, the pastors, the small group leaders, the singers, the greeters, or your accountability partner will disappoint you. What will you do? You will be tempted to complain.

In our young church plant I have watched people come and go in two-and-a-half short years. Often people come in with great enthusiasm for all that's involved in a church plant—the sacrifices, the challenges, the relationships, the risk, the vision. Then over time, the honeymoon ends, seasons change, and disappointment and discontentment set in. The temptation to complain and argue becomes very strong. This is also a temptation for the pastors! The challenges of leading a church could tempt one to live in self-pity and despair, spewing out Israel-like grumblings.

Sometimes complaining expresses itself in whispers of grumblings against someone, and at other times it rises to vocal arguments. We find examples of grumbling and arguing in the wilderness narratives found in Exodus and Numbers (Exod 16:7-12; Num 14:2,26; 17:5-25). You might just pause and go read those accounts. Paul told the Corinthians to consider their sad example and do the opposite (1 Cor 10:10). The question is not, Will you be tempted to complain? You will be tempted to complain by others, since complaining is the common language of the culture—and it always has been. We live in a world filled with complainers! When you are tempted, what will you do? Will you downplay this sin, as many often do, or will you remember this verse? Maybe a better question is How can you maintain a joyful attitude in the face of these problems?

Once again, we must go to the gospel for joy. The gospel tells us that we are far better off than we deserve. Considering what we deserve and what we've been given should keep us from complaining. When we lose sight of the gospel, we will go down the dark hole of murmuring. Keep your focus on Philippians 2:6-11 and 3:7-11 and you won't disobey Philippians 2:14. The Israelites complained when they lost sight of

God's redemption, and we will complain if we lose sight of the greater exodus found in the death and resurrection of Jesus.

John Piper reported a vivid illustration of the need to meditate on what we have in Christ and what we have coming in the future in order to put trials in their proper perspective. Newton likened complaining to the folly of the following scenario:

> Suppose a man was going to New York to take possession of a large estate, and his [carriage] should break down a mile before he got to the city, which obliged him to walk the rest of the way; what a fool we should think him, if we saw him ringing his hands, and blubbering out all the remaining mile, "My [carriage] is broken! My [carriage] is broken!" ("John Newton")

We must remember that we only have a mile to go. Soon we will see Christ. Soon we will be with Christ. We don't deserve such an inheritance. So if we have to walk a mile, we can do it with a song.

The Reason to Avoid Grumbling and Arguing (2:15-16)

Obviously, we should avoid grumbling because it's offensive to God. Grumbling is an awful sin. This alone should serve as sufficient reason to avoid it; but Paul's reason in the next verse, indicated by the "so that," goes beyond this reason. Paul has the world in view. He says that grumbling and arguing damage our witness.

Shining as children of God (v. 15). If you want to shine like stars in the world, you must resist the temptation to grumble. When our conversations with other believers, or among outsiders, are filled with negative murmuring, we lose our distinctiveness. Paul says that we should instead be "blameless," "pure," and "faultless" in this generation, which he characterizes as "crooked and perverse." Grumbling causes us to lose our distinctive character, or in the words of Jesus, our "saltiness" (Matt 5:13-16). Consequently, we will lose our effectiveness. Realize, then, that others are watching you. Others are listening to you. What are they seeing, and what are they hearing? Are we standing out like bright stars in a dark sky? This is Paul's concern as it pertains to grumbling. He has the watching world in view. We will shine like stars, and like a city on a hill, when our conversation remains blameless, pure, and faultless.

Consider what an opportunity we have for making an eternal difference in someone's life simply by speaking a different language from that of the culture—by going through the day, avoiding the temptation to grumble, and replacing that practice with gratitude and praise. When my friend C. J. Mahaney enters a coffee shop or some public space and they ask him, "How are you doing?," he often responds with, "I'm doing far better than I deserve." Yes, we are! When we pepper our ordinary days with expressions of gratitude instead of expressions of complaining, we get our shine on! We can make a difference in people's lives simply by obeying this verse. The fact is we are indeed "doing far better than we deserve." This is indicated here in this passage and throughout Philippians. Paul reminds the church that they are "children of God" (2:15). We don't deserve to be adopted children of the Father, but that's what we are as Christians. Our Father loves us, hears us, and provides for us. Marvel at this, and fill your conversations with gratitude.

As you consider the challenge to shine in the world, remember again that God is at work in us. We aren't alone in this battle. God empowers His children to speak in a way that glorifies Him and attracts others. Are you relying on His grace to speak in ways that are gracious and appropriate (see Col 4:2-6)? Paul is drawing a sharp distinction between the type of speech we should have and that of the rest of this "crooked and perverted" generation. Is your speech different? Do you see how important it is to avoid complaining and arguing?

Also, remember this passage if you ever find yourself being persecuted. When one avoids complaining in the face of persecution, he or she stands out like a radiant light. That person is saying, "Christ is worth it. Christ is better." When our language is like that instead of murmuring, it gets people's attention. May God empower us to light up the night with such words and attitudes.

Holding firmly to the message of life (v. 16a). In verse 16a Paul develops his argument further as he explains a particular way one should shine: "Hold firmly to the message of life." In contrast to complaining, Christians should be defending and proclaiming the word of life. Don't turn loose of God's Word in a dark culture, and don't stop proclaiming it to a perverse culture. Let the Word of Christ dwell in you richly (Col 3:16) so that it will permeate your heart and spill out into praise and proclamation. The word of life is our source of vitality, and it is the message we hold out to the world.

We could summarize this section with Mahaney's statement, "Paul wants the church to be a proclaiming church, not a complaining church" ("Better Than I Deserve"). If we complain but try to proclaim, we become confusing to others. Let us fill our speech with gratitude and grace as we hold out the word of life to a dark world. This is a life worthy of the gospel of Christ (1:27).

Anticipating the day of Christ (v. 16b). Paul moves from his exhortations to a personal reason for the church to shine that involves an eternal outlook on this life. He says, "Then I can boast in the day of Christ that I didn't run or labor for nothing." Paul's images of running and laboring remind us of the strenuous nature of ministry. Paul uses such images elsewhere (e.g., 1 Cor 3:11-15; 9:24-26; 15:10; Gal 2:2). Why endure the difficulty? Paul labors for "the day of Christ" (cf. 1:6,10). This is instructive for us. We often minister with very shortsighted goals, but Paul takes the long view. Paul knew that the only One who mattered would one day evaluate his work. Because of this reality, he worked hard and sought to finish his race well (2 Tim 4:6-8). Our goal shouldn't be to gain popularity or to grow a huge church, but to be faithful to Jesus.

Don't misunderstand the phrase "Then I can boast" as a statement of personal pride and self-exaltation. That would be entirely inconsistent with the whole letter of Philippians. Paul's boasting will be a boasting in the grace of God, who worked in his life and his labor and in the lives of the Philippians. The Philippians' fruitfulness will prove on the final day that he didn't run in vain. He tells the church to persevere in light of this eternal perspective.

Rejoice
PHILIPPIANS 2:17-18

In verses 17-18 Paul changes the image from running and working to being a sacrificial offering. The previous images of a runner and a laborer imply endurance, but this image implies more. It implies the giving of one's own life.

Look at how much Paul loves this church. His main focus is on the church's faithfulness and fruitfulness; what's secondary is his own suffering and situation. Paul isn't complaining about serving as a drink offering. He leads by example. What's impressive about this drink offering analogy is that Paul says, "I am glad and rejoice with all of you." Just as wine was poured out in ancient (Greek and Jewish) sacrificial ceremonies, Paul says he is *happy* to pour out his blood for the advancement of the gospel. Just as Christ emptied Himself, Paul is glad to pour out himself for the glory of God. He's a glad offering.

In addition, Paul urges the church to follow his example of pouring out their lives in service and to rejoice with him. Here we find another text on imitation, a theme running through Philippians. Jesus was the ultimate example for us (2:5-11), and here Paul serves as an example. In the next passage we find two more examples worth following (see also 3:17). Paul gives the church, and us, an amazing picture of rejoicing through trying times. How can he rejoice? Jesus is Lord. Jesus is worth it. Jesus will bring to completion what He began. In Jesus and through Jesus, we are doing better than we deserve! Root your joy in Jesus.

How do we live in light of the truths of the Christ hymn of Philippians 2:6-11? In the shadow of the cross, and before the throne of God, work out your salvation with fear and trembling; give a shining witness to a dark world by not grumbling but holding out the word of life; and rejoice through sacrificial service, rooted in the grace of God and anticipating the coming day of Christ Jesus.

Reflect and Discuss

1. There is a significant difference between "working *for* your salvation" and "working *out* your salvation." Why is this an important distinction to make?
2. What does it mean to have "a long obedience in the same direction"?
3. How does living with an awareness of the holy presence of God compel you to live a life of holiness?
4. Underneath our work is God's work. How does this bring comfort to your life as a Christian?
5. How does grumbling and complaining damage your witness?
6. We are all tempted to complain and grumble. How can you maintain a joyful attitude in the face of the problems of life?
7. What do Paul's images of running and laboring teach you about the nature of your ministry to others?
8. How does the reality of "the day of Christ" affect how you live your life and make disciples?
9. Paul also uses the image of being a "sacrificial offering." What does this image teach you about the nature of your ministry to others?
10. What do you find encouraging about Paul's sacrificial mind-set? How can you cultivate this type of mind-set for the advancement of the gospel?

Model Servants

PHILIPPIANS 2:19-30

Main Idea: As Paul gives the travel plans of Timothy and Epaphroditus, he holds them up as Christlike examples worth watching and following.

I. Understanding the Importance of the Travelogue
II. The Example of Timothy (2:19-24)
    A. Timothy's compassion (2:20-21)
    B. Timothy's companionship (2:22-24)
III. The Example of Epaphroditus (2:25-30)
    A. The type of man he was (2:25)
    B. The type of love he displayed (2:26)
    C. The type of help he needed (2:27)
    D. The type of welcome he deserved (2:28-30)
IV. In Humility Consider Others as More Important than Yourselves.

If you're not a Christian, you may have various thoughts about Christians. Maybe you've been turned off by the phony religiosity of people who say they're Christians. Maybe you've detected nothing different about their lives compared to yours. I want you to look at some better examples in this passage. Here we see the type of believers that we're supposed to be like. Don't reject Christ and the church based on a poor representation from those who, in the words of Bonhoeffer, embrace "cheap grace"—that is, those who claim the name *Christian* but seem no different from anyone else. Take a look at an authentic version of Christianity here in Philippians in these two men who have been radically transformed by God's saving grace in Christ.

At first glance, verses 19-30 are a bit of a downer. C. J. Mahaney quips, "No one's favorite verse is found in this passage!" ("Whom Should We Follow?"). Paul opens the letter with a heart-stirring thanksgiving and prayer. He proceeds with his inspiring Christ-centered ambition and vision described in 1:12-26. Next, he moves into the weighty exhortation of the letter, challenging the Philippians to "live worthy of the gospel" (1:27a). This exhortation is followed by a plea for unity that comes through humility (1:27b–2:4). Paul illustrates what a humble mind-set

116

looks like with the motivating and majestic Christ hymn of Philippians 2:5-11. Then, after commanding the Philippians in 2:12 to "work out [their] own salvation with fear and trembling" by doing "everything without grumbling and arguing" (2:14), Paul describes his own inspiring example of being "poured out as a drink offering" (2:17-18). In chapters 3–4 we see more popular and powerful passages. But before we get to chapter 3 . . . we find a *travel itinerary*. Seriously? Should we just skip this and move on to Paul talking about our union with Christ and what it means to live in the power of the resurrection (3:10)? Should we just skip over to Philippians 4:6-7 and learn about how we might have the peace of God? We could do that, but we would bypass some important material. This passage is calling us to Christlikeness, and we need to consider it carefully.

Understanding the Importance of the Travelogue

To see the importance of this passage, consider two questions. First, why do we have a travel itinerary at all? This is probably obvious to you, but I'll mention it. Paul includes this section because communication was important. He didn't have access to technological advances like FaceTime. The church was supporting Paul, and Paul wanted to extend thanks to the church and outline his plans. Further, Epaphroditus, who delivered a gift to Paul, was being sent back to Philippi sooner rather than later, and Timothy was being sent later rather than sooner. Paul needed to alert the church to these dynamics. "That's clear enough. Good for them," you might say. So why is it important for us? Next question . . .

Why is this travel itinerary in the middle of the book? While there are exceptions (as in 1 Cor 4:1-19), a travelogue in the Epistles normally appears at the end of the book. For example, at the end of Colossians 4 Paul says, "Tychicus . . . will tell you all the news about me. I have sent him to you for this very purpose" (Col 4:7-8). Because of this unusual placement in Philippians 2, some have concluded that Philippians is more than one letter. But I don't think that's the best answer. The best reason for including this travelogue here is that it fits perfectly within the flow of the whole letter. By speaking about Timothy and Epaphroditus, Paul provides concrete examples of what he's been talking about in the previous two chapters.

And this is why this passage lays claim on our lives. Paul moves from *instructions* and *imperatives* to *living illustrations*. We need illustrations and examples of a Philippians type of life! D. A. Carson gives numerous cases of the need for examples in matters such as prayer, language, life-style, entertainment, and he says, "Much Christian character is as much caught as taught—that is, it is picked up by constant association with mature Christians. . . . Modeling, modeling; it takes place all the time, whether we take it into account or not" (*Basics*, 69–70).

These men exemplify Philippians 1:5, for they had a "partnership in the gospel." God began a good work in them, and He was carrying it out (1:6). These men show us what it looks like to have affection for Christ's church (1:7-8). We could also say that they illustrate what it looks like to live "worthy of the gospel" (1:27), and that they illustrate the impera-tives of 2:12-16. The most obvious text that should come to our minds now is found here in the immediate context:

> Do nothing out of rivalry or conceit, but in humility consider others as more important than yourselves. Everyone should look out not only for his own interests, but also for the interests of others. (Phil 2:3-4)

Timothy and Epaphroditus are humble, others-focused servants who provide a shining example of working out their salvation in practical acts of serving without grumbling (2:12-14). Remember that we said "J.O.Y." comes when you get things in the right order: "**J**esus, then **O**thers, and then **Y**ourself." As a student said, there's a "whole lot of J.O.Y. in this passage!" These two men love Jesus and others. We shouldn't elevate them beyond reason, but we must see them as Paul is using them—as examples worth watching and as men worth following.

As we read through the text, we should seek to *imitate* such servants. We should seek to *honor* such servants (2:29). We should seek to *send* such servants or *go* like these servants. Regarding imitation, we should say, "Imitate them, as they follow after the example that is in Jesus" (2:5-11; cf. 3:17). Regarding honor, we're reminded of the need to show appreciation and respect for those that build up Christ's church. Regarding going and sending, we see the need to send our best and to be ready and available to go serve others ourselves.

So there's more than a travel itinerary here; Paul commends the character of these two brothers in Christ. He holds them up as model servants. Practically, these brothers show us what it looks like to have a changed heart. Jesus transformed them into compassionate, self-forget-ful, sacrificial servants worthy of emulation. When a church like the one in Philippi, or a church today, follows such selfless examples, they will grow united (1:27–2:4).

What about the person who reads this section and says, "It's kind of mundane"? We could say, "Indeed, you won't find anything super-sensational here, and that's probably why you need to read it closely!" There are no light shows, mega conferences, or acrobatic stunts here. There are no hobbits disappearing or Chihuahuas doing tricks. But faithful Christian living doesn't always look extraordinary.

We are drawn to the dramatic. The church gets sucked into the extraordinary as a product of the culture, in which everything gets sensationalized around us; even the nightly weather report is often sensationalized! As a result of our addiction to sensationalism, we get bored easily, we can't be still to study or listen, and we tend to downplay faithful, normal Christian service that honors Jesus. God normally meets us and uses us in the ordinariness of life.

Let me use an illustration. Fred Craddock once said,

> To give my life for Christ appears glorious. To pour myself out for others . . . to pay the ultimate price of martyrdom—I'll do it. I'm ready, Lord, to go out in a blaze of glory. . . . We think giving our all to the Lord is like taking a $1,000 bill and laying it on the table—"Here's my life, Lord. I'm giving it all." But the reality for most of us is that he sends us to the bank and has us cash in the $1,000 for quarters. We go through life putting out 25 cents here and 50 cents there. Listen to the neighbor kid's troubles instead of saying, "Get lost." Go to a committee meeting. Give a cup of water to a shaky old man in a nursing home. Usually giving our life to Christ isn't glorious. It's done in all those little acts of love, 25 cents at a time. It would be easy to go out in a flash of glory; it's harder to live the Christian life little by little over the long haul. (Quoted by Darryl Bell, "Practical Implications of Consecration")

Faithful Christian living might mean martyrdom for some, and if so, then we should rightly honor those believers. But for many others, those like Epaphroditus, faithful Christian living involves pouring our lives out, little by little, in practical acts of service over the long haul. It involves "giving out quarters every day": having a lonely person over for dinner; babysitting for a single mother; inviting some international students over; doing foster care; praying with a friend; helping someone move; visiting those in the hospital; and so on. This passage in Philippians 2 involves a guy delivering a gift to Paul and getting sick along the way. Paul says essentially that he spent some quarters and should be honored.

So let's look at the examples of Timothy and Epaphroditus. (I would like to call them "Timbo" and "Ephro," but I'll refrain!) Let's consider how we might imitate them, honor others like them, go like them, or send others like them.

The Example of Timothy
PHILIPPIANS 2:19-24

Paul tells the church that he's not sending Timothy right away. Maybe the church was expecting him to come soon. Timothy might be waiting until Paul's trial is concluded. If the verdict is favorable, then Paul plans on coming shortly after Timothy gets deployed. But Paul is not certain about everything, and he recognizes that he is subject to God's will, as indicated by the phrase "I hope in the Lord Jesus" (v. 19, cf. v. 24). In his travels he knows that Jesus is Lord over all things. In the middle of this itinerary, you will notice a heart-felt commendation of Timothy. Consider two aspects of Timothy's example: his compassion and his companionship.

Timothy's Compassion (2:20-21)

Paul says that he has "no one else like-minded" as Timothy is. Of course, Paul knows other believers in Rome, but no one is quite like Timothy in attitude, character, and closeness to the apostle. Apparently, Luke and Aristarchus are no longer with him in Rome (cf. Col 4:10,14; Phlm 24). What makes Timothy special among those present? Paul says that *Timothy genuinely cares about others.* Timothy is truly concerned for the well-being of others. He is a compassionate servant who loves the church. Like Paul, Timothy has a concern for the health of churches (2 Cor 11:28).

Paul says that many others seek "their own interests" (Phil 2:21). Already in chapters 1 and 2, Paul mentioned that some in Rome served out of envy and rivalry (1:15,17; cf. 2:3). But Timothy is in the group that served Christ out of goodwill and love (1:15-16). Notice the shift from verse 20 to verse 21. In verse 20 Paul says that Timothy is concerned for "your interests," and in verse 21 he says that he seeks after the interests "of Jesus Christ." Serving Christ involves serving others in the church. Serving Christ's church flows from our love for others and Jesus' glory, not our own selfish agendas.

By highlighting the warm, selfless, Christ-centered character of Timothy, Paul might also be preparing the congregation to listen to his son in the faith. Remember, there are tensions in Philippi. Paul informs the church that Timothy is the type of guy they can trust and listen to in order to resolve the matter. They can be assured that Timothy won't serve with self-centered motives but will serve the interests of Christ, who longs for unity in His church. Timothy's arrival will be worth the wait (O'Brien, *Epistle*, 320). Let us pursue the same type of compassion that flows from a heart enthralled by Jesus. Don't serve for the admiration of others, but for the adoration of Christ. Serve out of compassion for people, not to make a name for yourself. Let us humbly seek the good of others in light of how Jesus has poured out His life for us.

Throughout the years, the church has had many shining examples of selfless, Christ-exalting service. For instance, historians tell us that in AD 252 a plague hit Carthage, and people were leaving the city because of the threat of contamination, losing everything. The Christian leader Cyprian drew all the other Christians together in the middle of the town—in a town that persecuted Christians and blamed them for the problems—and said, "Fan out through this town to give to all according to their need." And they would not abandon the city in the midst of the plague. The Christians earned a reputation for showing charity to all people, regardless of status or background.

What kind of leader do you follow? What kind of leader will you be? Follow compassionate servant-leaders who are following Christ, like Timothy. Listen to these types of leaders. Hear their hearts. Watch their lives. And if you become a leader, be this type of leader. Don't insist on the finest accommodations. Don't become self-absorbed. Don't live for the admiration of others. Look to the interests of others for the glory of Christ.

Timothy's Companionship (2:22-24)

Next, Paul says, "But you know his proven character, because he has served with me in the gospel ministry like a son with a father." Paul loves Timothy as a spiritual son (1 Cor 4:17; 2 Tim 1:2; cf. 2 Kgs 2:12). His words about Timothy highlight the familial nature of the church. Timothy wasn't merely a volunteer in an organization; he was Paul's son in the faith. Paul mentions that Timothy had proven his character to others. He was devoted to Christ's cause and Christ's church. Together, Paul and Timothy were "slaves of Christ Jesus" (1:1). They had been through the fire of testing and trial, advancing the gospel in the midst of hardship (Acts 16:1,3; 17:14).

The striking note about the loyal companionship of Timothy is highlighted in the next verse: "Therefore, I hope to send him as soon as I see how things go with me" (2:23). Paul couldn't dispatch Timothy immediately. Perhaps he needed his help in a legal or pastoral matter; we don't know. But we do know that Paul treasured Timothy's companionship. Timothy was a true friend who helped sustain the apostle during this time. What made Timothy a great friend? The best friends are those who serve and care for you like Christ would serve and care for you. Do you have friends like that? I hope you do. Are you a friend like that? I hope you are. Care for others as Christ would care for them. That means being present, speaking the truth, strengthening them in weakness, praying for them, and providing support and resources when needed.

So Paul is sending Timothy, his spiritual son, his companion, his fellow servant in the gospel. He was an extension of Paul to minister to the Philippians. In sending Timothy to the church, Paul is also displaying selfless service. He is sending his beloved companion for the good of others. Paul, too, is an example of selfless service that we should emulate.

The Example of Epaphroditus
PHILIPPIANS 2:25-30

Paul isn't sending Timothy immediately, but he is sending Epaphroditus. (He shouldn't be confused with Epaphras; cf. Col 4:12.) The name "Epaphroditus," which was common in the era, is derived from "Aphrodite" (the Greek mythical goddess). His family may have worshiped this goddess, and he was likely a Gentile convert (O'Brien, *Epistle*, 329). What happens when Jesus transforms an idol worshiper? We read about it here.

According to chapter 4, Epaphroditus brought Paul financial help from the church in Philippi. The church probably expected Epaphroditus to stay and minister to Paul, but Paul tells them that he's sending him back because Epaphroditus had fallen ill. We don't know what this illness was; perhaps it was a terrible fever or the flu. Whatever it was, he almost died. The events may have happened like this: He got sick *en route*, not after his arrival in Rome. Since Epaphroditus was carrying money, he probably didn't travel alone (cf. 2 Cor 8:16-22). One of the companions may have returned to the Philippian church with the alarming news, or someone traveling in the opposite direction could have reported the situation to the church (Witherington, *Friendship and Finances*, 80). Then one of his companions may have nursed him along as they journeyed to deliver the gift (see Hughes, *Philippians*, 113–14).

Paul wanted the church to welcome and honor Epaphroditus. Kent Hughes claims he was a layman, not an official leader in the church (*Philippians*, 115). Indeed, no position is mentioned here or in chapter 4. It's certainly true that you don't have to have a position to be useful or worthy of honor. Paul also sent him back because he didn't want the additional stress of keeping him in Rome.

Why the emphasis on *honor*? This emphasis is probably due to the fact that this was a culture based more on honor and shame than our American culture is. Think about it. The church sends their representative to the famous apostle. When he arrives, he has been sick, he almost dies, and he has to go home sooner rather than later. The church might think of him as an embarrassment. "We should have sent someone else!" they may have said. But Paul covers for him and says Epaphroditus deserves a hero's welcome.

Paul mentions five descriptions for Epaphroditus that underscore his character and partnership. The first three descriptions relate to his relationship with Paul and the next two his relationship to the Philippians. Then he mentions the compassion of Epaphroditus, his experience of God's restoring mercy, and the type of welcome he deserves when he returns to the church.

The Type of Man He Was (2:25)

Brother. This first description reminds us how we become partners in the gospel. Through Christ, we have been adopted by the Father. And when you become a Christian, not only do you have a new relationship with God, but you also get a new relationship with other believers. You are now brothers and sisters. The term *brother* may not mean much to you if you grew up in a church where you heard it regularly. Christians often use the term because they can't remember each other's names! But it's a miracle that we're brothers and sisters. Our identity has changed; God is our Father, and we are adopted family members. In calling him "brother" Paul is also highlighting his affection for Epaphroditus, not just this identity change. When you go through hard times with Christian brothers or sisters at your side, you form a deep relationship with them. Such was the case here. Praise God for brothers and sisters in Christ!

Coworker. Paul also labored in the same mission as Epaphroditus. Though Paul was more up front, in a position of leadership, he recognized that they were equals. Paul didn't assume some position of superiority. They worked together for the cause of Christ. Epaphroditus, you could say, nearly "worked himself to death."

Fellow soldier. Paul changes the image to one of his favorite pictures of the Christian life. He goes to the battlefield and calls him a "fellow soldier" (cf. 2 Tim 2:3-4). He and Epaphroditus had been through a spiritual war together (cf. Eph 6:10-20). As in the case of the term *coworker,* Paul sees himself as an equal, on the same mission together. As is the case with many good soldiers, Epaphroditus had been wounded, and he was being sent home to rest (Hughes, *Philippians,* 115).

Messenger and minister. Moving from their relationship with each other, Paul mentions the relationship between Epaphroditus and the Philippians. With two words he explains what Epaphroditus was called to do. He was their "messenger" (*apostolon*). Like the apostle Paul, he was "sent" with a mission to convey the love of the church and to give a gift to Paul. And he was also their "minister" (*leitourgon*), a word that carries the idea of priestly service in the Greek version of the Old Testament. This term doesn't refer to a position, but to a particular function. All believers are God's priests, and all believers are called to worship God through sacrificial service (Rom 12:1-2). Epaphroditus worshiped God by serving Paul and others. While it's good to discuss various aspects of corporate worship, we shouldn't limit our discussion of worship to merely what happens on Sunday. We need worshipers like Epaphroditus.

Wouldn't these five terms be wonderful on a tombstone? Wouldn't you like to be known as a brother, coworker, fellow soldier, messenger, and minister? What would people say should go on your tombstone? Emulate Epaphroditus.

The Type of Love He Displayed (2:26)

Paul notes Epaphroditus's compassionate sensitivity in the next phrase: "since he has been longing for all of you and was *distressed* because you heard that he was sick" (emphasis added). This verse is remarkable because Ephaphroditus is the one who is sick, yet we don't read of any self-pity—rather, quite the opposite! He's not concerned about himself; he's concerned about the anxiety of the Philippians! I must admit that this is a challenging example. When you get sick, do you turn inward?

Do you want to call your mom and have her make chicken soup? Well, Epaphroditus's sickness was much worse than the common flu. Yet he "consider[s] others as more important" even in his sickness (2:3).

The Greek word for "distressed" is used elsewhere only in the garden of Gethsemane passage, describing the great anguish of our Lord prior to His death (Matt 26:37; Mark 14:33). Even with death at his doorstep, Epaphroditus, like Jesus, is concerned about others more than himself. Jesus was obedient to death (Phil 2:8); Epaphroditus was obedient to the point of death (2:27), yet another way Epaphroditus points us to Jesus.

Perhaps someone has asked you, "As a Christian, what's different about your life compared to mine?" You could stop and teach them theology. But you could also say, "Come watch me live for a month, and you can tell me. See if there's anything different." In Philippians 2:5-11 we see the theology of a Christian, but in 2:19-30 we see the type of lifestyle that should mark a genuine Christian. Would someone see Epaphroditus's type of love in you if they watched your life for a month? To live this type of life, we need help (2 Cor 12:7-10). That's exactly what Epaphroditus received.

The Type of Help He Needed (2:27)

Just how sick was he? Paul says that he was so sick that he "nearly died." Three times Paul mentions his severe condition (vv. 26,27,30). How did Paul's fellow soldier survive? We don't have all of the details, but we do know this: "God had mercy on him." Did medicine help to cure him? Was he restored as a result of prayer? Did he experience a divine miracle apart from medicine? Was it a combination of all of these? We don't know. The significant thing to Paul was that his recovery was due to the sovereign act of a merciful God (O'Brien, *Epistle*, 337). Epaphroditus needed God's mercy in his weakness.

Paul adds that he, too, had experienced the mercy of God. If Epaphroditus had died, Paul would have had "one grief on top of another." Paul knows that "dying is gain" (1:21), but this doesn't mean he wouldn't mourn over his brother. Our world is filled with grief, but the believer can say with Paul, we are "grieving yet always rejoicing" (2 Cor 6:10). Paul would have wept over Epaphroditus; he wasn't an emotionless leader. This passage shows how much Paul loves people, and when you love people, you grieve over their absence. But we don't grieve as those without hope (1 Thess 4:13).

Does this little phrase, "However, God had mercy on him," move you? His mercies are new every morning (Lam 3:22), and we *need* new mercies every morning! We experience God's mercy in manifold ways. In His mercy He has covered our sin, and in His mercy He heals our bodies (Ps 103:1-5). Believers rejoice in the saving mercy of God, who has raised us up spiritually ("But God, who is rich in mercy"; Eph 2:4). We experience traveling mercies regularly. David said it well: "Surely goodness and mercy shall follow me all the days of my life" (Ps 23:6 ESV). God had been good to Paul, to Epaphroditus, and to the church in Philippi. And He's been good to us. May God fill your heart with gratitude for His bountiful mercies, and may your heart not be filled with entitlement. We don't deserve blessings.

The Type of Welcome He Deserved (2:28-30)

Paul says that he's eager to send Epaphroditus back to the Philippians so that everyone may experience peace. Paul wouldn't have to worry about him. The church would know that he was okay, and Epaphroditus wouldn't have to worry about the Philippians worrying! On arrival, Paul says there should be not only joy, love, and peace but also *honor*. Paul commands the church to welcome their messenger because he made a huge sacrifice. Paul says of him that he was "risking his life to make up what was lacking in your ministry to me" (v. 30). What was lacking was the Philippians' presence. Epaphroditus represented them in their absence. In so doing, he almost died. He deserves to be welcomed as Christ will welcome those who faithfully labor in service to others (Matt 25:14-46).

This command to honor Epaphroditus is so refreshing. In Paul's day, and in our day, it's usually the famous, the talented, and the powerful who are praised. But here's a simple messenger who took a gift to Paul in humble service and sacrifice, and Paul says to honor him. Similar language is found in 1 Corinthians, where Paul commends Stephanas and his family.

> *Brothers, you know the household of Stephanas: They are the firstfruits of Achaia and have devoted themselves to serving the saints. I urge you also to submit to such people, and to everyone who works and labors with them. I am pleased to have Stephanas, Fortunatus, and Achaicus present, because these men have made up for your absence. For they have refreshed my spirit and yours. Therefore recognize such* people. (1 Cor 16:15-18; emphasis added)

This sounds a lot like Epaphroditus, doesn't it? O'Brien notes, "Paul's teaching in both passages is consistent with that of Jesus, who said that the greatest honor among his followers belongs to the one who renders the lowliest service (Mk 10:42-45; Lk 22:24-27; cf. Jn 13:13-15)" (*Epistle*, 341).

I (Tony) am a Kentucky basketball fan. In 2014 we made it to the championship game only to lose to Connecticut. Almost 80,000 people showed up to watch that game. When Kentucky returned from the airport during their wins throughout the tournament, they were extolled by fans. Even after defeat, people welcomed them and honored their team. I don't have a problem with fans honoring players. Unfortunately, we fail to recognize the type of greatness exemplified in Ephaphroditus. We underappreciate faithful service to Jesus. Who's greater, the person who serves the least of these, or the person who wins a championship? Sports are wonderful gifts, but games are games. There are much more important battles to engage. When you see someone serving Christ faithfully, you should encourage them and thank them. Don't deify them, but honor them. Paul says this person is worthy of an appreciative and thoughtful welcome.

The Christian life should be filled with honoring one another (Rom 12:10; Eph 6:2; 1 Tim 5:3,17; 6:1; Heb 13:4; 1 Pet 2:17). Ultimate honor goes to Jesus, but under that honor we should have deep appreciation for the hard work of those who build up Christ's church. Let's step back and gather a few profitable points of application from the life of Epaphroditus.

Serving Jesus and others will cost you, but it's worth it! The call to put the needs of others above your own will mean that you might have to change your schedule this week. You might have to travel somewhere. You might get sick along your journey and have to minister in weakness. You might have to open your home or your wallet. You might encounter great conflict or persecution. If we're going to follow after these model servants, who are following Jesus' example, then we must acknowledge that the Christian life involves sacrifice—varying degrees of sacrifice. But it's worth it because we get to bless others and because it glorifies Jesus, who notices every small act of obedience and will reward it (see Matt 25:14-46; Luke 14:12-14).

Deep relationships are formed when you are on mission with other brothers and sisters. We're made for relationships—not superficial relationships based on fleeting affinities but for something much deeper, namely, gospel partnerships. We have pointed out already that the "partnership of the gospel" (Phil 1:5) involves more than potluck dinners. It involves a common mission of advancing the gospel. These two servants were coworkers with Paul, and as a result they shared a deep relationship that few experience. Let's remember this. Deep and abiding community is formed in the church as we serve together, not just when we sit together once a week in a Bible study or a worship event (as important as these are!).

The church has always been sustained, enriched, and built up by unsung heroes. Consider Romans 16. This particular postscript includes a list of unsung heroes. These postscripts, including the one in 1 Corinthians 16, demonstrate that Paul didn't just love books, theology, and ministry. He also loved people. When Paul talks about unsung heroes in the church, he does so with honoring and familial language, as he does with Timothy and Epaphroditus. I have highlighted a few of the ways that Paul honors them:

> *I commend to you* our sister Phoebe, *who is a* servant *of the church in Cenchreae. So you should welcome her in the Lord in a manner worthy of the saints and assist her in whatever matter she may require your help. For indeed she has been a benefactor of many—and of me also. Give my greetings to Prisca and Aquila,* my coworkers in Christ Jesus, who risked their own necks for my life. *Not only do I thank them, but so do all the Gentile churches. Greet also the church that meets in their home. Greet my dear friend Epaenetus, who is the first convert to Christ from Asia. Greet Mary, who has* worked very hard for you. *Greet Andronicus and Junia, my* fellow countrymen *and* fellow prisoners. *They are noteworthy in the eyes of the apostles, and they were also in Christ before me. Greet Ampliatus, my* dear friend *in the Lord. Greet Urbanus, our* coworker *in Christ, and my* dear friend *Stachys. Greet Apelles, who is* approved *in Christ. Greet those who belong to the household of Aristobulus. Greet Herodion, my* fellow countryman. *Greet those who belong to the household of Narcissus who are in the Lord. Greet Tryphaena and Tryphosa, who have* worked hard *in the Lord. Greet my dear friend Persis, who has* worked very hard *in the Lord. Greet Rufus, chosen in the Lord; also his mother—and* mine. *Greet Asyncritus, Phlegon, Hermes, Patrobas, Hermas, and* the brothers *who are with them. Greet Philologus and Julia, Nereus and his sister, and Olympas, and all the saints who*

are with them. Greet one another with a holy kiss. All the churches of Christ send you greetings. (Rom 16:1-16; emphasis added)

Those are some beautiful words—"brother," "mother," "sister," "coworker," "servant," those who "worked very hard." Let me ask you, based on all of these names, did the apostles do all the work in the church? No. Were they the only people worthy of honor? No. The church was filled with missionaries, with fellow servants of Jesus, who were laboring in their own ways to build up the church and reach out in mission. So don't get the impression that you don't have an important role to play in your church. You do! The church has been blessed throughout the centuries by unsung heroes like these.

In Humility Consider Others as More Important Than Yourselves

Timothy and Epaphroditus (and Paul!) give us living examples in the book of Philippians, particularly in 2:3-4. To summarize, let me repeat Paul's exhortation: "Do nothing out of rivalry or conceit, but in humility consider others as more important than yourselves." All three men show us what happens when the gospel really transforms us from the inside out: we begin to live like Jesus (2:5-11).

What about you? Is this the nature of your Christian life, a life of considering the needs of others above your own? The only way that happens is by trusting in Christ, who emptied Himself on behalf of sinful people like us, and by pursuing through the Spirit this attitude and these types of actions, which include everyday acts of love, little by little, over the long haul. Go spend some quarters today for the good of others and the glory of Jesus in the ordinariness of life.

Reflect and Discuss

1. In what ways does phony religiosity (those who claim the name "Christian" but seem no different from anyone else) hurt the credibility of Christ and the church?
2. What are some reasons we have a travel itinerary in Philippians?
3. Who are the people in your life who model Jesus? In what ways do they model Christlikeness?
4. Who are the people in your life to whom you model Jesus? In what ways would they say you model Christlikeness?

5. Does faithful Christian living always look extraordinary? Why or why not?

6. How do you cultivate a servant heart of selflessness rather than selfishness?

7. What made Timothy a great friend to Paul? Do you have friends like that? Are you a friend like that?

8. Consider each description. Why does Paul call Epaphroditus his "brother," "fellow worker," "fellow soldier," and "messenger and minister"?

9. Consider the ways God has had mercy on you today. Pause and thank God for the evidences of His grace.

10. What are some practical ways you can "honor" servants of the gospel like Timothy and Epaphroditus at your church?

The Glory of Knowing Christ

PHILIPPIANS 3:1-11

Main Idea: Paul warns the church about false gospels and reminds them of the means and the glory of knowing Christ.

I.   **No Trouble to Me, Safe for You (3:1)**
II. **Marks of Those Who Know Christ (3:2-6)**
    A. Mark 1: We serve by the Spirit of God (3:3b).
    B. Mark 2: We boast in Christ Jesus (3:3c).
    C. Mark 3: We put no confidence in the flesh (3:3d-6).
       1. Don't put your confidence in a ritual.
       2. Don't put your confidence in your ethnicity.
       3. Don't put your confidence in your rank.
       4. Don't put your confidence in your tradition.
       5. Don't put your confidence in your rule keeping.
       6. Don't put your confidence in your zeal.
       7. Don't put your confidence in your obedience to the law.
III. **How to Know Christ (3:7-11)**
    A. Justification: Trust Christ alone as your righteousness (3:9).
    B. Sanctification: Know Christ more and become more like Him (3:10).
    C. Glorification: Anticipate your resurrection (3:11).

My (Tony) parents recently brought me four tubs of stuff that I used to value. The contents included baseball cards, trophies, a letterman's jacket, and more sports-related material. They were tired of having my former treasures fill up their storage space. As I looked through the things, I was at first excited. Then I stepped back and evaluated the whole. Here was 18 years of my life placed into four plastic tubs. It was pretty sobering. I used to spend countless hours playing sports and trading baseball cards. While I'm thankful for my childhood days and for my days playing sports, I really wish I had some different goals growing up. I wish I had lived with Philippians 3 in mind.

What do you treasure? Is there anything of surpassing value? Is there anything that deserves our life-long, passionate pursuit? The answer is yes. Paul describes it in verse 8:

> More than that, I also consider everything to be a loss in view of the surpassing value of knowing Christ Jesus my Lord.

Paul reminds us that nothing on earth compares to knowing Jesus Christ as Lord and Savior. You will never regret pursuing Christ.

I (Francis) took my wife with me to Memphis for a speaking engagement. Nothing is more romantic than being near Elvis, right? It's amazing how crazy people are over this person, who is dead. In Philippians 3 Paul has crazy love for Jesus, who is alive. This is the love we need also.

This passage is extremely important because it tells us what it means to know Jesus, what it means to find eternal salvation and ultimate satisfaction in life. Paul describes what a Christian isn't, what a Christian is, and how one can become a Christian. So, if you're reading this commentary and you're unsure whether you are a Christian, I pray this passage will change your life as you consider it carefully.

Elsewhere in the Bible the idea of "knowing Christ" or having the "knowledge of God" involves the idea of salvation. Jesus said these very important words in John 17:

> This is eternal life: that they may know You, the only true God, and the One You have sent—Jesus Christ. (John 17:3)

So salvation is about knowing Jesus. It doesn't mean merely to know *about* Him; it means that you have a relationship with Him. And those who know Christ want to know Him better and better.

Consider Paul. The risen Christ appeared to him and totally changed his life (Acts 9:1-9), as he describes in several places (e.g., 1 Tim 1:12-17; Gal 1:11-17). Now, some 30 years later, he still wants to know Christ more and more.

No Trouble to Me, Safe for You
PHILIPPIANS 3:1

This passage is also important because it reminds believers of their need to stay focused on the true gospel of Jesus. As mentioned, salvation isn't about knowing some things about Jesus. But it's also not about doing religious things to earn acceptance before Jesus. This text really speaks against the problem of *legalism*, that is, the temptation to derive your justification before God, your acceptance by God, and your forgiveness from God by your own religious works. We're reminded here that you can't earn salvation. It's a gift to be received. But even dedicated Christians have a tendency to forget the gospel daily. They have a tendency to revert back to legalism, as the book of Galatians so powerfully points out (see Gal 3:1-9). Legalism is self-atonement. It's a self-salvation project that only leads to pride or despair. We must resist the gospel of human achievement.

Paul begins the chapter saying, "Finally, my brothers, rejoice in the Lord. To write the same things to you is no trouble to me and is safe for you" (ESV). Many like to compare Paul's word "Finally" to contemporary preachers who seem to never know when to end a sermon. But the word could be translated something like "So then" (Carson, *Basics*, 80). Paul isn't indicating that he's finished with the letter. He's only halfway through it. He's picking up the theme of "rejoicing" (2:17-18) and carrying on the idea of emulation. He's providing an example that includes a passion to know Christ Jesus as Lord.

Paul says that he's told the Philippian congregation the "same things" before. He's probably referring to what he taught them in person. Previously, he taught them the gospel. Now he's still teaching them the gospel. Paul says it's no trouble for him to repeat these things, and it's safe for the congregation. In other words, the church will be protected from legalism and false gospels by studying the true gospel regularly.

Every church should be a "same things church." Oh, we must change some ministry methods, but the message must never change. And the "same thing" has numerous implications, but we must be about the same things, namely the truths of the gospel. We must constantly remind one another of the gospel, rehearse the gospel, sing the gospel, and proclaim the gospel—not only for the good of the unbeliever but also for the building up of the believer. Repeating the gospel is an expression of love for other believers. If you're a teacher, don't grow cold to the gospel. Look at Paul's example here. It doesn't trouble him to remind them of what it means to know Christ. It's an expression of his love for the Philippian congregation, as it serves to protect them.

To understand what it means to know Christ and to understand what we must avoid, let's look at this text in two parts: three *marks* of those who know Christ, and *how* to know Christ. By understanding these things, and by embracing Christ, we, too, can "rejoice in the Lord."

Marks of Those Who Know Christ
PHILIPPIANS 3:2-6

Paul provides three distinguishing marks of a genuine Christian in verse 3. They are contrasted with what he says in verse 2. For those of you who like dogs, you must realize that Paul lived in a different context. Dogs weren't viewed as cute little pets. They were nasty, unclean, and dangerous. They often wandered where they didn't belong. Paul viewed these false teachers like feral dogs. They were entering the church and damaging it.

These particular teachers were known as "Judaizers." During the time of the early church many devout Jews were willing to accept Jesus as Messiah, but they wanted to hold on to forms of Judaism. They believed that Gentiles had to become Jews before becoming Christians. This involved the act of circumcision and taking on the law of Moses (Carson, *Basics*, 81). We read about them in Acts 15. They were saying, "Unless you are circumcised according to the custom prescribed by Moses, you cannot be saved!" (Acts 15:1). But the leaders of the church, including Paul, Barnabas, James, and Peter, denied this claim and preserved the gospel of grace. Salvation comes through Christ and Christ alone, apart from works of the law.

The reference to dogs is striking because the Jews often called the Gentiles "dogs," since they viewed them as unclean (e.g., Mark 7:27-29). But Paul states that a dramatic reversal has taken place through the work of Christ. Now it's the Judaizers who must be regarded as dogs. He also calls the Judaizers "evildoers" and "mutilators of the flesh" (ESV). They were evildoers because their mission was evil, not good. Their mission wasn't heroic, but hellish. We're reminded here that false teachers have missionaries too. Someone shouldn't be commended just because they go on a mission trip. If they're exporting a distorted gospel, then they're dangerous; they're deadly.

The phrase "mutilators of the flesh" speaks against the value of circumcision. They were trusting in a physical operation instead of in God's gracious work of salvation in Christ. Silva says, "Here in Philippians Paul takes the Judaizers' greatest source of pride and interprets it as the surest sign that they have no share among God's people" (*Philippians*, 148). When Gentiles accepted this pressure to be circumcised in order to gain God's blessing, they were acting like pagans, who also mutilated the flesh in order to gain the favor of the gods (Hanson, *Letter*, 220). They didn't need mutilation; they needed regeneration.

About 15 years ago we used to sing "Who Let the Dogs Out?" It was a sort of light-hearted chorus, but the verse lyrics were awful. Much like the false teachers—the song's message might appear attractive on the surface, but after you examine it, it's perverted.

Who let these dogs out? Answer: the evil one. The Devil wants to destroy people's confidence in Christ's sufficient work. He would like nothing more than to have people believe in a false gospel. So beware of dogs. Like physical dogs, there are all sorts of spiritual dogs. Many do the same thing that these Judaizing dogs were doing, namely, adding to the gospel. When you add to the gospel, you lose the gospel! It's not Jesus *plus* your good works (whatever your own version of good works may be). It's Christ and Christ alone.

In verse 3 Paul says "We are the circumcision" to speak not of a circumcision of the flesh, but that of a changed heart. At the end of his letter to the Galatians, he says it like this:

> For both circumcision and uncircumcision mean nothing; what matters instead is a new creation. (Gal 6:15)

While Paul was a circumcised Jew, most in the Philippian congregation were Gentiles. Paul is saying that those who trust in Christ are the true people of God; they are the true circumcision. Following this statement, he provides three distinguishing marks of a Christian, of the true people of God. The first two statements are positive and the third is negative.

Mark 1: We Serve by the Spirit of God (3:3b)

Paul tells the church that true believers "worship by the Spirit of God" (ESV). When Paul uses the word *worship*, he isn't speaking simply of what we do in a Sunday morning gathering. He's speaking of "service," as the HCSB translates it. He's talking about a life devoted to God in spiritual service (cf. Rom 12:1).

True Christians possess the Spirit. Paul says to the Christians in Rome, "You, however, are not in the flesh, but in the Spirit, since the Spirit of God lives in you. But if anyone does not have the Spirit of Christ, he does not belong to Him" (Rom 8:9). When Jesus spoke to the woman at the well in John 4, He said something very similar: "True worshipers will worship the Father in spirit and truth" (John 4:23).

Does the Spirit of God dwell in you? Do you worship and serve God by the Spirit? On what are you basing your assurance of salvation? Don't base it on attendance at meetings or on involvement in social work. Rest and rejoice in the fact that the Spirit of God dwells in you, enabling you to worship and serve God for the praise of His glory.

Mark 2: We Boast in Christ Jesus (3:3c)

Paul adds that the true people of God "boast in Christ Jesus." Our glory is in Christ alone! Again our minds are drawn to Galatians, particularly where Paul famously says it like this:

> But as for me, I will never boast about anything except the cross of our Lord Jesus Christ. The world has been crucified to me through the cross, and I to the world. (Gal 6:14)

We don't glory in our earthly status, in our achievements, or in our gifts. Personal boasting in salvation is excluded for the Christian, for salvation has come to us through the work of another, a gift of the sovereign and gracious God (Rom 3:27; Eph 2:8-9). We must then boast only in Christ. To the Corinthians Paul says, "The one who boasts must boast in the Lord" (1 Cor 1:31).

If you meet someone who claims to be a Christian but isn't making much of Christ, then you have reason to be suspicious of their claim. The Christian life is a Christ-exalting life. Do you boast in Christ around your friends? Do you glory in Christ Jesus in your ministry publicly? Do you use your platform to make much of Christ Jesus our Lord? Churches can be known for all sorts of things. Let's be known for boasting in Christ!

Mark 3: We Put No Confidence in the Flesh (3:3d-6)

The final mark is related to the second. Paul says that the people of God "do not put confidence in the flesh." This is simple enough. Everyone has their confidence somewhere, and the Christian's confidence is in Christ, not his own effort or goodness. That is why the Christian boasts in Christ and rejoices in Christ. The human heart is prone to trust in other things, instead of Christ, for salvation. But this important passage reminds us that our tribe doesn't provide us with any confidence of being able to stand before God's awesome presence. When it comes to being accepted before a holy God, your nationality doesn't matter, your rituals don't matter, your education doesn't matter. We can stand safely, securely, and confidently before God because of the work of another, namely, Christ.

Where is your confidence? What will enable you to stand before God and receive His grace instead of His judgment? In what are you trusting? There's only one place to look, according to Paul. So here are three marks of a Christian: We serve by the Spirit of God. We boast in Christ Jesus. We put no confidence in the flesh. If you aren't a Christian, consider the testimony of Paul, as he details his former life before meeting the risen Christ. You, too, can turn from trusting in false saviors and place your faith in Christ alone for salvation.

The Judaizers appealed to their impressive Jewish credentials, so Paul now flashes his own credentials, which were unparalleled. He effectively says, "If you want to brag, I can brag even more!" His point in doing this is to show the Philippians the emptiness of fleshly confidence. He will contrast this salvation by human achievement with a salvation by Christ's achievement and call his former life of Judaism "filth."

Paul could boast in his own religious privileges and accomplishments, for he had many! His list includes four items pertaining to his birth privileges as a Jew, and the next three draw attention to his own religious achievements. These qualities were impressive to those like the Judaizers, but Paul says he has no confidence in them for providing salvation. As we briefly consider them, we can identify seven sources of false confidence. While we can't make a one-for-one correlation between Paul's self-portrait and contemporary non-Jewish religious people, we can make some general applications for people today who aren't trusting in Christ alone for eternal life.

Don't put your confidence in a ritual. Paul says that he was "circumcised on the eighth day" (v. 5 ESV). Paul was an "eighth-dayer." He wasn't a Jewish proselyte. His circumcision was done in a first-class way (Gen 17:12). Those who were converts to Judaism could never claim to have been circumcised on the eighth day. Today, people may put their confidence in other spiritual rituals, like being baptized as an infant or attending religious meetings. These experiences aren't grounds for spiritual confidence. Paul went through this famous Jewish ritual, but he considered it of no advantage. Salvation is about becoming a new creation in Christ, not about going through a particular ritual. Look to the One who is the substance of the shadows (Col 2:17).

Don't put your confidence in your ethnicity. Next in his self-portrait, he says that he was "of the nation of Israel" (v. 5), which means he was of the "race of Israel" (Hanson, *Letter*, 223). Paul was a physical descendant of Abraham. He was no Gentile convert to Judaism, but the real thing.

Yet this special privilege didn't give him reason for assurance of salvation. He had to look to the offspring of Abraham, namely, Christ.

Don't put your confidence in your rank. He goes on to add that not only was he an Israelite, but he also belonged to "the tribe of Benjamin" (v. 5). Paul didn't come from a disrespected Israelite tribe, but from this distinguished tribe. When the promised land was divided among the 12 tribes, Jerusalem, the holy city, was in Benjamin's territory. When the kingdom split, Judah and Benjamin remained loyal to the Davidic dynasty. Yet Paul says, as proud as that could make a Jew, it was of no ultimate value for granting anyone salvation. Many who are exalted in the world today will one day be humbled because they've failed to bow down to Christ. Salvation isn't by your rank. It comes by trusting in David's greatest Son, Jesus Christ.

Don't put your confidence in your tradition. Traditions can be fine as far as they go, but you should place no confidence in them when it comes to salvation. Being a traditionalist is of no more value than being a progressive if you aren't focused on Jesus. Paul calls himself a "Hebrew of Hebrews" (v. 5 ESV). While he was fluent in Greek, he didn't abandon his Hebrew culture. He was also fluent in Hebrew and devoted to his traditional culture. We also cannot rely on our cultural heritage or family tradition for salvation. I've met a lot of people whom I've invited to corporate worship over the years, who have claimed that their entire family was of a particular religious group. We must tell them, don't trust in tradition. You must trust in the ultimate Hebrew, Jesus Himself.

Don't put your confidence in your rule keeping. Paul says regarding the law he was a "Pharisee" (v. 5). They loved their rules. Their name comes from an Aramaic term denoting "the separated ones" (Hanson, *Letter,* 226). They even added to the commands of the Old Testament—so much so, that it was hard to know what the actual biblical commands were. That's who Paul was. He adopted a Pharisaical lifestyle. He belonged to a morally superior group of Jews.

You will meet people today who think that salvation comes by being a moral person. To be clear, I'm not encouraging rule breaking. We must simply note that rule keeping won't earn salvation. Many have the idea that moral people will go to heaven. It's still around today, and it's the default mode of the human heart.

I was at the bedside of a family member recently. In his dying days, I was trying to explain the gospel to him. I read to him Ephesians 2:8-9 and talked about salvation as a gift of grace. His response was at first,

"I was in the Boy Scouts." That's fine, but keeping the code of some group doesn't merit eternal life. It didn't for Paul as a Pharisee, and it won't for us either. Salvation isn't by rule keeping.

Don't put your confidence in your zeal. We certainly hear this claim today: "It doesn't matter what you believe, as long as you are sincere and really believe it." Well, it would be hard to fathom anyone more "sincere" than Saul of Tarsus. He wasn't a Pharisee in name only; he was zealous. He says, "regarding zeal, persecuting the church" (v. 6). Regarding his pre-conversion life, to the Galatians he says, "I was extremely zealous for the traditions of my ancestors" (Gal 1:14). His zeal was expressed through his persecution of the church (Acts 8:3; 9:1; 22:4-6; 26:10-11). To the Corinthians he said that only by the grace of God could he be forgiven of such sin (1 Cor 15:9-10).

Salvation doesn't come by passion. People are passionate about lots of things. Salvation comes by knowing the real man of zeal, Jesus Christ. People can be sincere but be sincerely wrong. Paul told the Romans that some have "zeal for God, but not according to knowledge" (Rom 10:2). One must know Christ; one must be "found in Him" (Phil 3:9).

Don't put your confidence in your obedience to the law. Paul wraps up his religious résumé, saying, "regarding the righteousness that is in the law, blameless" (v. 6). While Paul isn't claiming sinless perfection, he is saying that his life was exemplary when it came to obeying the Old Testament law. He was a self-righteous person, who boasted in his ability to keep God's law, like the rich young ruler (Luke 18:18-23). Later in verse 9, however, Paul will talk about the need for the righteousness of another—Christ. Salvation comes through the obedience of another, through the work of another—Christ. While Paul's public record of moral performance was stellar, he later placed it in the loss column.

This phrase contrasted with verse 9, "the righteousness from God that depends on faith" (ESV), summarizes the difference between Christianity and other world religions. Other systems promote works-based righteousness, but the gospel is about imputed righteousness. It's about receiving Christ's righteousness as our own. The most sincere religious person can't keep God's law. We need Christ. He lived the life we should have lived, and then He died the death we lawbreakers should have died. Let me ask you again, Where is your confidence? Are you trusting in your rituals, your ethnicity, your rank, your tradition, your rule keeping, your zeal, or your obedience to the law? Paul says that a genuine Christian puts no confidence in these things. Our confidence lies in another, namely, Christ. Put your trust in Him! Paul goes on to tell us more about what this means in the next four verses.

How to Know Christ (3:7-11)

Paul transitions with some remarkable statements on knowing Christ. Silva calls this section "the essence of Pauline theology" (*Philippians*, 155). At the center is Christ. Paul mentions Christ by name or pronoun nine times in five verses; his supreme ambition is knowing Christ. In verse 7 Paul says that everything he thought was in the credit column (his list of privileges and accomplishments in verses 5-6) has been transferred to the debit column. Only Christ remains in the credit column. He repeats himself more forcefully in verse 8. He didn't just count all lost; he lost it all!

Paul calls his religious accomplishments "filth" or "rubbish" (ESV) or "dung" (KJV) compared to knowing Christ. Paul uses a term that sometimes referred to animal or human excrement. At the risk of sounding crass, he says it's all "dog crap" compared to knowing Christ. The vulgarity of the term is deliberate, as Paul wants to strike us with the worthlessness of life apart from Jesus. You can have the Bread of Life that will eternally satisfy or you can have a pile of dung. Which do you prefer: the dung of religious self-efforts and earthly praise and possessions or the eternal joy of knowing Christ as your Savior and Lord? Paul made his decision, and he's trying to help others choose wisely. One may hear an echo from Jesus' question, "What will it benefit a man if he gains the whole world yet loses his life? Or what will a man give in exchange for his life?" (Matt 16:26).

This zealous Pharisee turned into a zealous missionary for Christ. This same Christ he had persecuted (Acts 9) became his Savior, Lord, and treasure. Because of his conversion to Christ, Paul "suffered the loss of all things." You might say he traded a list of accomplishments for a list of afflictions. He lost friends, intellectual peers, his home, his security, his status, and more. In place of these things, he received the following:

> *Are they Hebrews? So am I. Are they Israelites? So am I. Are they the seed of Abraham? So am I. Are they servants of Christ? I'm talking like a madman—I'm a better one: with far more labors, many more imprisonments, far worse beatings, near death many times. Five times I received 39 lashes from Jews. Three times I was beaten with rods by the Romans. Once I was stoned by my enemies. Three times I was*

shipwrecked. I have spent a night and a day in the open sea. On
frequent journeys, I faced dangers from rivers, dangers from robbers,
dangers from my own people, dangers from the Gentiles, dangers in
the city, dangers in the open country, dangers on the sea, and dangers
among false brothers; labor and hardship, many sleepless nights,
hunger and thirst, often without food, cold, and lacking clothing. Not
to mention other things, there is the daily pressure on me: my care for
all the churches. Who is weak, and I am not weak? Who is made to
stumble, and I do not burn with indignation? (2 Cor 11:22-29)

Now that's a list! Understand that Paul isn't complaining here. Paul was
committed to Christ, and he viewed everything done in Christ's name as
"gain." On one side of the page is *loss* or *filth*—his former life of Judaism
with all its privileges and accomplishments. On the other side of the
page is *gain*—where Christ alone stands. The gain side of the page is
infinitely better to Paul, even though it means great sacrifice.

Verse 9 is extremely important for understanding how one becomes
a Christian—you need Christ's righteousness. Verses 10-11 are extremely
important for understanding what a Christian pursues—you need to
know Christ more and more. To use theological language, verse 9 speaks
of *justification.* Verse 10 speaks of *sanctification.* Verse 11 speaks of *glorification.* If you aren't a Christian, you need to be justified, counted righteous
before God. Otherwise, you face condemnation. If you're a Christian,
you, like Paul, need to pursue a better knowledge of Christ in this life-
long process of sanctification, which culminates in eternal glorification.

Justification: Trust Christ Alone as Your Righteousness (3:9)

In his list of accomplishments Paul said that with regard to righteousness he was "blameless" (v. 6). However, he couldn't live up to sinless
perfection. He, like us, needed someone else's righteousness in order
to be justified before God.

You see, here's the problem. Only righteous people are going to
heaven. Yet none of us are righteous (Rom 3:9-18). Therefore, we need
another source of righteousness, and that's why the gospel is good news.
As Paul says here in Philippians 3 and elsewhere, believers have received
the righteousness that comes from God through faith in Christ alone
(cf. Rom 3:21-26); we call this "imputed righteousness." This is the
opposite of works-based righteousness or self-righteousness. That's all
dung. We need the righteousness of another, an alien righteousness. We

need God's righteousness. To the Corinthians, Paul says, "He made the One who did not know sin to be sin for us, so that we might become the righteousness of God in Him" (2 Cor 5:21). What a glorious exchange! Christ received our punishment though He never sinned, and we received His righteousness though we didn't deserve it. Consequently, we are found in Christ. That means that God sees us through the righteousness of Christ. Believers are now protected from judgment, and we can know that we have forgiveness from God and are accepted by God. No better news exists.

Some define "justification" as "just as if I never sinned." But we should add that it's more than this. It's "just as if I've always obeyed." For we haven't just gone from negative to neutral; we have gone from negative to positive. We have not just received forgiveness; we have been given the perfect righteousness of Jesus.

Paul quickly makes two important points in Philippians 3:9 regarding this "justification" or this "righteousness." *First, justification is a gift from God.* Paul says that this righteousness comes "from God." We can't earn it, and we don't deserve it. God, in infinite grace, gave His only Son to live and die for law-breaking people that they might be saved.

Second, justification is received by faith. Paul says it clearly, doesn't he? And he actually says it twice: "but one that is through faith in Christ—the righteousness from God based on faith" (v. 9). Salvation doesn't depend on your record, your rank, your ethnicity, your religious attendance, your good deeds, and such. It depends on faith alone in Christ's perfect work alone. Justification is God's work, secured by Christ's death, and appropriated by faith.

This is what it means to be a Christian. This is what it means to know Christ. This is what it means to have your values in the right place. Carson says, "Paul recognizes that in God's universe, the most important thing is to know God" (*Basics*, 86). Knowing Christ as your Lord is more important than politics, sports, movies, social media, and even family. And we come to know Him by looking away from ourselves and looking to Christ as our righteousness. You should see now how infinitely different Christianity is from other religions. In other systems, *you have to do* the work. In Christianity, *Christ did* the work. We rejoice in those wonderful words, "It is finished!" (John 19:30). They are a translation of just one word in Greek, but it's loaded with meaning, and I dare say we will be pondering it for all eternity.

So, will you look to Christ as your righteousness? Do not trust in your own goodness. Many people think they're somewhere between Mother Theresa and Ted Bundy, assuming that God somehow grades on a curve. Consider Paul: he said as to righteousness under the law, he was blameless, yet he discovered that he was under the judgment of God and needed Christ's righteousness. We need this righteousness also. If you are a Christian, then remind yourself of this good news daily by reading the Bible, meeting with other Christians, meditating on good books, and singing gospel-saturated songs. Isaac Watts wrote "When I Survey the Wondrous Cross," a beautiful hymn that calls this passage to mind:

> When I survey the wondrous cross
> On which the Prince of glory died,
> My richest gain I count but loss,
> And pour contempt on all my pride.
>
> Forbid it, Lord, that I should boast,
> Save in the death of Christ my God!
> All the vain things that charm me most,
> I sacrifice them to His blood.
>
> See from His head, His hands, His feet,
> Sorrow and love flow mingled down!
> Did e'er such love and sorrow meet,
> Or thorns compose so rich a crown?
>
> Were the whole realm of nature mine,
> That were a present far too small;
> Love so amazing, so divine,
> Demands my soul, my life, my all.

I think the apostle Paul would have enjoyed this song! I pray you can sing it as well.

Sanctification: Know Christ More and Become More Like Him (3:10)

In verse 10 we find that Paul didn't adopt an attitude like, "I've arrived spiritually." He never got bored with knowing Jesus. As believers, we, too, need to press on to know Him. Of course, Paul does know Christ, but because of his love for the Savior, he wants to know Him more. Is there a better example for believers than this? Paul says, "Join in imitating me" in Philippians 3:17. As we observe his life, we see an all-consuming passion to know Christ. He sounds like David in Psalm 63; his passion was to seek God and to be satisfied in Him.

Dr. Stan Norman was one of my (Tony) favorite professors in seminary. His Systematic Theology class was magnificent! I used to say, "We should type notes on our knees," because the content was so worshipful at times. In one of Dr. Norman's classes, the subject of the day involved Jesus' resurrection from the dead and the deep implications of it. In the midst of dealing with this subject, a frustrated student said, "I didn't come here to study this stuff. All I want to do is know how to pastor a big church." Dr. Norman didn't like this response, to put it mildly—nor should he. To think that you can pastor and not need to know about the Christ, His resurrection, and how it applies to people's lives is foolish. Paul says this is of first importance (1 Cor 15:3-5)! This student's attitude didn't reflect the life of the apostle Paul, who considered everything as dung compared to knowing Jesus. He should have realized that the very reason he was in seminary was to know Christ more and to become more like Him.

J. I. Packer put it well: "Once you become aware that the main business that you are here for is to know God, most of life's problems fall into place of their own accord" (*Knowing God*, 34). What is your main business in life? Is it to pastor a big church? Is it to make money? Is it to get married? Is it to be entertained? Everything in life flows from this fountain: knowing Christ. What do you want to pass on to your kids? Alistair Begg said a man once quipped to him, "When I was young I had six theories and no kids. Now I have six kids and no theories" (in DeYoung, *Crazy Busy*, 74). It only took me (Tony) five kids to realize this! Let's give them what they must have: a knowledge of Christ.

Specifically, Paul mentions knowing Christ and "the power of His resurrection" and "the fellowship of His sufferings, being conformed to His death." Let's unpack this.

Note first, believers have the same power that raised Jesus from the dead (see Eph 1:19). This power is at work within us so that we may desire to work according to God's pleasure (Phil 2:13). This power is at work within us to make us holy. This power is at work within us to help us understand God's great love and mercy. This power gives us strength to endure life's hardships (Col 1:11-12).

But Paul wants more. At this point, everyone may be "amening"! You might say, "Yeah, I want to know Christ. Yeah, I want the power of Christ." But we may be tempted to skip this next line and jump to the resurrection part. We must not skip over this line about suffering because we'll miss something very important. Paul says he wants to know the fellowship of Christ's sufferings. Earlier, he told the Philippians that we have been given the gift of suffering for Christ (1:29). This flies in the face of prosperity theology, which says if you have faith you will be healthy, be wealthy, and have no trials. Many don't understand the truth about Christianity. When I (Francis) became a Christian in high school, no one told me about suffering on behalf of Christ. I was raised with a version of Christianity that adopted a view that one could be a disciple but not look like Jesus. Paul corrects our understanding and gives us an inspiring example to follow.

To be clear, we shouldn't read this as if Paul enjoyed suffering in and of itself. That's not what he means. Rather, he understands that in following the Man of Sorrows, we, too, will encounter suffering and sorrow, and as we follow along this Calvary Road, we will know the Master better. If you want to know Christ more than anything in life, and it's through suffering for Him that you'll know Him better, then you won't mind suffering. It will be worth it! You will actually find joy in it (Acts 5:41).

Glorification: Anticipate Your Resurrection (3:11)

At first glance, Paul seems to be uncertain about his resurrection, but we should reconsider that assumption. Rather, he's either speaking modestly—over against the Judaizers and others who held to an over-realized eschatology (Witherington, *Friendship and Finances,* 91), thinking the perfected state was in the present—or he is using "somehow" as Carson thinks:

> The word "somehow" in the original probably suggests that
> Paul is uncertain as to *the timing* and *circumstances* of this
> experience. Might it come to him in his lifetime, so that he
> receives a transformed, resurrection body without passing
> through death? From his letter to the Thessalonians we
> learn that this is what Paul teaches will befall those believers
> who are alive when Jesus returns (1 Thess 4:13-17). Or will
> he die and then rise from the dead? Either way, "somehow,"
> he will "attain the resurrection of the dead." And in Paul's

mind, attaining that glorious end, the final resurrection,
the new heaven and earth, the home of righteousness, is
bound up with persevering in the knowledge of Jesus Christ.
So for that knowledge of Christ he yearns. (*Basics*, 88–89;
emphasis added)

We, too, should long for this "glorious end, the final resurrection" when
we will see Christ. Paul concludes this chapter by giving us this hope:

> But our citizenship is in heaven, from which we also eagerly wait for a
> Savior, the Lord Jesus Christ. He will transform the body of our humble
> condition into the likeness of His glorious body, by the power that
> enables Him to subject everything to Himself. (Phil 3:20-21)

We have a taste of this glory now, but we have not experienced the
fullness of it yet. Paul writes to the Corinthians, "For God who said, 'Let
light shine out of darkness,' has shone in our hearts to give the light of
the knowledge of God's glory in the face of Jesus Christ" (2 Cor 4:6).
When God redeems a person, He uses the same creative power that He
used when He spoke the universe into existence. He shines in our hearts
to give us the knowledge of Christ. Later, more glory will be revealed.
Habakkuk says, "For the earth will be filled with the knowledge of the
LORD's glory, as the waters cover the sea" (Hab 2:14). We await our resurrected bodies, our new home, and an increased knowledge of Christ.
Let this hope purify you (1 John 3:1-3). Let this hope encourage you
in your sufferings (Rom 8:18-39). Let this hope help you put all things
into perspective.

My (Tony) first mission trip was to Australia. I know: it was a hard
location. Our team went to Sydney to do street evangelism during the
Olympics. After a few days, our leader asked me and three other guys on
our team to go lead a basketball clinic in a small town about five hours
south, along the beautiful coast. We went and had a very fruitful ministry there. Our hosts were locals. They treated us wonderfully. When
we arrived, they showed us our rooms and then took us to the ocean. I
looked at this majestic ocean and the beautiful countryside behind me.
I saw dolphins jumping in this stunning scene of endless waves. The
youngest member of the family then asked me if I wanted to get in. Of
course I did. I began, like many do, by putting one toe in the water.
Then I put in a foot. Then I walked out into the ocean until I was swim-
ming. But I never covered the bottomless glory of this ocean. There was
so much more to know and to experience.

Paul is showing us in this passage that there's an ocean of glory in Christ Jesus for us to know and experience. He never grew stagnant or bored with knowing Christ. Instead, he wanted to know Him better and better. He traded his self-righteousness for God's perfect righteousness through faith in Christ. He possessed Christ's resurrection power. He knew Christ better and better by suffering for Christ, and he thus rejoiced in suffering. He anticipated a glorious resurrection that would enable him to know his Savior even more. Let's not be content with putting a toe in the water. Let us pursue a deep relationship with Jesus Christ, and let's long for the day in which we see Him, the One with scars on His hands, who defeated death through His resurrection. Nothing on earth compares to knowing Christ Jesus our Lord.

Reflect and Discuss

1. Consider the things that people treasure. Why do they treasure these things?
2. Why is it important to resist legalism and false gospels?
3. How can your church be protected from legalism and false gospels?
4. According to 3:3, what are the three distinguishing marks of a genuine Christian?
5. On what are you basing your assurance of salvation?
6. Consider the seven sources of false confidence (ritual, ethnicity, rank, tradition, rule keeping, zeal, and obedience to the law). Which source is most enticing for you? Why?
7. Why do you need Christ's righteousness?
8. Believers have resurrection power. What is this power within you working to bring about?
9. How does suffering for Christ enable us to know Christ more?
10. How does the hope of your resurrection encourage you in the Christian life?

Making Every Effort to Know Christ

PHILIPPIANS 3:12-21

Main Idea: Paul urges the church to pursue Christian maturity with humility, passion, and gospel-centeredness.

Five Challenges for Growing in Maturity

I. **Humbly Acknowledge That You Haven't Arrived (3:12a,13a).**

II. **Passionately Pursue a Greater Knowledge of Christ (3:12-14).**
   - A. A passionate pursuit
   - B. Forgetting and reaching
   - C. One thing I do.

III. **Never Lose the Wonder of the Gospel (3:12b,14b).**

IV. **Follow Cross-Centered, Heavenly Minded Examples (3:15-19).**
   - A. Follow faithful examples (3:17).
   - B. Avoid the patterns of pretenders and earthly minded people (3:18-19).

V. **Live in Light of Your True Citizenship (3:20-21).**

On April 19, 2014, more than 36,000 runners hit the pavement for the 118th Boston Marathon. Following the tragic events of the bombings at the previous year's race, in which three people were killed and many were wounded, this particular race was filled with emotion. And in storybook form, the winner added even more drama. For the first time since 1983, an American won the race. At age 38, he became the oldest person to win the race in 83 years. With the names of the victims killed in the previous year's violent attack written on the corner of his bib, Meb Keflezighi crossed the finish line in first place. As he crossed the line, people in the crowd were going crazy, many chanting, "USA" He lifted his hands upward with joy and triumph. It's hard to watch the highlights without being moved to tears by the dramatic scene.

In Philippians 3:12-21 Paul uses an intense running analogy to describe the Christian life. Having described his passionate, all-consuming desire in verse 10—to know Christ—the apostle now tells the Philippians that he's not stagnating. He's not slowing down. He's still running hard after Christ. Kent Hughes says, "There is nothing in Scripture quite like this explosion of spiritual longing" (*Liberating Ministry*, 145). As Paul explains this explosion of spiritual longing, he tells the Philippians that they should follow his example and take his perspective on spiritual progress. In verse 15 he says, "Therefore, all who are mature should think this way." Every Christian, then, should take a close look at this passage because *Paul provides an inspiring and instructive path for growing in spiritual maturity.*

As you study this text, you should be provoked. You shouldn't feel *condemned* if you're a Christian, but you should be *convicted.* There's a huge difference between conviction and condemnation! The Christian is free from judgment (Rom 8:1), but we should feel conviction. When God convicts us, it's evidence of His love for us. It's evidence that He's working in us (Phil 2:13). It's proof that He will bring our salvation to completion (1:6).

Five Challenges for Growing in Maturity

Let's consider five particular applications from Paul's example and explanation of spiritual maturity. (I [Tony] was greatly helped by a sermon on this passage from my friend C. J. Mahaney, who gave me some ideas that I've built upon in this exposition.)

Humbly Acknowledge That You Haven't Arrived
PHILIPPIANS 3:12A,13A

Twice Paul uses a negative to *correct* any misunderstanding that the Philippians might have regarding spiritual maturity in general or with Paul's Christian life in particular. Some false teachers in Philippi had adopted a *perfectionistic* view of spirituality. Paul says that even though he has counted everything as loss for the sake of Christ, that doesn't mean he has arrived. He isn't perfect. He hasn't entered the resurrected state yet. He's straining ahead for that day. Mature people humbly acknowledge that they haven't arrived. Be careful of an attitude that makes you think otherwise. If Paul could have this mature attitude, how much more should we?

The gospel humbled Paul. Look at the way Paul talks about his life here, compared to his pre-conversion experience in verse 6, where he said, "in the law, blameless." He previously thought of himself as having arrived, but the gospel has a humbling effect. In telling the Philippians that he wasn't perfect, Paul not only corrects any misunderstandings that they might have had regarding legalism or perfectionism, but his words surely brought *hope* to them as well! How so? Paul is identifying with them as a fellow Christian. He doesn't want them to think that he is somehow superhuman and superior. He's made some remarkable statements about his life in the book of Philippians, but he's admitting that he hasn't arrived. So you and I shouldn't despair. Keep running with Paul!

Paul wants them to know that he's with them on the journey, and this is one of the marks of true Christian leadership. Leadership is not lordship, and it's not about being superior. It's about following Jesus, becoming more like Him, and bringing others along on the journey. What happens when you humbly realize that you need to grow in Christ-likeness? Your view of others will change. You will grow less smug and less critical of others because you will believe you need to grow as well. You will use your words differently. You will grow less self-righteous, and you will be quicker to identify evidences of grace in the lives of others. Also, your love for the Savior will grow because you will realize how much you need His grace!

I mentioned C. J.'s message on these verses earlier. He really embodies this first point regarding maturity. I sent him a text message to thank him for his ministry to me. In response he sent me a typically humble, joyful, and encouraging text back. He then asked me to give him some feedback on his preaching! He was very serious about this. I mention it only to highlight that this mature Christian and wonderful preacher realizes that he still has room for growth in life and ministry. I have watched C. J. at various times, and his life exudes this idea of humble *teachability*. When someone else is preaching, he's always taking notes, engaged in the sermon, normally on the front row. He's always reading new books. He's always quick to confess his need for growth. That's a mark of maturity.

Passionately Pursue a Greater Knowledge of Christ
PHILIPPIANS 3:12-14

Many Christians can identify with the first point. We're not perfect. Check. But many Christians use this point as an excuse to be complacent. That's not the case for the apostle Paul! Even though he knows he isn't perfect, that doesn't mean he isn't exerting passion to grow in his knowledge of the Savior.

Notice the passion in verse 12: "I make every effort to take hold of it," and in verse 13: "But one thing I do: Forgetting what is behind and reaching forward to what is ahead." If that were not enough passion, he adds in verse 14, "I pursue." This isn't a man coasting; he isn't loafing. He's running hard after the prize.

What's the "prize"? What goal is Paul pursuing? Based on the previous passage, it's a fuller knowledge of Christ. It involves gaining Christ. That's what Paul wants—to know Christ more and more; and in knowing Him more, he will become more like Him. This pursuit is a lifetime adventure. To illustrate this pursuit, Paul uses athletic imagery to convey his passion for the Savior.

A Passionate Pursuit

Be careful that you don't adopt a passive attitude about the Christian life. Growth in Christlikeness isn't an impassive stroll. The New Testament uses disciplined athletic imagery elsewhere to describe the effort involved in growing in Christ. Consider just two of them:

> *Don't you know that the runners in a stadium all race, but only one receives the prize? Run in such a way to win the prize. Now everyone who competes exercises self-control in everything. However, they do it to receive a crown that will fade away, but we a crown that will never fade away. Therefore I do not run like one who runs aimlessly or box like one beating the air. Instead, I discipline my body and bring it under strict control, so that after preaching to others, I myself will not be disqualified.* (1 Cor 9:24-27)

> *Therefore, since we also have such a large cloud of witnesses surrounding us, let us lay aside every weight and the sin that so easily ensnares us. Let us run with endurance the race that lies before us, keeping our eyes on Jesus, the source and perfecter of our faith, who for the joy that lay before Him endured a cross and despised the shame and has sat down at the right hand of God's throne.* (Heb 12:1-2)

Now that's passion! Running, exercising self-control, not running aimlessly, not boxing the air, disciplining one's body—all of this displays the apostle's passion. Then the writer of Hebrews, in a book that emphasizes Christian perseverance, speaks of laying aside anything that doesn't help us run, as we fix our eyes on Jesus. Paul and the author of Hebrews are under no illusion that the Christian life is lived passively and effortlessly. If you want to grow in maturity, you need passion and discipline. *Earning* is *not* a good word for Christians because we can't earn any acceptance before God, but *effort* is a good word for those who have already been made new creations in Christ. We must pursue holiness (Heb 12:14) in this life by God's power.

Forgetting and Reaching

Consider Paul's running image closely. This passionate run involves *forgetting* and *reaching* (v. 13). Both are essential for running a good race, and both are essential for spiritual maturity. Every good runner knows that you can't look over your shoulder, or you will get distracted, stumble, or lose momentum. You have to forget "what is behind." O'Brien notes that *epilanthanomai* means "to forget" (Matt 16:5; Mark 8:14; Jas 1:24), or "to neglect, overlook, or care nothing about" (Luke 12:6; Heb 6:10; 13:2,16; *Epistle*, 428). What exactly is Paul to forget? O'Brien puts it succinctly and powerfully:

> He will not allow either the achievements of the past (which God has wrought) or, for that matter, his failures as a Christian to prevent his gaze from being fixed firmly on the finish line. In this sense he forgets as he runs. (*Epistle*, 429)

I love that expression: "He forgets as he runs."

This really should encourage us. Modern wisdom focuses on your past, often forcing you to place too high a value on your past. You need a better path. Sure, your past affects your life—either for good or for ill. But don't make too much of it. Your past doesn't have to determine your future. If you had an awful childhood or made some bad mistakes, you've certainly experienced consequences, but they don't have to determine the rest of your life. The gospel is more powerful than that! Look at the guy who is writing this letter! He persecuted Christians "to the death" (Acts 22:4)! Yet we don't find Paul saying, "Oh, I'm limited now. My previous experiences have made me damaged goods." You don't even find him saying anything like, "I need to pay God back now." He simply forgets as he runs, and you can too! The gospel really is good news!

So follow Paul's lead. *Forget failures and run.* Every Christian has failed God at some point. We could list the failures of many of our biblical heroes. Only One has never failed. We must also not over-interpret "forget about it" to mean avoiding making a situation right or not asking for forgiveness. We must deal with sin, but if you've been forgiven and sought to make wrongs right, then forget and run. Don't let Satan bring up accusations against you if Christ has forgiven you. Flee to Christ; remind yourself of the gospel and press on.

Follow Paul's lead in this way also: *Forget past achievements.* While we do find Paul occasionally relating some of his ministry achievements, we don't find him using past victories as an excuse not to press on in the present. We should be grateful to God for all of His blessings, recounting them like the psalmists (e.g., Ps 103:1-5), but don't use past victories as an excuse to live complacently today. Successes can create an unhealthy tendency to cling to the glory days. By constantly reminiscing, some live unprofitably in the present. Have you ever been around those who talk about the way church used to be in the glory days and how they used to share their faith and serve in the church? These "glory days" Christians remind me of Uncle Rico in the movie *Napoleon Dynamite.* He's a middle-aged former athlete who lives in a camper van and regularly videos himself throwing a football. Don't be Uncle Rico. Move on with life in the present season.

We must not let former victories create a relaxation and self-satisfaction in the present. Consider the NCAA tournament. When teams win games and advance, what do they often say? We hear something like this: "We will enjoy this victory for the moment, but we've got to get ready for the next game." Their victory yesterday doesn't mean they will win tomorrow. So it is in the Christian life. Every day brings new challenges and opportunities. Did Paul have some amazing victories? Could he have lived in the glory days? Could he have grown smug and self-righteous? Oh, yes! But he's not letting accomplishments make him lazy. He's forgetting accomplishments as he runs. Neither is he comparing himself with others. He's focused on remaining faithful until the race is over.

One Thing I Do

How can we do this? Paul tells us here. I love the simplicity of these words: "One thing I do" (v. 13). Here we find a "one-thing guy." He's passionately pursuing a greater knowledge of Christ. He is forgetting failures and achievements, and he is straining ahead to know Christ more. What's your one thing? If we asked people who know you well, "What's his or her one thing?," what would they say?

Mahaney asks a super-helpful question based on this idea: "What one change could you make in order to pursue the one thing that matters the most?" ("Straining for the Prize"). Negatively stated, what sin or habit or activity could you throw off in order to run the race better (Heb 12:1-2)? Positively, what could you begin doing that you aren't doing right now?

Don't underestimate the power of making one change. David Powlison notes that change in one area affects every area of our lives. We don't typically think this way. We tend to think of spiritual growth in boxes; that is, after we work on one area, we can move to the next. But when you change one area of life, by God's grace, it moves through the totality of your life (Mahaney, "Straining for the Prize"). I would add to this idea, that this one change not only affects your life, but it will affect others as well. Just one change in your life will affect you, your friends, your church, and your neighborhood.

If you want to see a discernible difference in your life, then think about how you are spending *time* and how you are spending *money*. These issues often reveal our one thing. With regard to time, are you making the most of your days (Eph 5:15-16)? Are you spending an inordinate amount of time on mindless activities or selfish pursuits? Have you taken a walk in your neighborhood recently in order to meet people and share your faith? Have you spent some unhurried and unhindered time in prayer lately? Are you working an excessive amount of hours? With regard to money, how are you stewarding God's resources? Are you spending any money on missions? Is the sin of greed and materialism weakening your life?

In addition to time and money, let me also encourage you to begin a spiritual practice of growing in *knowledge*. This passage is about knowing Christ, and you can't grow in knowledge without *thinking*! Perhaps you will use your commute to work as an opportunity to listen to the Scriptures or to good sermons. Perhaps you will begin a group that memorizes Scripture together, or you might even combine your athletic workout with an opportunity to listen to the gospel taught or to lectures on theology. Perhaps you want to get a new book that will help you grow in Christ. It has always struck me that at the end of Paul's life we find him requesting books (2 Tim 4:13). He had soared to places that we haven't seen, but he still wants books. Why? Because he was not satisfied with his knowledge of Christ. He wanted more. Do you? Let's grow in becoming one-thing people!

Never Lose the Wonder of the Gospel
PHILIPPIANS 3:12B,14B

Paul mentions two phrases that highlight the wonder of the gospel. In verse 12 he says, "I make every effort to take hold of it," and then he says this wonderfully rich gospel phrase, *"because I also have been taken hold of by Christ Jesus"* (emphasis added). Down in verse 14 he also speaks of "God's heavenly call," which is another beautiful statement about God's grace in salvation. God is calling us heavenward.

Paul never lost the wonder of the gospel, and we shouldn't either. Christian maturity involves going deeper into the gospel and never beyond the gospel. All of our growth comes from the outflow of the gospel. What was Paul in awe of? It was the fact that Christ took hold of him. What a concise and accurate statement of Paul's conversion. Jesus took hold of Paul. But that's not just Paul's story; that's our story too! Christ has taken hold of us! How did this happen? It happened by grace! Paul mentions "God's heavenly call" in verse 14. Christians are those who have responded in repentance and faith to the call of the gospel. God called us by grace. We heard the gospel as a gift of grace. We are sustained by grace. For all eternity, we will sing the praises of the God of all grace.

The problem with many people when they talk about spiritual maturity is that they talk about it apart from the gospel. They think the gospel is the ABCs of Christianity, not the A to Z of Christianity as Tim Keller says ("The Centrality of the Gospel," 1–2). In Colossians Paul says, "As you have received Christ Jesus the Lord, walk in Him" (Col 2:6). The Colossians were trying to move on to something else, and Paul effectively says, "There *is* nothing else!" Just as you received Jesus—desperately, and in faith—so walk in Him. Keep looking to Him. Keep treasuring His grace. Keep relying on His power. The Philippians faced the threat of false teachers who promoted a sort of maturity that was divorced from the gospel of grace. In verse 16 Paul says, "Only let us hold true to what we have attained" (ESV). Stay focused on this central truth, and keep marveling at God's great work of salvation through Christ Jesus.

As we grow in maturity, we must remember that it's only because Christ Jesus has taken hold of us that we *want to* make every effort! It's only because God has taken hold of us that we *can* make any effort! Revel in the good news of Jesus daily. Marvel at His redemption. Boast in His cross. Fill your affections with this: He seized you!

A picture comes to mind here of a child holding on to a parent. One time, my (Tony) daughter got pulled into the ocean by the surf while the other four kids and I were playing. No one was paying close attention except for my bride. She ran into the water to pull out little Victoria, screaming in panic. Kimberly seized her, and in turn, Victoria didn't want to turn her loose! Oh, we have been delivered out of death and from destruction because Jesus rescued us. Now we, in turn, embrace Him as our glorious, gracious Savior. Never lose the wonder of His rescuing love. Christian maturity involves loving the Savior.

Follow Cross-Centered, Heavenly Minded Examples
PHILIPPIANS 3:15-19

Whom you follow matters. Whom you hang out with matters. The book of Philippians has struck this theme of *imitation* several times now. Paul has pointed to himself as an example (2:17-18), to Timothy and Epaphroditus as examples (2:19-30), and to Jesus as example *par excellence* (2:5-11). Now Paul encourages believers to adopt his outlook and his values for growing in spiritual maturity and to seek God for increasing wisdom. Paul knows he, too, must persevere in these areas. He includes himself in the phrase, "We should live up to whatever truth we have attained" (v. 16). A faithful Christian leader pursues Christ alongside everyone else. That pursuit includes not departing from the progress already made, not abandoning central truths already learned.

Indeed, the pursuit of Christ is a lifelong journey. Take the Old Testament character Caleb as a faithful example worth watching. In Joshua 14 he is seeking his inheritance in Hebron, which Moses swore to give him years before. Despite being 85 years old, he maintains that he is willing and able to drive out the Anakim in the strength of God! As you read the following passage from this account, notice the repetition of how Caleb "wholly followed the LORD" (ESV; cf. Num 14:24; Deut 1:36).

> Then the people of Judah came to Joshua at Gilgal. And Caleb the son of Jephunneh the Kenizzite said to him, "You know what the LORD said to Moses the man of God in Kadesh-barnea concerning you and me. I was forty years old when Moses the servant of the LORD sent me from Kadesh-barnea to spy out the land, and I brought him word again as it was in my heart. But my brothers who went up with me made the heart of the people melt; yet I wholly followed the LORD my God. And Moses swore on that day, saying, 'Surely the land on which your foot

has trodden shall be an inheritance for you and your children forever, because you have wholly followed the LORD my God.' And now, behold, the LORD has kept me alive, just as he said, these forty-five years since the time that the LORD spoke this word to Moses, while Israel walked in the wilderness. And now, behold, I am this day eighty-five years old. I am still as strong today as I was in the day that Moses sent me; my strength now is as my strength was then, for war and for going and coming. So now give me this hill country of which the LORD spoke on that day, for you heard on that day how the Anakim were there, with great fortified cities. It may be that the LORD will be with me, and I shall drive them out just as the LORD said." Then Joshua blessed him, and he gave Hebron to Caleb the son of Jephunneh for an inheritance. Therefore Hebron became the inheritance of Caleb the son of Jephunneh the Kenizzite to this day, because he wholly followed the LORD, the God of Israel. (Josh 14:6-14 ESV)

Can't you hear this old man's passion as he says, "Give me that hill country"? This isn't a man coasting it out in his dying days. He's living with a vibrant faith in God. I picture an old grandpa who wants to wrestle with the young bucks at Thanksgiving! Caleb basically says, "When I was 40, Joshua and I were ready, but the others were scared. Now, I am still ready!" What a wonderful example of faithfulness and zeal.

Paul encourages the Philippians to look to faithful examples in the present in addition to such biblical heroes. He knows that he's not the only example the church has. He also warns them of cross-denying, earthly minded examples they must avoid. Let's consider these two applications.

Follow Faithful Examples (3:17)

Faithful examples are those who live out the values Paul promotes. These values include many of the practices here in the book of Philippians: putting the needs of others ahead of our own, not grumbling or complaining, pouring out our lives for the cause of the gospel, and more. It's essential to receive sound teaching, but we also learn by observing the lives of people who illustrate sound teaching. Christianity is not just taught; it's also caught.

While it is not an issue mentioned in Philippians, we can apply this to marriage. In a culture filled with broken marriages and distorted views of marriage, we really need godly marriages on exhibit before our young people. Many really haven't seen a healthy marriage lived out. In addition to marriage, many have never seen evangelism done well. They know they should do it, but they really don't know how. If that's you, attach yourself to someone doing it, and go with them. Watch them. Hang with them. Find faithful examples and watch them. Follow those who are showing you what it looks like to live out the Christian life in other ways, including prayer, giving, showing neighbor love, and studying the Bible. Find some "deceased mentors." Read the biographies of the saints of old and find fresh encouragement from their way of life.

Allow me to share a few excerpts from one deceased mentor, George Mueller. Known for his great love for orphans and his exemplary prayer life, Mueller provides wonderful counsel for us in trusting God and growing in maturity. This spiritual giant once said, "I saw more clearly than ever, that the first great and primary business to which I ought to attend every day was, to have my soul happy in the Lord" (in Piper, "George Mueller's Strategy"). What did it mean to be "happy in the Lord"? He said this:

> The more we know of God, the happier we are. . . . When we
> became a little acquainted with God . . . our true happiness
> . . . commenced; and the more we become acquainted with
> him, the more truly happy we become. What will make us so
> exceedingly happy in heaven? It will be the fuller knowledge
> of God. (Ibid.)

Take this seriously. The reason there's little happiness in the world is there's little knowledge of Christ in the world. This passion to know the Lord continued for Mueller. At age 71 he wrote this to some younger believers:

> Now in brotherly love and affection I would give a few hints
> to my younger fellow-believers as to the way in which to keep
> up spiritual enjoyment. It is absolutely needful in order that
> happiness in the Lord may continue, that the Scriptures be
> regularly read. These are God's appointed means for the
> nourishment of the inner man. . . . Consider it, and ponder
> over it. . . . Especially we should read regularly through the
> Scriptures, consecutively, and not pick out here and there
> a chapter. If we do, we remain spiritual dwarfs. I tell you so
> affectionately. For the first four years after my conversion I
> made no progress, because I neglected the Bible. But when I
> regularly read on through the whole with reference to my own

located at the pulpit, being colored red. This red represents this short life. The rest of the rope represents eternity. Now, based on this illustration, what should occupy our hearts the most, this life or heaven? How should we live in light of this reality? How should we spend money in view of heaven? Will we not live differently if we really embrace what Paul is saying here, and what he will say in verses 20-21? Yes. Don't live like these enemies of the cross. Don't set your mind on earthly things. Set your gaze on Christ and on our heavenly citizenship!

Before we consider this heavenly mind-set in more detail, notice here that Paul doesn't despise these enemies of the cross. He sheds "tears" over them. It's a sad thing for those who act like they are Christians never to boast in the cross, to see them only set their minds on earthly things, and to see them mainly get excited about satisfying their lustful appetites. That should grieve us. It should lead us to tears in prayer for them.

Remember the proverb: "Whoever walks with the wise becomes wise, but the companion of fools will suffer harm" (Prov 13:20 ESV). Don't become a fool by observing and following the ways of foolish people. Find examples of those who are walking the way of the cross and finding a superior joy in knowing Christ more and more. Whom you follow matters. Follow those who are following Jesus passionately.

Live in Light of Your True Citizenship
PHILIPPIANS 3:20-21

Paul concludes by reminding the church of the heavenly mind-set they should possess. People walking and growing in maturity realize that this world is not their home. We should have certain "groanings" in this life because we aren't from here (Rom 8:18-27)! Paul reminds us that our citizenship is in heaven.

Philippi was a Roman colony. It was a little Rome. When people visited Philippi they said, "This reminds me of Rome." We noted this previously as we observed Paul's exhortation in 1:27, which could be rendered, "Only conduct yourself as a citizen, in a manner worthy of the gospel." Paul is telling the Philippians that the church is a little colony of the kingdom of heaven. When you are in the presence of God's people, their values and their lives should point to heaven.

When you see people taking care of the vulnerable, caring for orphans, doing all that is good and right and true, giving to the poor, speaking edifying words to one another, outdoing one another in show-ing honor, showing no partiality or racism, putting the needs of others ahead of their own, you should say: "This smells like heaven!" We should be giving the world a glimpse of what's coming in the future. We can show them what the King is like and what the kingdom is like. People should look at the words and deeds of believers and say, "You aren't from around here, are you?" You can tell them, "My citizenship is in heaven. I'm just passing through."

Bad examples set their minds on earthly things. Faithful examples live in light of their true citizenship. C. S. Lewis said this about the latter:

> If you read history you will find that the Christians who did the
> most for the present world were just those who thought most
> of the next. . . . It is since Christians have largely ceased to
> think of the other world that they have become so ineffective
> in this. (*Mere Christianity*, 134)

We can endure trials in this life when we remember this wonderful real-ity. A close family member is going through an awful ordeal. I (Tony) recently texted her to express my sympathy and assure her of my prayers. She responded, "Thanks. The tomb is empty. The rest is just small stuff." What a heavenly mind-set!

Paul tells us that not only should we be living out the kingdom's val-ues, but we should also be awaiting heaven's Lord. He says we "eagerly wait for a Savior." Who is this Savior? He says, "the Lord Jesus Christ." In saying this, Paul is saying that Caesar isn't Lord. Oh, Caesar might have thought he was Lord. He might have taken the title "Savior." He might have tried to build a kingdom that won the praise of people. But all leaders pale in comparison to the coming King of heaven. We eagerly wait for His arrival. We welcome His arrival. We must live in light of His arrival.

Additionally he tells us, the church, that the Lord "will transform the body of our humble condition into the likeness of His glorious body." Christian maturity is about growing in Christlikeness, and the culmination of this will happen when Christ appears. Paul and John write the following:

> *And just as we have borne the image of the man made of dust, we will*
> *also bear the image of the heavenly man.* (1 Cor 15:49)

Dear friends, we are God's children now, and what we will be has not yet been revealed. We know that when He appears, we will be like Him because we will see Him as He is. And everyone who has this hope in Him purifies himself just as He is pure. (1 John 3:2-3)

What hope this is! This hope should motivate us, assure us, purify us, and center us on what's most important. The believer has the most encouraging news in the world. This is as bad as it will ever be. Soon we will see Him. Soon we will receive a new body, fitted for the new heaven and new earth!

How will this happen? Paul says that Christ will transform us "by the power that enables Him to subject everything to Himself." If Jesus can subject everything, then He can easily transform our lowly bodies! Therefore, let us make every effort. Let us make every effort to know Christ, and in knowing Him more intimately, become more like Him. Let us make every effort by heeding these five challenges for growing in maturity:

- Humbly acknowledge that you haven't arrived.
- Passionately pursue greater knowledge of Christ.
- Never lose the wonder of the gospel.
- Follow cross-centered, heavenly minded examples.
- Live in light of your true citizenship.

Perhaps you're familiar with the movie *Chariots of Fire*. It's about two runners in the 1924 Olympics, one being Eric Liddell, a Christian. He makes the often-quoted statement, "I believe that God made me for a purpose. But He also made me fast, and when I run, I feel His pleasure." Paul, too, felt the pleasure of running for the prize, and he's commending this way of life to us. Eric Liddell would later serve on the mission field, running for something greater than a gold medal. As you run for the prize, may you feel God's pleasure too. Fix your eyes on Jesus, the One who ran for "the joy that lay before Him" (Heb 12:2). Run for the pleasure of Christ, the One who took hold of you. Let us reach forward until we see Him. When we see Him, we won't regret having made every effort to know Him more and more in this life. We won't regret having lived in view of our true citizenship. Every day we are getting closer. Keep running until you see Him.

Reflect and Discuss

1. How does the gospel humble you?
2. What is the prize that Paul pursues in verse 14?
3. Why do we need passion and discipline to grow in spiritual maturity?
4. Do you use past victories and successes as an excuse not to make every effort in the present? Pause and ask the Lord for freedom from this sin.
5. Paul was a "one-thing" guy (v. 13). What would people who know you well say is your "one thing"?
6. What one change could you make in order to pursue the one thing that matters the most?
7. What does it mean to say that the gospel is the ABCs of Christianity, not the A to Z of Christianity?
8. What are some characteristics of the "enemies of the cross" in verse 18?
9. In what ways is your church a little colony of the kingdom of heaven?
10. How should the promise of Jesus' return affect the way you live your life?

Shepherding a Church's Heart

PHILIPPIANS 4:1-9

Main Idea: In love, Paul shepherds the church by urging them to be united, to rejoice in the Lord, to be gentle, to replace anxiety with God's peace through prayer, and to think on praiseworthy things.

I. **Receiving Paul's Love (4:1)**
   A. Endurance
   B. Empowerment
II. **Receiving Paul's Counsel (4:2-9)**
   A. Pursue like-mindedness with other true believers (4:2-3).
   B. Rejoice in the Lord (4:4).
   C. Be known for graciousness (4:5).
   D. Relieve anxiety through prayer (4:6-7).
   E. Think on praiseworthy things (4:8-9).

I almost titled this section "Stuff Christians Deal With" because Paul addresses several common problems Christians face. So, do you have at least one problem in your life? How about one problem in your church? If you can answer "yes" to these questions, then you can identify with Philippians 4:1-9! The apostle Paul speaks about some serious struggles that Christians encounter in this fallen world. These struggles include disputes, joylessness, lack of graciousness, anxiety, and impure thoughts.

Remember, the Philippian church was a great church—indeed, an impressive church—but even great churches, made up of wonderful believers, still struggle with sin and need God's Word to correct them. We need to take our seat in Paul's pastoral study (in prison!) and heed his counsel—for our good and for the good of other believers.

Receiving Paul's Love

PHILIPPIANS 4:1

Perhaps you're familiar with Tedd Tripp's wonderful book *Shepherding a Child's Heart*. It's a tremendous blessing to the church. The good doctor talks about our need to apply the gospel to our children's hearts carefully and consistently. Here in Philippians 4 we have the tremendous blessing of being addressed by the apostle Paul, who is "shepherding the church's heart." He supplies us with gospel-filled instruction for our souls.

In verse 1, a transitional verse, Paul piles up tender expressions to convey his love for the Philippians: "my brothers," "you are dearly loved and longed for," "my joy and crown," and "dear friends." Clearly, Paul loves the Philippians. This church was his crowning achievement, according to some scholars. His heart soared with joy when he thought about them (1:3-4). As he finishes this joyous letter, he again reassures them of his care for their souls.

All of us who are Christians should also feel loved when we read these verses. The Good Shepherd leads us and ministers grace to us through His inspired Word. Because He loves us, He won't leave us the same. He convicts us because He loves us, and He wants to complete the good work that He's started. So as we look at this text, let us say, "Savior, like a shepherd lead us."

Endurance

Verse 1 looks back to what's just been said, and it looks ahead to what follows. In light of all that has been said ("So then"), especially in light of 3:17-21, Paul urges the church to "stand firm," that is, "stick with it," "endure," or "never give up the Christian walk" (Carson, *Basics*, 98). It's an appeal to persevere in light of our heavenly citizenship and the Lord Jesus' climactic return. Because our citizenship is heaven, don't give up. By God's grace, keep your eyes on faithful examples, and don't adopt the patterns of those who are self-absorbed. Don't adopt the patterns of those who glory in their shame, who set their minds on earthly things. Paul is encouraging the church to keep living the Christian life faithfully, and we need to apply his counsel to our souls. In your marriage, with your finances, in your parenting, in your struggle against temptation, in gospel mission, in prayer—never give up the Christian walk!

The transitional verse also looks ahead. Paul wants the Philippians to walk in the way that he's about to describe (Carson, *Basics*, 99). He wants them to persevere in their work toward unity, to continue showing graciousness, to continue rejoicing, to continue praying for God to relieve anxiety, and to continue thinking noble thoughts.

Empowerment

By what power do we endure? He doesn't simply tell the church to stand firm. He tells them the way in which they will persevere: "in the Lord." We need this reminder as well. Our strength isn't in how long we've been Christians, how much we know about the Bible, or how many mission trips we've been on. Our strength for standing firm is in our union with Christ. Take a moment to scan verses 1-9 and notice how often Paul mentions the centrality of a relationship with Jesus Christ for these exhortations to be lived out:

- "agree *in the Lord*" (v. 2)
- "Rejoice *in the Lord*" (v. 4)
- "the peace of God . . . will guard your hearts and minds *in Christ Jesus*" (v. 7)

This means if you're not a Christian, look no further for application to your life. You need to be "in Christ." Paul mentions having your name in the "book of life" (v. 3). That's what you need! You need to know Jesus. If you are a believer, then realize Paul isn't calling you to simply "try harder." The exhortations that follow do require effort, but they are empowered through our union with Jesus, and they are "supercharged" through our communion with Jesus. So let's heed these instructions with hope, believing that we can change in these areas because of Christ.

Receiving Paul's Counsel
PHILIPPIANS 4:2-9

In verses 2-9 Paul strings together several exhortations (though one could treat vv. 2-3 separately). In other letters Paul piles up exhortations, as in Romans 12:9-21 and 1 Thessalonians 5:12-22. Sometimes he piles up various virtues or vices (Gal 5:19-24). Given the nature of these rapid-fire points, commentators outline such passages differently. The same is true here. We've decided to outline it in five parts, paying attention to five challenges.

There's nothing really new here, though. The themes in this section have already been touched on previously in the letter. Paul urges *unity* among believers in 4:2-3. This theme was also in 1:27–2:4. The theme of *rejoicing* in 4:5 has been highlighted several times (1:18; 2:17; 3:1). The idea of *gentleness, graciousness,* or *forbearance* in 4:5 was touched on in 2:1-3. Paul mentions *prayer* in 4:6-7, and he underscores the importance of prayer in 1:3-11. Paul's appeal to *noble character* in 4:8-9 reminds us of character qualities highlighted in 2:3,14-15 and elsewhere in the letter (Witherington, *Friendship and Finances*, 110–11). Additionally, in these exhortations Paul continues to emphasize the gospel, the Lord's presence, and the idea of being "in Christ." It's as though Paul were collecting and restating many of his central ideas from the letter in these exhortations. Let's look at each of these Christian struggles and apply Paul's counsel to our own souls.

Pursue Like-Mindedness with Other True Believers (4:2-3)

The problem. Paul makes a final call for unity in these verses. The obvious problem has to do with a disagreement between two ladies. The most striking thing about Paul's appeal is its *directness*. So far his appeals for unity have been general, but here he calls out specific people! Can you imagine these two ladies sitting in the congregation, listening attentively to the letter being read to the church corporately, when all of a sudden—"I urge Euodia and I urge Syntyche to agree in the Lord." Talk about an awkward moment! Apart from the Pastoral Epistles and the book of Philemon, the only other personal exhortation like this is found in Colossians 4:17, where Arichippus is encouraged to complete his ministry, which suggests an indirect criticism from Paul. Unlike that example, however, Paul expresses a clear rebuke to these ladies (Silva, *Philippians*, 192).

This is a serious issue for Paul. He can't speak in vague generalities. He cuts right to it and to them. Why? Because he loves them and he loves the church.

Not much is known about these women or the cause of their strife. Women played a prominent role in the early church—as they do in every church—especially in Philippi (Acts 16:11-15). These two seem to have had an influential role, for Paul mentions how they labored with him in the cause of the gospel (4:3), but we don't know how they exerted influence exactly. What about the cause of the rift in their relationship? Did the problem arise out of problems with leadership structure? Was it merely a preference issue? Were they guilty of envy and rivalry (2:3)? We don't know. It doesn't seem to be a doctrinal issue, given what Paul says about them. My guess is that the problem dealt with leadership.

The solution. While we don't know the exact cause of the problem, we can note the process for solving the problem, provided by Paul.

First, Paul instructs the women themselves to resolve the matter by having the same mind (v. 2). He repeats his plea ("urge," "beg," or "entreat") before the mention of each name. Paul isn't taking sides. He "urges" both sisters to agree in the Lord. The best solution for resolving differences is simple: solve the problem with one another.

After his plea, Paul provides the attitude in which Euodia and Syntyche should work toward unity, with this word "agree." This Greek phrase *autos phroneō*, which appears several times in Paul's writings (Rom 12:16; 15:5; 2 Cor 13:11; Phil 2:2), means "to have the same mind" or literally "to think the same thing" (O'Brien, *Epistle*, 478; see also Carson's discussion in *Basics*, 101–3). Once again the phrase is used in the context of unity. Paul is urging them to have right attitudes toward each other so that they may work together faithfully.

Such like-mindedness can only come by imitating the humility of Jesus, who gave up His rights for the good of others (2:5-11). To resolve differences, we need the attitude of Jesus. Paul points them to Jesus with the phrase "in the Lord." It's because of the Lord's power, because of their commonality in the Lord, and because they are willing to submit to the Lord, that they can agree in the Lord. Both ladies are called to bow before the lordship of Jesus and to put on His mind, that they may resolve their differences.

Agreement like this doesn't mean that you throw out basic, sound doctrine; that's not what Paul has in mind. Nor does he tell them to agree on absolutely everything, including their preferences. Paul is encouraging a common attitude of Christ and gospel-centeredness. If the ladies can center on the gospel and pursue the attitude of Christ, they will be able to go on with the work. Philippians 2:1-11 really seems to be in view here; it's an amazing, helpful text when thinking about resolving differences. These two ladies are living examples of how that text can work.

Second, Paul calls for intervention (v. 3a). Paul alerts the whole church to the problem and urges one called a "true partner" to "help these women." We don't know who this person is (unless the Greek word for partner, *syzygus*, is his actual name), but Paul and the church do know him, and he urges this servant to play the peacemaker. These ladies may have begun already to work out their differences, and Paul is now calling on this servant to help them resolve things completely (see O'Brien, *Epistle*, 481).

In asking for help, Paul reminds us of the importance of the church family assisting in the reconciliation process. Kent Hughes says, "The apostle didn't lay out a precise remedy for Euodia and Syntyche but handed it over to the church family in Philippi. He gave them tender guidelines and was diplomatic and encouraging" (*Philippians*, 164). As members of the church, we must eagerly maintain the unity of the Spirit (v. 3). Don't let your fear of "meddling" keep you from seeking to reconcile people. There's a difference between meddling and seeking to do gospel-centered reconciliation.

Further, if you, as a believer, are acting wrongfully toward your brother or sister, you shouldn't think, *It's none of anyone's business.* It is the church's business because you're a part of the body and your sin affects the whole body. Paul has no problem alerting the church to the problem and asking for someone to help mediate (cf. 1 Cor 6:1-8). Why? Again, it's because he loves the church, and he wants the church to be healthy and to flourish.

Third, Paul reminds everyone why these two sisters should be reconciled (v. 3b). The reason is simple: the gospel. Here we see a wonderful pattern for a peacemaker to follow. Paul commends as he corrects; he affirms as he admonishes; he reminds as he rebukes. Paul believes they're *genuine sisters*. He can confidently say their "names are in the book of life" (cf. Luke 10:20; Heb 12:23). The church on earth should reflect the church in heaven. How sad is it when two genuine believers can't resolve nondoctrinal issues! He also believes that they're *genuine servants*. He says they have "contended for the gospel" at Paul's side, along with many faithful co-laborers like Clement and others whom he doesn't name. Not only were their names in the book of life, but they together also told others about how to live among God's people— through faithful gospel mission. Yet they're divided, and because such disagreement shouldn't exist between fellow sisters and fellow servants, Paul says, "Agree in the Lord."

Let me ask you three application questions. First, *Do you see yourself as a threat to the unity of your church?* You should! So should I! Here are two wonderful servants of Jesus who are at odds with each other. Every member can be a threat to unity. That should sober us and make us want to apply Philippians 2:1-11 to all of our relationships.

Next, *Will you ask for help when you have a conflict?* How fortunate we are to have the church, filled with co-laborers, as in Philippi, who can apply the gospel to our lives. Call a small group leader, a wise Christian friend, or a pastor to help you when necessary.

Finally, *Are you prepared to give help?* While not everyone will be a Paul Tripp, everyone can counsel with Scripture and prayer. Based on this text, I think you have a good plan! If two people are at odds, begin with Philippians 4:2 and say, "Agree in the Lord." Explain what this means. Then you may have them read Philippians 2:1-11 aloud. Unpack that passage a bit for them. Then perhaps you could have them leave for a day or so, meditate on this particular passage, and see if they might be able to come back and agree to pursue like-mindedness with each other. See if they might humble themselves, as Jesus humbled Himself, and unite in the gospel.

We often say at Imago Dei Church that we encourage "awkward conversations" to take place. If you're going to have a real relationship with others, you will have conflicts. So plan on having these "Euodia-and-Syntyche conversations" for the good of the church and for the glory of Christ. Seek to submit to the lordship of Christ, to put on the mind of Christ, and to deal with the issue. If you can't resolve it, then ask for someone to help you do it.

All of this requires grace-filled humility. Division in the body like this not only damages the health of the church but also affects our witness to the world. No one wants to join a group of people who don't like one another! Further, disunity keeps us from exercising forward energy in the mission. Petty differences demand sideways energy; they occupy far too much time—time that individuals could be using to spread the gospel.

Rejoice in the Lord (4:4)

Another common Christian struggle is maintaining a joyful heart.

The need. Paul once again finds it necessary to issue this command to "rejoice." He obviously thought these Christians in Philippi needed to hear it. Can exemplary Christians like the Philippians struggle to maintain joy? Yes! Why did George Mueller say, "The first great and primary business . . . every day was to have my soul happy in the Lord"? Because we don't always wake up ready to sing. When you read Christian biographies, you'll actually be encouraged that some of our greatest heroes wrestled through seasons of dryness, despair, and discouragement.

The causes. Many things can rob us of joy. One of them is mentioned in verse 6—anxiety! But doubt, loss of a loved one, work, illness, relational difficulties, and numerous other problems can cause Christians to lose their song.

The solution. Notice what Paul says about rejoicing. He doesn't say, "Rejoice when your circumstances are going well." He says, "Rejoice *in the Lord* always" (emphasis added). Joy comes from our relationship with Jesus, not our circumstances. Paul isn't writing this letter from a sweet beach house. He's writing in prison. Surely some of the Philippians remembered when he and Silas sang hymns in prison despite being beaten and bruised. How then can he say this? Where did Paul's joy come from? It came from the Lord Jesus Christ.

Most people think you get joy when you *get* what you *desire*. But real joy comes when you *realize* what you *deserve*. The realization of what you deserve (judgment) and what you've received instead (salvation) should lead you to great joy. It's not about getting what you want; it's about being grateful for all that you have in Christ Jesus.

Recently Pharrell Williams's catchy song titled "Happy" made people "clap along" and sing and dance all over the world. For months it was the number one song in the land. You could see people sing it on talk shows, at sporting events, in public streets, and in countless other contexts. It first appeared as a single for the movie *Despicable Me 2*. Interestingly, the song plays when Lucy gives Gru (the former super-villain) a kiss. When the formerly despicable guy finds love, it makes him happy. That sounds like the gospel! When formerly despicable characters are seized and changed by the love of Jesus, it should make them happy. In Philippians the happiest man in Rome is in jail! What makes him rejoice? The good news of Christ rescuing him makes him rejoice. When we consider what we deserve because of our despicable sin and what we have because of the redeeming love of God through Christ, that realization should give rise to joy. When you ponder how the Savior has lifted you out of the miry pit, it should give you "a new song," as David says (e.g., Ps 40:1-3). Rejoice in the Lord—in the Savior and Lord, who loves to redeem and forgive despicable people.

Instruction. So when and how long should we rejoice in the Lord? Paul tells us: "always." Carson notes this is a command, not good advice (*Basics*, 106). We're commanded to rejoice. Certainly there will be occasions when we're grieved and filled with sorrow, but even in those times the Christian can say with Paul, "as grieving yet always rejoicing" (2 Cor 6:10). Paul doesn't teach that we should always be skipping around, totally detached from the real world. He teaches that even in hard times the Christian can drink deeply from the well of salvation that produces joy in the midst of struggle. You should always sing with joy because of the Savior, even in times when you have to sing with tears pouring down your face.

Effect. What would happen if you and others in your church lived lives of constant rejoicing? Think of all the sins that are overcome by a heart that rejoices in the Lord always. Would this practice not conquer sins like envy, gossip, stinginess, arrogance, discontentment, and complaining? These sins grow out of a heart that's not finding joy in Christ. Further, when we rejoice in the Lord while we serve the Lord, we honor Him. Our attitudes as we serve the Lord matter to Him. So, let's regularly reflect on how graciously the Lord has treated us, and may that lead us to live a life of joy.

Be Known for Graciousness (4:5)

The first part of Paul's next exhortation is translated in various ways:

- "Let your graciousness be known to everyone. The Lord is near" (HCSB).
- "Let your reasonableness be known to everyone. The Lord is at hand" (ESV).
- "Let everyone see that you are considerate in all you do. Remember, the Lord is coming soon" (NLT).
- "Let your gentle spirit be known to all men. The Lord is near" (NASB).
- "Let your gentleness be evident to all. The Lord is near" (NIV).

Scholars tell us that this Greek word for "reasonableness" (ESV), "graciousness" (HCSB), or "gentleness" (NIV) isn't easy to translate. Having a "gentle forbearance with others" gets at the idea (Fee, *Pauline Christology*, 406). It's the opposite of being contentious and self-seeking (Carson, *Basics*, 106).

This spirit of graciousness was evident in Jesus' life and ministry (2 Cor 10:1), including His attitude toward those who reviled and crushed Him (1 Pet 2:23). In the Pastoral Epistles Paul says this is a qualification of a pastor (1 Tim 3:3). Here Paul says that believers should display this gracious, gentle spirit with one another and with the watching world. We need this spirit when we seek to reconcile with other people. We need a gracious, forbearing spirit. We need a willingness to give up our preferences and show grace to others. This call for graciousness is also important as we engage this world with biblical truth. It's especially important when speaking on the most volatile issues in the culture right now, namely, homosexuality and gay marriage. Nothing creates more criticism and outrage these days than teaching, or even saying, that there has been a historical position on marriage—one man and one woman in the covenant of marriage. As we take our stand on such issues, we need courage, but that courage must also be mingled with graciousness.

Is your graciousness evident to your friends, family, neighbors, and fellow church members? Maybe a better question is, Do you even desire this character quality? What do you want to be known for—fame, success, beauty? May we all aspire to have a reputation, as individuals and as a church, for being gracious and gentle in our dealings with both those inside and those outside the church.

Paul then adds, "The Lord is near." There's division over how this should be received. Is it temporal or spatial? That is, is Paul referring to the Lord's *return* ("soon," temporal), or to the Lord's *presence* ("close," spatial)? If he's speaking of the Lord's return, then perhaps he's saying something like, "Jesus is returning, so live appropriately. Do you want Him to return and find you being harsh and self-promoting?"

But if he's referring to the Lord's presence, he may just be calling their attention to the fact that God is close to the Philippians and He's ready to assist them in their pursuit of Christlikeness. His nearness should certainly inspire one to pray, as the next verse commands. This idea of God's presence supplying sweet assurance to the believer can be found throughout the Old Testament, especially in the Psalms, and Paul may be echoing the psalmists. We read passages like, "The LORD is near the brokenhearted" (Ps 34:18).

Both interpretations—temporal and spatial views—are theologically correct, and Paul may have both in mind (O'Brien, *Epistle*, 489). Christ's return should cause us to live differently in the present, and Christ's closeness should encourage us and cause us to call on Him for blessing and help in the areas of resolving differences, rejoicing, being gentle, and overcoming anxiety.

Relieve Anxiety through Prayer (4:6-7)

If the first three issues didn't provoke you, surely number four will! The writer of Proverbs says, "Anxiety in a man's heart weighs it down" (Prov 12:25). Anxiety is like carrying a huge pack for miles. We can all identify with this and affirm its truth, but perhaps deep down we don't want to believe Philippians 4:6-7. Can you really relieve your anxiety through prayer and experience God's unspeakable peace? Yes, you can. Let's look closely at what Paul says about this common problem and his solution. Paul's teaching here is not only consistent with Jesus' instruction in Matthew 6:25-34, but it also sounds very similar to it. One can hear an echo from the Shepherd Himself.

What is worry/anxiety? We worry when we imagine the future in a terrible way. John Piper says, "Anxiety seems to be an intense desire for something, accompanied by a fear of the consequences of not receiving it" ("Is There Good Anxiety?"). This desire normally involves something we really value, like money or relationships. Worry involves imagining the future in a worst-case scenario and then freaking out about it. We can freak out about how we think our kids will turn out, how we will pay the rent next year, who we will marry, and so on.

To be clear, there's a difference between what we might call "alarm" and "worry." Things that alarm us may be helpful. We even call our clocks "alarm clocks." These are good inventions because they wake people up. I do wish they had a different name, like "daily-resurrection-practice clocks" or "opportunity clocks," but it is, nevertheless, a positive invention. Sometimes alarms in our minds will go off, telling us to take out the trash, make a phone call, or go talk to a person in need. One may call this "good anxiety" or a "good burden."

Paul mentions having "anxiety for all the churches" (2 Cor 11:28 ESV) as a desirable trait. What did he mean by anxiety for churches? Paul meant that he cared; he was concerned for their spiritual future. We, too, should have a burden for people's souls (cf. Rom 9:1-3). Remember also that Jesus wept over Jerusalem and was a man of sorrow, but He never sinned by worrying and taught that we shouldn't worry. So the problem of anxiety doesn't mean we live unconcerned, dispassionate lives. Indeed, some worry is positive. This good anxiety calls us to perform our responsibilities.

Negative worry is different. I remember hearing a John Ortberg sermon in which he described worry as carrying around an alarm clock all day! Can you imagine what kind of day that would be? Maybe you live like that. Do you live with self-defeating, persistent thoughts filled with worry? This type of anxiety, which Jesus and Paul talk about, is sin. This form of worry is pagan; it could be called "functional atheism" because you're living as though God doesn't exist, as if He's not the all-sovereign ruler over all.

This line of thinking leads us to how one can live with a good form of anxiety and avoid sinful anxiety—you have to broaden your vision. You have to step back and observe the big picture, as Paul did (cf. Rom 8:28), and realize that no anxiety should immobilize us and squeeze the joy out of us, because we have an eternal perspective of God's goodness (Piper, "Is There Good Anxiety?"). Crushing anxiety happens when I believe lies. You might think of your worries as false prophets. They're telling you that God isn't good, sovereign, and wise. You need to listen to another sermon. Every day the birds are preaching another one, and we should watch and listen to them.

Why were the Philippians anxious? There are many causes of anxiety, and the Philippian church faced several of them. They faced external threats. Paul tells them not to be frightened by their opponents (1:28). They were dealing with internal opposition (4:2-3). They were concerned for their beloved missionary-church planter, Paul (4:10), as well as their representative, Epaphroditus (2:26). They also may have been a bit worried about God's provision, so Paul reassures them of God's providence (4:19). We can surely identify with these causes, right?

Is some external threat causing you to be anxious? Is there conflict within your church that's creating anxiety? Do you have a concern for someone that's creating anxiety? Are you worried about wealth and provisions? There may be a number of other causes such as noise, traffic, isolation, interruptions, family crises, envy, and loneliness. There are many threats to peace.

What does anxiety do to you? Anxiety is a joy killer. Anxiety will also make you self-absorbed. When you're consumed with your worries, you will be less likely to serve others wholeheartedly. Worry distracts you and keeps you from mission. It also robs you of peace, which Paul says will fill the hearts of praying believers. All of these results are spiritual issues. There may also be physical results that display the signs of anxiety. Here are just a handful of them: unusual mood swings, irritability, anger, sweating, rapid heartbeat, chest pain, exhaustion, nervous twitching, decreased concentration and memory, nausea, shortness of breath, hair loss, weight gain or loss, panic, indecisiveness, canker sores, muscle tension, insomnia, self-medicating, high blood pressure, eating comfort foods, and reckless driving.

What should we do about anxiety? Here's the real question for us, right? We may be given many recommendations, including acupuncture, whiskey, exercise, aromatherapy, yoga, medicines, and deep breathing. While God blesses us with many evidences of His common grace through some of these means, we should start with what He's said to us about the issue specifically in His Word. We need God's Word to know God's peace. Since Paul is echoing the words of Jesus, let's go back and briefly highlight the Good Shepherd's instructions and allow His teaching to minister to our anxious hearts. Moisés Silva says, "That the apostle is here reflecting, or even directly alluding to, Jesus' teaching seems very likely indeed" (*Philippians*, 195). Jesus says,

> *This is why I tell you:* Don't worry *about your life, what you will eat or what you will drink; or about your body, what you will wear. Isn't life more than food and the body more than clothing? Look at the birds of the sky: They don't sow or reap or gather into barns, yet your heavenly Father feeds them. Aren't you worth more than they? Can any of you add a single cubit to his height by worrying? And why do you worry about clothes? Learn how the wildflowers of the field grow: they don't labor or spin thread. Yet I tell you that not even Solomon in all his splendor was adorned like one of these! If that's how God clothes the grass of the field, which is here today and thrown into the furnace tomorrow, won't He do much more for you—you of little faith? So* don't worry, *saying, "What will we eat?" or "What will we drink?" or "What will we wear?" For the idolaters eagerly seek all these things, and your heavenly Father knows that you need them. But seek first the kingdom of God and His righteousness, and all these things will be provided for you.* Therefore don't worry *about tomorrow, because tomorrow will worry about itself. Each day has enough trouble of its own.* (Matt 6:25-34; emphasis added)

This passage comes immediately after Jesus' teaching on treasures and money in the previous paragraphs. Notice "This is why" in verse 25; it seems that this particular cause of anxiety is on our Lord's mind. In this amazing passage where Jesus tells us three times, "Don't worry" (Matt 6:25,31,34), He then gives five reasons why we shouldn't be consumed with anxiety.

The Good Shepherd tells us that **God provides for birds and flowers; He will surely provide for us** (Matt 6:26,28-30). Here we have two illustrations. God feeds the birds and clothes the wildflowers. I (Tony) love to sit outside of my house and watch the birds eat and the flowers blossom. Every day a sermon is being preached, saying, God provides; God sustains. I find it easy to pray outside. The universe is not a clock running by itself. God didn't wind up the universe and say, "Go for it." No, God provides for His creation, as many of the psalms point out (e.g., Ps 104). The point is clear: If you're more valuable than birds, you'll be okay. Relax in His promises.

Martin Luther once described his favorite preacher, a bird:

> I have one preacher that I love better than any other. It is my little tame robin, who preaches to me daily. I put his crumbs upon my windowsill, especially at night. He hops onto the sill when he wants his supply, and takes as much as he desires to satisfy his need. From there he always hops to a little tree close by, and lifts up his voice to God, and sings his carol of praise and gratitude, tucks his little head under his wings, and goes fast to sleep, to leave tomorrow to look after itself. He is the best preacher I have on earth. (Tan, *Encyclopedia*, 1,649–50)

Let the birds preach a better sermon to you. God feeds the birds, which are less valuable than you. God clothes the wildflowers, which are temporary; He will provide for you who are eternal (Matt 6:28).

The Good Shepherd also tells us that **worrying is pointless** (Matt 6:27,34). This is the pragmatic side of worry. It's worthless. You can't add any more days to your life, and you can't control tomorrow. Your worries aren't helping; rather, they're adding to the problems.

Next, the Good Shepherd tells us that **worrying is a pagan practice, not a disciple's practice** (Matt 6:31-32). He says that "the Gentiles seek after all these things" (ESV). We should be seeking something else, namely, the kingdom, not being overwhelmed with worldly things. Your name is in heaven's book. Rest in God's grace, and stop freaking out like one who doesn't know God.

Additionally, the Good Shepherd reminds us that **God knows our needs more than we do** (Matt 6:32). Nothing catches Him by surprise. Trust in His sovereign care.

Finally, the Good Shepherd tells us that **God will provide everything we need when we seek His kingdom and His righteousness** (Matt 6:33). Jesus doesn't promise a drama-free life. He tells us elsewhere that we may have to give our lives for the kingdom. But He will give us what we need as we seek His kingdom. In Luke He says, "Fear not, little flock, for it is your Father's good pleasure to give you the kingdom" (Luke 12:32 ESV). We can sell our possessions, store up treasures in heaven (Luke 12:33-34), and pour ourselves into mission (Luke 12:4-12) with confident trust that God provides for His flock as they seek His kingdom. What are you seeking first? Are you seeking the kingdom?

In Philippians 4:6-7 Paul tells us three things about dealing with anxiety. They're quite simple and reflective of the Savior's words.

Accept the truth that you shouldn't have a heart filled with pagan anxiety (v. 6). Paul simply says, "Don't worry about anything." It shouldn't be part of our lives. He's merely echoing Jesus' three-time exhortation in Matthew 6. Do you understand this? You shouldn't worry in a sinful way any more than you should gossip, envy, covet, or commit sexual sin. The first step to tackling this sin is realizing it's not an acceptable habit or personality trait. It's sin, and this is a commandment: "Do not be anxious" (ESV).

Cast all of your cares on God who cares for you (vv. 6-7). The first and most basic remedy for anxiety is prayer. Paul says that peace comes only through prayer. He says to relieve your anxiety in this way: "In everything, through prayer and petition with thanksgiving, let your requests be made known to God." Don't worry about anything; pray about everything. This is a commandment. So pray, and know God's peace! Luther quipped, "Pray and let God worry." D. A. Carson says, "I have yet to meet a chronic worrier who enjoys an excellent prayer life" (*Basics*, 112). Here's the antidote to anxiety. This is basic Christianity, but how are you doing in this discipline of unhurried, unhindered time with God? Do you know the peace that comes from being in God's presence (see Ps 91:1-2)?

Paul says we should pray with thanksgiving and intercession. Paul isn't denying that we will have hard times; instead, he understands that in those hard times we can offer up the sacrifice of thanksgiving. Hard times can serve as occasions to offer our requests to God. Remember from where Paul is writing this! We can be thankful as we reflect on the manifold mercies of God, even in a prison. We should also offer up our petitions to God when in need. We should ask and keep on asking, as Jesus instructed us, because our Father loves to give good gifts to His children (Matt 7:7-11). You can seek Him about any care you have, from needing daily bread to going overseas on mission.

Peter says that we should cast all of our cares on God because He cares for us (1 Pet 5:7), which is an echo of Ps 55:22, "Cast your burden on the LORD, and He will sustain you; He will never allow the righteous to be shaken." I liken this to the great game of bowling. Have you ever watched the bowler after he or she releases the ball? It's often quite humorous. I (Tony) grew up in a bowling alley (my dad was a "commissioner"), and I've seen all sorts of things. People contort their bodies after they roll a ball down the lane, hoping that a side lean will somehow affect where the ball goes. Some talk to the ball. Others tip toe, leap, or slide to the side, hoping that the ball will land in the pocket. The fact is, once you let go of the ball, nothing you do will change the course of the ball! Just let the ball go. Do this with your burdens as well; release them to God. Don't release a burden and then worry about it. Cast your burden on the Lord; He will sustain you. Let God deal with it.

The psalmist says many need to trust God and go to sleep at night. He says, "In vain you get up early and stay up late, working hard to have enough food—yes, He gives sleep to the one He loves" (Ps 127:2). God never worries. God is in control. God loves His people and tells them to go to sleep at night. May God grant us grace to enjoy the peace that comes from casting our cares on Him.

Fight anxiety with faith in God's promises (4:5-7,19). I get this idea from a few places in Philippians 4. The next verse is one of these promises, "And the peace of God, which surpasses every thought, will guard your hearts and minds in Christ Jesus" (v. 7). Paul doesn't say that prayer will keep us from having problems; rather, once we pray and give our burden to God, we can have peace in the midst of the problem. He says that we can be garrisoned by the peace of God. Like a Roman soldier standing watch over a building, so the peace of God will guard our hearts when anxious thoughts and fears arise. Paul adds that this peace "surpasses every thought," which sounds a bit like Ephesians 3, speaking of God's ability "to do above and beyond all that we ask or think" (Eph 3:20). One reason God's peace is so extraordinary is that you can have it when it doesn't make sense to have it! Why should you have peace when you're in a Roman prison? It doesn't make sense unless God's peace really does flood your soul through prayer. And it does. This peace transcends understanding.

So while medicine, a massage, and other practices have their place, they will never give you this type of peace because this peace only comes from God. How do you get it? You have to know the Prince of Peace. It's only through a relationship with Jesus that you can know what Paul's talking about. But if you are a Christian, then fight your anxiety with God's promise of peace. He promises to give you unexplainable peace when you pray. So believe this promise!

There are other encouraging truths, promises, and applications in chapter 4 in which we can rest. We find that the Lord is near us (v. 5). Fight your anxiety by believing that He is with you and that the Lord Jesus will return for you. Paul mentions "thanksgiving" in 4:6. How can we live thankfully all the time? One cause for thanksgiving is the fact that God keeps His promise, and as we look across the page, we find this sweet assurance: "And my God will supply all your needs according to His riches in glory in Christ Jesus" (v. 19). Believe that promise.

We grow anxious when we fail to remember God's promises. So take God at His Word. Believe that He gives His peace to those who seek His presence. Believe that He will provide for His children. Fight fear with God's promises. Understand that this isn't prosperity theology. Paul is in prison. Many of the Philippians are poor (2 Cor 8:2). God's promises aren't material possessions and earthly treasures, but something much deeper, much more important, and much greater, namely, God's peace, God's presence, and God's provisions to do kingdom work. Seek first the kingdom, and trust Him.

Think on Praiseworthy Things (4:8-9)

The final issue that Paul addresses is the Christian's thought life. For Christians to grow in likeness to Jesus, we have to have a renewed mind (Rom 12:1-2; Eph 4:23). God has blessed His church with His Word as a primary means of purifying our minds. Jesus prayed, "Sanctify them by the truth; Your word is truth" (John 17:17). David prayed for God to examine his thoughts, saying, "Search me, God, and know my heart; test me and know my concerns. See if there is any offensive way in me; lead me in the everlasting way" (Ps 139:23-24). David knew that real change involves a change of one's thoughts. In the Sermon on the Mount, Jesus gets at the thoughts behind adultery and murder, calling attention to the sinfulness of lustful thoughts and malicious thoughts (Matt 5:21-22,27-30). What we think matters, and it matters more than we think. We need God's Word to saturate our minds that we may be renewed and kept from offensive ways.

In addition to this Paul highlights the need to think on admirable things. Think about what's true, not false. Think about what's honorable, not dishonorable. Think about what's just, not unjust. Think about what's pure, not impure. Think about what's lovely, not repulsive. Think about what's commendable, not wrong. Think about what's morally excellent, not filthy. Think about what's admirable, not shameful

(Carson, *Basics*, 116). Paul's verb, *logizomai*, means to "take into account carefully" or to "calculate" (Witherington, *Friendship and Finances*, 117). We are to dwell, think, ponder, consider carefully, and reflect on virtuous things in this life.

Paul's virtuous things may appear in various places in the culture. God is the Creator and Giver of all good gifts, so we shouldn't be surprised to find many praiseworthy qualities in our world. What we must do is *sift* things through the grid of Scripture. This text doesn't give us a license to be "worldly" or to determine our own morality, but it does encourage us to ponder things that the God of the Bible finds worthy of our thoughts. We must seek to take "every thought captive to obey Christ" (2 Cor 10:5). Surrender your thought life to Jesus, and don't allow it to drift into the gutter. One may find such traces of admirable qualities in the arena of agriculture, in the plant and animal kingdoms, in the arts, in music, in the military, among parents, in children, and in sports. Think biblically and in a Christ-centered, Christ-exalting way about these and other things in our world.

In addition to thinking praiseworthy thoughts, Paul also mentions following godly examples. He writes, "Do what you have learned and received and heard and seen in me, and the God of peace will be with you" (v. 9). Once again the theme of imitation appears, and so does the theme of peace. Emulate leaders who think holy thoughts. Emulate leaders who set their minds on their Creator and Redeemer. Watch them. Watch how they view creation, what they read, what they talk about, what they value. As a result, Paul says, the follower will know more of God's peace. The prophet Isaiah wrote, "You will keep the mind that is dependent on You in perfect peace, for it is trusting in You" (Isa 26:3). How true this is. Set your mind on praiseworthy things, give your burdens to God, and know the perfect peace of God.

To conclude, Paul shepherds the church lovingly, wisely, and faithfully, urging them to be united, to rejoice in the Lord, to be gentle, to replace anxiety with God's peace through prayer, and to think on praiseworthy things. As we meditate on these things, we should remember the hope we have in Christ. Jesus never broke these commands, and He solved all these problems. Christ is the reconciler, the gentle Savior. His gift of salvation gives us cause to rejoice. He removed our greatest fear and relieves our deepest anxiety through His victorious death and resurrection. He paid the penalty for those who sinned with their thoughts, and He grants them a new mind in turn. Look to the Savior for your righteousness and for daily renewal, and go imitate Him. As you do, the peace of God will be with you.

Reflect and Discuss

1. What was Paul's solution to the dispute between Euodia and Syntyche?
2. Why is division in the body of Christ so dangerous?
3. How might you encourage unity rather than division?
4. Why are "awkward conversations" sometimes necessary to have with others?
5. What would happen if you and others in your church lived lives of constant rejoicing?
6. What does Paul mean by "The Lord is near" (4:5)?
7. What does anxiety do to you? How does it affect others around you?
8. What are the three things Paul tells us in Philippians 4:6-7 about dealing with anxiety?
9. What does Paul mean when he says to think about admirable things? How do you do this?
10. How are you doing in the discipline of spending unhurried, unhindered time with God? Do you know the peace that comes from being in God's presence?

Models of Giving and Receiving

Main Idea: As Paul expresses his gratitude to God for the church's support, he carefully highlights some important Christian aspects of giving and receiving.

I. **Six Words on Giving and Receiving (4:10-20)**
   A. Gratitude: Thank God for the generosity of other believers (4:10).
   B. Contentment: Pursue this rare jewel (4:11-13).
      1. Contentment is unconnected to our circumstances (4:11-12).
      2. Contentment is learned (4:11-12).
      3. Contentment flows from union with and reliance on Christ (4:13).
   C. Partnership: See the inseparable relationship between financial support and gospel partnership (4:14-16).
   D. Fruitfulness: Understand the spiritual and eternal importance of giving (4:17).
   E. Worship: Bring pleasure to God through sacrificial giving (4:18).
   F. Faith: Trust in God's provision (4:19-20).

II. **Warm Greetings and Gospel Encouragement (4:21-23)**

Many pastors are hesitant to talk about money in the local church. There are several reasons for this reluctance. Pastors know that some people are suspicious of pastors, especially those who talk about money. Pastors don't want to appear greedy; neither do they want to be associated with prosperity preachers. While pastors should always be careful when teaching on any subject, they shouldn't avoid talking about a subject that the Bible addresses frequently: money. In this particular passage we find a wonderful theology of giving and receiving that everyone, pastor and member alike, should consider closely. The Philippians are models of giving, and Paul is a model of receiving. We should pay close attention to them both.

I (Tony) haven't known extreme poverty; neither have I known great prosperity (at least in an American way). My dad worked in a factory my whole life, and while we had plenty, we weren't super-wealthy. I went to college on a full baseball scholarship, and somehow (by God's grace) I made it through seminary without debt. Now I'm a pastor and professor, and I have plenty, but I have no anticipation of making an appearance on *MTV Cribs*. I can't identify with all the hardships of the apostle Paul, but I can't identify with Bill Gates, either. Maybe you can identify with me.

However, I have struggled throughout my life with treasuring Christ more than anything. I have struggled to be content in Christ. I have wrestled with thinking that I have too much money and that I'm not doing enough with it. I have also worried about not having enough money at times. In my most recent move I left a very large church in order to plant a church and teach at a seminary. This caused quite a reduction in income. I need to pay off five international adoption expenses, and I still own a house in another state that I'm trying to sell. Because of these very real challenges, I love this passage of Scripture and need it greatly.

I (Francis) have also wrestled with the issue of wealth and possessions at various points in my life. Regarding cars, I have asked, "Would Jesus drive?" "If so, *what* would Jesus drive?" I struggled for years with taking a salary from the church. I have also agonized over the state of the American church, which seems to be more consumer-driven than mission-driven. Perhaps you think you don't struggle with money; you might want to reconsider that assumption. Jesus says, "Watch out and be on guard against all greed" (Luke 12:15). We have to watch out for it because greed is sneaky. Few people think they're greedy. If you think you don't need to read about this subject, then you probably do!

Another misguided assumption is that either the rich or the poor are spiritually superior to the other. Those who think the wealthy are more spiritual may either believe in a radical prosperity theology (if you have enough faith, you'll be healthy and wealthy), or a low-level prosperity (if we keep the moral system of the Bible, God is obligated to bless us materially). Both are wrong of course; many of our international brothers and sisters are being killed for preaching the same message we're preaching. Their obedience to Christ has not brought riches, but hardship and persecution.

Those who think the poor are spiritually superior assume that wealthy people are always less spiritual than the poor. For these, the pathway to maturity involves selling everything and moving to a mud hut in Africa. While the Lord may call some to do this, such a comprehensive view is misguided and simplistic. Many great spiritual leaders in church history were poor, and many were wealthy. So both groups need to reconsider this assumption. We need to trade *prosperity theology* and *poverty theology* for *Pauline theology*. Because of the sensitive nature of the subject and the need to clarify one's motives, Paul addresses money matters here with wonderful pastoral grace. He has carefully selected his words. His theology is something we can build our lives on. Let's consider what Paul says in six parts.

Six Words on Giving and Receiving
PHILIPPIANS 4:10-20

Gratitude: Thank God for the Generosity of Other Believers (4:10)

Paul begins the final portion of the letter with another explosion of joy. Once again, the apostle is rejoicing! This time he adds the adverb "greatly." Why is he so happy? He's thrilled by the Philippians' renewed support. He doesn't say why they went for a period of time without giving. Perhaps it was due to their poverty (2 Cor 8:1-2) or due to Paul's inaccessibility. Paul simply says that they lacked opportunity, but they never lacked concern. Bottom line: Paul is super-grateful for the Philippians' concern about him and for their generosity.

As you scan through verses 10-20, you will notice something interesting. Paul never *explicitly* says "thank you" directly to the Philippians. Some think Paul is saying, "Thanks . . . sort of." Does Paul lack gratitude for them? Absolutely not! Paul conveys his gratitude in a triangular fashion, between himself, the Philippians, and the Lord. By communicating gratitude in this fashion, he avoids three common pitfalls associated with talking about money: manipulation, flattery, and silence.

In regard to **manipulation**, Paul doesn't want his thanksgiving to be interpreted as a request for more money. Sometimes nonprofits can come off this way: "Thanks for the check. But you haven't sent anything recently. Do you really hate orphans? Then write us another check!" The letters don't actually say it like that, but the message may contain a guilt-driven request. Paul doesn't want his thankfulness to be portrayed as a clever way of asking for more. Twice in this passage he says "not" (vv. 11,17 ESV) in order to emphasize that he's not rejoicing because of the gift itself, nor does he want them to think he needs more help. He's interested in the church bearing fruit and pleasing God.

Paul also avoids **flattery**. He doesn't go over the top in his commendation. He doesn't tell the church, "I'm dedicating this prison cell to you, Philippians. I'm putting a plaque up with your names on it." Paul doesn't go over the top with thanks.

Finally, he avoids **silence**. Some people fear that if they show *any* gratitude, the recipients will become puffed up. This is the hyperspiritual person. Paul knows that those who serve and give faithfully should be honored.

How then does Paul avoid these pitfalls? He avoids manipulation by reminding them *why* he's happy: it's because the church is bearing fruit and because of the relationship he has with them. He's not rejoicing because of the gift.

He avoids flattery by rejoicing in *the Lord* for the Philippians. He doesn't go on and on about *them*, but praises *the Lord* for their faithfulness.

He avoids the silent treatment by actually rejoicing in the Lord *in front of the Philippians* (Carson, *Basics*, 122). Paul thus ends the letter the way he opened it: "I give thanks to my God for every remembrance of you" (1:3). Scholars have pointed out that there are striking parallels between the thanksgiving in 1:3-11 and the thank-you section of 4:10-20, forming nice bookends to the letter (see O'Brien, *Epistle*, 513–14).

Follow Paul's example here. If someone has blessed you, thank God for them—in front of them. You might do this with a letter or face-to-face. Thank God for those who care for you. Thank God for those who bless you in various ways.

Contentment: Pursue This Rare Jewel (4:11-13)

As Paul seeks to avoid manipulation and clarify his motivation, he spends three verses explaining Christian contentment. While he's grateful for the Philippians' faithfulness, he doesn't want to come across as a poor beggar, and he doesn't want them to misinterpret his joy. He looks to exalt Jesus as his source of joy and his ultimate source of strength. As a result, we have some extraordinary reflections on the undervalued grace of contentment. The philosophies of Paul's day talked about contentment as "self-sufficiency." Paul transforms the idea to describe contentment as "Christ-sufficiency." Christian contentment is about believing that *Christ is enough*. Contentment was rare in Paul's day, and it is rare in ours.

Two particular books in the Puritan period reflected on this passage and subject. Jeremiah Burroughs wrote a book titled *The Rare Jewel of Christian Contentment*, and Thomas Watson wrote *The Art of Divine Contentment*. I (Tony) love both titles, especially Burroughs' title. I actually took this book with me when my wife and I left for a 40-day trip to Ukraine for our adoption process. I had three outfits and Jeremiah Burroughs! It ministered to my soul. Contentment is like a rare jewel. It's uncommon. If it was uncommon during days of the Puritans, then how much more rare is it today? We should gaze at this jewel for a bit, behold it, and pursue it (Mahaney, "A Rare Jewel"). Paul tells us three truths about Christian contentment.

Contentment is unconnected to our circumstances (4:11-12). Paul stresses in this text that his contentment didn't increase or decrease based on his material provision. More stuff won't bring a Christian deeper satisfaction, and neither will less stuff. Yet many in our day often think they need a change of circumstances in order to experience more joy. Perhaps you can identify with this poem:

It was spring, but it was summer I wanted,
The warm days, and the great outdoors.
It was summer, but it was fall I wanted,
The colorful leaves, and the cool, dry air.
It was fall, but it was winter I wanted,
The beautiful snow, and the joy of the holiday season.
It was now winter, but it was spring I wanted,
The warmth, and the blossoming of nature.
I was a child, but it was adulthood I wanted,
The freedom, and the respect.
I was 20, but it was 30 I wanted,
To be mature, and sophisticated.
I was middle-aged, but it was 20 I wanted,
The youth, and the free spirit.
I was retired, but it was middle age that I wanted,
The presence of mind, without limitations.
My life was over, but I never got what I wanted.
(Lehman, "Present Tense")

What do you think you need in order to be content? Do you need more stuff? Do you need a bigger house that makes it on HGTV? Do you need a car with a pool in it? Do you need a different place to live? Or do you think a mud hut in Africa would make you more content? Paul is teaching us the hard, sobering truth that the rare jewel of Christian contentment has nothing to do with our circumstances. It's found in Christ. We need Him.

Contentment is learned (4:11-12). Twice Paul says that he learned contentment. Contentment wasn't "zapped" into his heart. Through many experiences, Paul learned that Christ was enough. Paul knew abundance. He knew what it was like to be hosted by the wealthy Lydia in Philippi. Surely he had some wonderful dinners with some wealthy Christian friends in Ephesus and Corinth. But he was no more content during such experiences. One might argue that it's harder to be content in abundance than in need. Calvin writes,

> He who knows how to use present abundance soberly
> and temperately with thanksgiving, prepared to part with
> everything whenever it may please the Lord, giving also a
> share to his brother according to his ability, and is also not
> puffed up, that man has learned to excel and to abound. This
> is an excellent and rare virtue, and much greater than the
> endurance of poverty. (Cited in Hughes, *Philippians,* 185)

Paul also knew hardship. Lest we think he's blowing smoke, just read through the New Testament! Here's a sample of his hardships from his Corinthian correspondence:

> *Up to the present hour we are both hungry and thirsty; we are poorly clothed, roughly treated, homeless; we labor, working with our own hands.* (1 Cor 4:11-12)

> *. . . by great endurance, by afflictions, by hardship, by difficulties, by beatings, by imprisonments, by riots, by labors, by sleepless nights, by times of hunger . . .* (2 Cor 6:4-5)

> *Three times I was shipwrecked. I have spent a night and a day in the open sea. On frequent journeys, I faced . . . hardship, many sleepless nights, hunger and thirst, often without food, cold, and lacking clothing.* (2 Cor 11:25-27)

Paul knew what abundance was like, but he also *often* went without food. He knew what it was like to sleep in the cold. He really did know what it meant to be brought low. Paul learned contentment as he followed Jesus; he learned what mattered. We might wish that a certain crisis would break us from our love affair with this world, but contentment isn't learned in a single crisis. It's learned through exposure to times of need and times of plenty. It involves a regular struggle to believe that Christ is enough. It involves us going through the school of need and the school of plenty. Both schools offer various tests that we must take.

In the *school of prosperity*, we will encounter the test of greed. Will having possessions create in us an insatiable desire for more? Solomon wrote, "The one who loves money is never satisfied with money, and whoever loves wealth is never satisfied with income. This too is futile" (Eccl 5:10). Additionally, Paul tells Timothy that those who are "rich" have other temptations:

> But those who want to be rich fall into temptation, a trap, and many foolish and harmful desires, which plunge people into ruin and destruction. For the love of money is a root of all kinds of evil, and by craving it, some have wandered away from the faith and pierced themselves with many pains. (1 Tim 6:9-10)

> Instruct those who are rich in the present age not to be arrogant or to set their hope on the uncertainty of wealth, but on God, who richly provides us with all things to enjoy. Instruct them to do what is good, to be rich in good works, to be generous, willing to share, storing up for themselves a good reserve for the age to come, so that they may take hold of life that is real. (1 Tim 6:17-19)

Paul calls attention to the temptations of arrogance, misplaced trust, not enjoying God's free gifts, not doing good works, stinginess, making poor investments, and living an empty life.

What about *the school of poverty*? This school also presents various tests. The poor too are tested by greed—though this may surprise people. The poor aren't immune to greed. Greed may cause the poor to be tempted to sin in order to get rich (through lying, stealing, relying on others instead of working, or manipulating). They may grow envious of their neighbor, even if their neighbor is also poor. The person with a mud hut could easily grow envious of the person who has a metal roof. If you visit orphanages, you will see greed and envy at work, as kids want the trinkets of their peers, despite the fact that all the kids are in poverty. Greed isn't removed when one becomes rich or poor. It's a heart issue. The poor also have the temptation of losing contentment in Christ if they should ever become wealthy.

The writer of Proverbs reminds us that in every situation, we should long for a content life that glorifies God:

Two things I ask of You;
don't deny them to me before I die:
Keep falsehood and deceitful words far from me.
Give me neither poverty nor wealth;
feed me with the food I need.
Otherwise, I might have too much
and deny You, saying, "Who is the LORD?"
or I might have nothing and steal,
profaning the name of my God. (Prov 30:7-9)

The rich are tempted to deny God. The poor are tempted to want to be like the rich or to steal in order to gain. The writer says, "Give me a content life. Give me what I need. Help me see You are most important, O Lord." Contentment is learned.

Contentment flows from union with and reliance on Christ (4:13). Paul now tells us the "secret" of contentment. The secret is a public secret. It's an open secret. What's the secret? Here it is: Christian contentment is rooted in our relationship with Christ. It flows from our union and communion with the Savior. Paul says, "I am able to do all things through Him who strengthens me." This particular verse is one of the most often quoted verses in the Bible, but unfortunately, it's one of the most misapplied verses in the Bible! Paul isn't making a categorical, comprehensive statement here. He isn't saying that "I can break these chains, body slam these guards, and run out of this prison with 4.4 speed—through Christ who strengthens me!"

Many athletes love to quote this verse for inspiration to achieve their dreams. Often they are well intentioned, but they are uninformed. I don't question their motive, just their exegesis. I (Tony) can't dunk a basketball. And it doesn't matter how often I quote Philippians 4:13, this fact will not change! The only time I can dunk is when someone lowers the goal to about seven feet (which Francis and I recently did in Austin, Texas). It's not a problem with my unbelief; it's a problem with my height and ability!

The phrase "all things" must be governed by the context. The context is about contentment and material possessions. The NIV translates it well: "I can do all *this* through him who gives me strength" (NIV; emphasis added). If the ESV and HCSB added the word "these," then they would convey Paul's thoughts exactly, "I can do all [these] things through Christ who strengthens me" (ESV). Paul is saying that through Christ he's able to be content in every situation. This is the secret: Christ is enough. Christ empowers us to be content. C. J. Mahaney says it well: "Paul learned the secret because he learned to give attention to the Savior" ("A Rare Jewel"). Paul isn't preoccupied with his situation; he's preoccupied with Jesus. This is the secret. When you focus on Jesus, you can be content.

Are you preoccupied with your circumstances or with your Savior? To quote NASCAR driver Jeff Gordon, "Either you focus, or you end up hitting something really hard!" (in Mahaney, "A Rare Jewel"). This simple and true statement also illustrates the nature of the Christian life. Either you focus on Jesus, or you will crash into discontentment, complaining, deceit, distrust, or greed. The secret is focusing on Jesus and communing with Him daily. Find your strength in Him.

Think about this question also: Has a lack of contentment made you less flexible to live on mission? Contentment makes you *adaptable*. How can people leave it all for the foreign mission field? Here's how: they're preoccupied with Jesus, not their circumstances. They've chosen to live out Philippians 4:11-13. They don't need a bunch of stuff and familiar, comfortable surroundings.

Christian contentment makes us flexible, able to go anywhere. If you're from the South and you decide to join a church plant in the North, you will face many cultural challenges. You won't get any more sweet tea! If you move to another country, in an impoverished place, you might have to drink instant coffee! That's a real test of contentment! More seriously, overseas living will require you to learn another language, adopt new customs, and reorient your whole way of life. Can you do this? You can't if you aren't content in Christ. Those who are content in Christ have learned to say with Paul, "But if we have food and clothing, we will be content with these" (1 Tim 6:8).

I have met some people who say, "I'll serve anywhere as long as it's in Georgia." Or, "I can go anywhere as long as I'm close to my family." So do you need Jesus plus something else, or is Christ enough? Paul is showing us that contented Christians haven't made this world their home. They have found contentment somewhere else, in Someone else! The writer of Hebrews says,

> *Your life should be free from the love of money. Be satisfied with what you have, for He Himself has said, "I will never leave you or forsake you."* (Heb 13:5)

Apply this text. Don't love money; be content with what you have. Realize that the Lord will never forsake you. That's Great Commission language (Matt 28:18-20). Christian contentment makes us adaptable, flexible, open to wherever the Lord wants to send us because what we must have is Him. If we have His presence, then we have enough.

Partnership: See the Inseparable Relationship between Financial Support and Gospel Partnership (4:14-16)

In these verses Paul resumes the subject of verse 10 and adds to his point by highlighting more details of the Philippians' exemplary support. Paul highlights the Philippians' *sympathy* and *authenticity*. They were kind to share (fellowship) in his troubles. Their kindness went beyond mere sentiment, though. They were authentic partners, sharing in Paul's mission through financial support.

Paul shows us here the inseparable relationship between financial giving and gospel partnership. If you aren't giving, you aren't a partner. You're more like a consumer or a customer. But Paul doesn't view the Philippians as customers. He views them as co-laborers. They put skin in the game. Even though many of them weren't wealthy, they earned a reputation for giving sacrificially, generously, and cheerfully to support the mission (2 Cor 8–9).

Paul's relationship with the Philippians was special. No wonder he loved this church so much! He says that from the very early days of the church, they supported the mission of advancing the gospel and planting churches. When he left Philippi for Thessalonica (Acts 16–17; cf. 2 Cor 11:9), this young church was already helping him. He says that no other church entered such partnership (Phil 4:15). Apparently, some were enjoying the benefits of Paul's teaching and pastoral care but not assuming the responsibility of giving. How common this is in local congregations—receiving benefits but giving nothing in return. When a person is receiving sound instruction, which leads to life and godliness, and when a person is receiving pastoral care, they have the privilege and the responsibility of giving to support the mission of the church.

As individuals, don't be customers; be co-laborers. Join as partners through financial giving. See the relationship between being a partner and giving financially. Don't be a ninja. Don't simply appear on a Sunday, and then vanish mysteriously. Become a partner. Surely, partnership involves more than money, but money is important; we can't carry out the mission with pure sympathy.

As a church, follow the Philippian example. Even though they were a young church, they were supporting work elsewhere, and they were participating in the planting of other churches. I (Tony) want our young church plant to scatter hundreds of communities of light into the dark nooks and crannies of the world. I long to see the multiplication of many churches, not just the addition of attenders to one local church. This will happen through sacrificial, generous support for the glory of our Savior, who is worthy of every sacrifice we make.

Fruitfulness: Understand the Spiritual and Eternal Importance of Giving (4:17)

Next Paul adds to his theology of giving and receiving by highlighting the spiritual and eternal significance of living a generous life. Paul again says, "Not." He's being very careful as to what he says and what he doesn't say. After talking about the privilege and responsibility of giving, he says, "Not that I seek the gift." Paul wants them to know that his joy isn't due to the fact that they've given him a gift. He's not pressing the importance of giving because he wants to get rich. That's not his motive. Why then is Paul so happy about the Philippians' partnership? He says, "I seek the fruit" (ESV). That's what Paul is after! He wants the Philippians to bear fruit—he wants them to profit spiritually. He's happy because the Philippians are acting like Christians. Paul opened the letter praying that the Philippians would be "filled with the fruit of righteousness" (1:11). Here is one form of fruitfulness: generous giving.

Every pastor should feel free to talk about money because every pastor should care about the fruitfulness of God's people. As pastors, we have a responsibility to see that people grow spiritually and invest eternally. We should want to see growth and faithfulness in every area of their lives, including financial stewardship. This doesn't mean we know everyone's salary or the balance of their bank accounts. But we should teach on it and hold people accountable because we care for God's people and because we will give an account for shepherding them.

Earlier, Paul told the Philippians that he's laboring for their "progress and joy in the faith" (1:25). He wants progress. That involves, in part, seeing progress in giving. Are you seeking to bear fruit? Are you bearing fruit in this area? Paul prays for the Colossians that they would be "bearing fruit in every good work" (Col 1:10). Here's a good work: bearing fruit by giving financially to advance the gospel.

When I (Tony) was in college, two particular teammates really mentored me. They showed me how to bear fruit in various graces, including the area of giving to the mission of the church. I remember walking into the bedroom of one of my friends after baseball practice, and I noticed above his desk was a Post-it note that said, "This week's offering: [amount]." My 21-year-old self said, "Hmm. That's interesting. He's already thinking about what he's giving this Sunday." That example and many other examples of generosity really impacted me. Do you have a disciplined plan for giving to the mission of the church?

Paul also points out the eternal importance of giving; he says, "I seek the fruit *that increases to your credit*" (4:17 ESV; emphasis added). Paul is pleased because he knows God will bless the believers for laying up treasures in heaven, not on earth. We need to live with this divine perspective. God will honor people's faithfulness and fruitfulness in this life. Jesus taught this subject in several places (e.g., Matt 6:19-24; Luke 12:32-34).

Alistair Begg notes that while it's not a bad idea to have an IRA (Individual Retirement Account), every believer should have an *IEA* (Individual Eternal Account); that is, we should be laying up treasures in heaven. Regarding one's IEA, he asks, "What's in it?" and "When did you make your last contribution?" (Begg, "Everyone Needs One"). The safest and surest investment is to steward your resources faithfully for the good of the kingdom. Paul is thrilled because the Philippians are contributing to this eternal account, showing that their treasure isn't here on earth, demonstrating that they are citizens of heaven.

Worship: Bring Pleasure to God through Sacrificial Giving (4:18)

Paul drops the financial metaphor and moves to Old Testament imagery. He uses the language of the sacrifice of worship. (His language also sounds like Romans 12:1-2, where he talks about offering up our lives to God as an act of worship.) Just as the Old Testament sacrifices made a pleasing aroma that would ascend skyward, Paul says sacrificial giving pleases God. Indeed, Paul places the highest possible value on giving—a means of worshiping God.

What scents attract you? I'm attracted to the smell of a grill, baseball fields, French press coffee, and of course the sweet scent of my bride's perfume! Sacrificial obedience is a pleasing aroma to God. This is why you should give faithfully: because you want to please God. You should want to give because you want to worship Him. We get to give! We get to worship! Our offerings actually please God. Please understand that our giving cannot score us points with God. We can't earn salvation by giving a check. We aren't pleasing God in that sense. We give because we are saved, not in order to be saved. We give as a response to the marvelous grace that God has shown us. We give because Jesus is a giver! He gave His life for us. So the mature believer knows that giving is no burden; it's pure joy. It's a glad act of worship. Every week when we give our offerings, we should say, "This is only by Your grace, Lord. Receive this as a joyful offering of worship to the One who made me His own!"

Whether you're a pastor, teacher, small group leader, or parent, you should teach the importance of giving because you want people to please God. It's not because you want their money; giving is important because you want them to worship God in a way that honors Him. Money is a great tool, but a terrible master. Worship God with your money, but don't worship money.

Faith: Trust in God's Provision (4:19-20)

Paul now encourages the Philippians with a magnificent promise. The Philippians "supplied" Paul's needs sufficiently, and now Paul assures them that God will supply all their needs out of His infinite resources. Paul doesn't promise the church that God will provide for their *greed*, but for their *need*. While Paul surely has material provision in view here, we shouldn't limit the application to this dimension. God also supplies every spiritual need, including the ability to be content and to find sufficient strength in Christ. Paul is saying that God will provide everything we need to live for Christ.

Those motivated like the Philippians should marvel at this extraordinary promise. Those giving like the Philippians should treasure this promise. Those giving and living like the Philippians should trust in God's provision (2 Cor 9:6-15). Paul is a living testimony of this promise. Through abundance and need, he found that Christ is enough; we can trust in the Father's care.

We have many fears when it comes to money. We need to fight fear with the promises of God. God loves His children. Believe this. He has taken hold of us; we're His. Treasure Jesus, and trust the Father. He's good to His kids. We should go to Scripture and remind ourselves of His promises. We should fix our eyes on the cross in moments of doubt and anxiety, remembering that God has already solved our greatest problem. He gave His own Son for us; He can provide daily bread for us (Rom 8:32).

We should learn to apply Philippians 4:6-7 to the matter of money. Pour out your heart to your Father in prayer as you encounter anxiety. We have a young couple in our congregation who served in youth ministry prior to moving to seminary. They tell a story that I think even George Mueller would find impressive! The couple was living on a meager salary. On one particular night, they were down to 13 cents in their bank account. They were getting paid the next day, but they were out of lots of supplies, including toilet paper! After a period of frustration, they decided to pray for God to provide. They took Philippians 4:6-7 seriously: Don't worry about anything, but pray about *everything*. That night their youth group did what many youth groups do—they "rolled" their home. That means they threw toilet paper all over their house, yard, and trees. But this group didn't really know what they were doing, so they only used one roll. They left the rest of the package on the doorstep, knocked on the door, and ran off. When the young couple opened the door, they found that their prayer was answered!

I use this story simply to illustrate how we should pour out our hearts to God and give Him our burdens. Whether you need a job, wisdom, bread, or baby formula, give it to God in prayer. Let's follow the pattern of Paul and the Philippians. Let's learn to rejoice in the Lord over our partners in the gospel. Let's thank God for them in front of them. Let's also learn the secret of contentment: Christ is enough. Let's see the relationship between financial support and genuine gospel partnership. Let's understand that giving is a way in which we bear fruit, store up treasures in heaven, and worship God. As we live in such a generous and sacrificial way, let's remember that we can trust God to take care of us.

Paul bounces out of this promise with praise to the Father (v. 20). This is the appropriate response to God, who has provided for our salvation and continues to sustain us spiritually and physically. Paul bursts into praise when thinking about the "glorious Father" (Eph 1:17). We have to admire Paul, who is confined in prison yet soaring with a heart full of praise! We would soar too if we pondered anew what the Almighty can do (and has done!). Great is His faithfulness!

Warm Greetings and Gospel Encouragement
PHILIPPIANS 4:21-23

Let's consider Paul's final words to his beloved partners in this inspired, joy-filled letter about gospel advancement. Paul tells the church to greet all the saints, who are saints due to their position "in Christ Jesus." He opened the letter with a greeting to the saints (1:1), and now he closes with a similar expression. They share a common bond because of their relationship with Christ. He also sends greetings from the "brothers." Once again, we see that Paul rarely lived an isolated life. He lived his Christian life in community, even when he was in prison. He then broadens his warm greeting by sending greetings from "all the saints." This reference reminds the church in Philippi, and us, about other genuine communities of faith and the solidarity that we share.

The most striking aspect of the final greeting is at the end of verse 22: "especially those from Caesar's household." Most believe that this expression refers to those who served in various ways in Caesar's home. This reference is a wonderful touch at the end of the letter, reminding the Philippians that the power of Rome can't ultimately stop the power of the gospel. Earlier Paul spoke about his desire for "the advance of the gospel" (1:12), and here we see that it is indeed advancing, even in his imprisonment. This must have been encouraging for the Philippians to hear as they were encountering opposition.

Paul closes with a word of blessing: "The grace of the Lord Jesus Christ be with your spirit." He opened with a grace blessing (1:2), and now he closes with one. This remarkable letter is saturated with grace from God's promise of completing what He started (1:6); to the promise we have of being with Christ (1:23); to the stunning self-emptying of Christ (2:7); to the imputed righteousness of Christ on believing sinners (3:9); to the fact that we have a heavenly citizenship (3:20); to the Father, who hears our prayers and gives us peace (4:6-7)—a Father who supplies all our needs (4:19). We need to know this grace more. We need relationships oiled in grace, and we, indeed, should praise God for His grace and favor that brings us great joy. Let us advance the gospel of grace faithfully and courageously.

Reflect and Discuss

1. Why are pastors sometimes hesitant to talk about money in the local church?
2. What are the differences between prosperity theology, poverty theology, and Pauline theology?
3. How does Paul avoid manipulation, flattery, and silence—the three common pitfalls associated with talking about money?

4. How do you define Christian contentment? From where does it derive?
5. What are the three truths about Christian contentment according to Philippians 4:11-13?
6. What is the actual meaning of Philippians 4:13? How does this apply to your life?
7. Has a lack of contentment made you less flexible for mission? Explain.
8. What is the relationship between being a partner and giving financially?
9. Why should you give faithfully? Do you have a disciplined plan for giving to the mission of the church?
10. Explain how Philippians 4:19-20 applies to the matter of personal needs.

WORKS CITED

Begg, Alistair. "Everyone Needs One: An IEA." *Generous Giving.* 2002. Accessed June 2, 2014. http://library.generousgiving.org/articles /display.asp?id=20.

Bonhoeffer, Dietrich. *Life Together.* New York, NY: HarperOne, 1954.

Bruce, F. F. *Philippians.* Understanding the Bible. Grand Rapids, MI: Baker, 1989.

Carson, D. A. *Basics for Believers.* Sixth printing. Grand Rapids, MI: Baker Academic, 2005.

———. "The Temptation of Joseph." Sermon at Evangelical Ministry Assembly, 1996. Accessed June 4, 2014. http://www.proctrust.org .uk/person/don-carson.

Chapell, Bryan. *Using Illustrations to Preach with Power.* Revised edition. Wheaton, IL: Crossway, 2001.

Christensen, Max L. *Heroes and Saints: More Stories of People Who Made a Difference.* Louisville: Westminster John Knox, 1997.

Craddock, Fred. Quoted by Darryl Bell, "Practical Implications of Consecration." Accessed June 3, 2014. https://bible.org/illustration /practical-implications-consecration.

DeYoung, Kevin. *Crazy Busy: A (Mercifully) Short Book about a (Really) Big Problem.* Wheaton, IL: Crossway, 2013.

Fee, Gordon D. *Pauline Christology.* Reprint. Grand Rapids, MI: Baker Academic, 2013.

———. *Paul's Letter to the Philippians.* The New International Commentary on the New Testament. Grand Rapids, MI: Eerdmans, 1995.

Gaffigan, Jim. *Dad Is Fat.* New York: Crown, 2013. Kindle edition.

Getty, Keith, and Stuart Townend. "How Deep the Father's Love for Us." Thankyou Music, 1995.

Grudem, Wayne. *Systematic Theology.* Grand Rapids, MI: InterVarsity and Zondervan, 1994.

Hanson, G. Walter. *The Letter to the Philippians*. Grand Rapids, MI: Eerdmans, 2009.

Hughes, R. Kent. *Philippians: The Fellowship of the Gospel*. Preaching the Word. Wheaton, IL: Crossway, 2007.

Hughes, R. Kent, and Barbara Hughes. *Liberating Ministry from the Success Syndrome*. Wheaton, IL: Crossway, 2008.

Keller, Tim. "The Centrality of the Gospel." Accessed July 14, 2014. http://download.redeemer.com/pdf/learn/resources/Centrality _of_the_Gospel-Keller.pdf.

———. *Church Planter Manual*. New York: Redeemer, 2002.

Lehman, Jason. "Present Tense." 1989. Used by permission.

Lewis, C. S. *The Four Loves*. In *The Inspirational Writings of C. S. Lewis*. New York, NY: Inspirational Press, 1994.

———. *Mere Christianity*. Harper Collins E-books. Kindle edition.

———. *Miracles*. New York, NY: Macmillan, 1947.

Lloyd-Jones, David Martin. *Spiritual Depression*. Grand Rapids, MI: Eerdmans, 1965.

Mahaney, C. J. "Better Than I Deserve." Sermon, Sovereign Grace Church, Louisville, KY, January 13, 2013. Accessed June 2, 2014. http://podbay.fm/show/572680977.

———. *Humility: True Greatness*. Sisters, OR: Multnomah, 2005.

———. "A Rare Jewel." Sermon, Sovereign Grace Church, Louisville, KY, April 28, 2013. Accessed June 2, 2014. http://podbay.fm /show/572680977.

———. "Straining for the Prize." Sermon, Sovereign Grace Church, Louisville, KY, February 24, 2013. Accessed June 2, 2014. http:// podbay.fm/show/572680977.

———. "Whom Should We Follow." Sermon, Sovereign Grace Church, Louisville, KY, January 20, 2013. Accessed June 2, 2014. http:// podbay.fm/show/572680977.

Martin, Ralph P. *Philippians*. Downers Grove, IL: IVP Academic, 2008.

Melick, Richard. *Philippians*. The New American Commentary. Nashville, TN: B&H, 1991.

Motyer, J. A. *The Message of Philippians*. Downers Grove, IL: InterVarsity, 1984.

O'Brien, Peter. *The Epistle to the Philippians*: The New International Greek Testament Commentary. Grand Rapids, MI: Eerdmans, 1991.

Packer, J. I. *Knowing God*. Downers Grove, IL: InterVarsity, 1973.

Peterson, Eugene. *A Long Obedience in the Same Direction: Discipleship in an Instant Society.* Downers Grove, IL: InterVarsity, 2000.

Piper, John. "And All the Earth Shall Own Him Lord." *Desiring God.* October 24,1982. Accessed July 14, 2014. http://www.desiringgod .org/sermons/and-all-the-earth-shall-own-him-lord.

———. "George Mueller's Strategy for Showing God." *Desiring God.* February 3, 2004. Accessed June 2, 2014. http://www.desiringgod .org/biographies/george-muellers-strategy-for-showing-god.

———. "Is There Good Anxiety?" *Desiring God.* April 21, 1981. Accessed July 14, 2014. http://www.desiringgod.org/conference-messages/is -there-good-anxiety.

———. "John Newton: The Tough Roots of His Habitual Tenderness." *Desiring God.* January 30, 2001. Accessed June 4, 2014. http://www .desiringgod.org/biographies/john-newton-the-tough-roots-of-his -habitual-tenderness.

Robertson, A. T. *Paul's Joy in Christ (Studies in Philippians)* and *Paul and the Intellectuals (The Epistle to the Colossians).* Nashville, TN: Broadman, 1959.

Silva, Moisés. *Philippians.* 2nd ed. Baker Exegetical Commentary on the New Testament. Grand Rapids, MI: Baker, 2005.

Stott, John. *Between Two Worlds: The Challenge of Preaching Today.* Grand Rapids, MI: Eerdmans, 1982.

———. "Pride, Humility and God." PDI—*Sovereign Grace Magazine.* September/October 2000. Accessed July 15, 2014. http://www .cslewisinstitute.org/webfm_send/375.

Tan, P. L. *Encyclopedia of 7700 Illustrations: Signs of the Times.* 6th ed. Garland, TX: Bible Communications, 1996.

Thielman, Frank. *Philippians.* The NIV Application Commentary. Grand Rapids, MI: Zondervan, 1995.

Timmis, Steve. "Christ Is Enough." Sermon preached at Imago Dei Church, Raleigh, NC. February 9, 2014.

Tozer, A. W. *The Knowledge of the Holy.* New York, NY: HarperCollins, 1961.

Tripp, Tedd. *Shepherding a Child's Heart.* Wapwallopen, PA: Shepherd, 1998.

Witherington, Ben, III. *Friendship and Finances in Philippi: The Letter of Paul to the Philippians.* New York, NY: Bloomsbury T&T Clark, 1994.

SCRIPTURE INDEX